MARCUS
TRESCOTHICK

MARCUS
TRESCOTHICK
Coming back to me

THE AUTOBIOGRAPHY

with Peter Hayter

HarperSport
An Imprint of HarperCollinsPublishers

First published in 2008 by
HarperSport
an imprint of HarperCollins
London

First published in paperback 2009

2

A CIP catalogue record for this book is
available from the British Library

ISBN 978-0-00-729248-6

Printed and bound in Great Britain by
Clays Ltd, St Ives plc

The HarperCollins website address is
www.harpercollins.co.uk

Mixed Sources
Product group from well-managed
forests and other controlled sources
www.fsc.org Cert no. SW-COC-1806
© 1996 Forest Stewardship Council

FSC is a non-profit international organisation established to promote the
responsible management of the world's forests. Products carrying the FSC
label are independently certified to assure consumers that they come
from forests that are managed to meet the social, economic and
ecological needs of present and future generations.

Find out more about HarperCollins and the environment at
www.harpercollins.co.uk/green

To the most important people in my life:
Hayley, Ellie, Millie, Mum, Dad and Anna

Contents

Acknowledgements

Hayley: Without you in my life it would have never been the same. I thank you for being there, for following me around the world and never asking for anything in return. I know I have been a pain in the arse at times and I am sure you have wanted to give me a clip now and again. The past couple of years have not been easy for us both, but without you by my side I do not know how I would have got through it. I love you.

Ellie and Millie: You are everything to me. I love seeing your smiling faces every morning and getting your big cuddles and kisses at the end of a long day, I will always be here for you. I love you both.

Mum, Dad, Anna: Thanks for being there, for not shouting when I crashed the car or when I hit another bouncy ball through the patio windows; thanks Anna for never minding having to go to another cricket match when we were young even if you did make me late for my last game that time. I'm sure that bits of this book have been hard to read for you all, but I hope you now understand how much I need you. We live counties apart but you are always close to my heart. I know I do not say it much but I want you all to know I miss you loads and love you very much.

Peter Hayter: Reg mate, thanks for helping me with this book. For our sins we have been blessed with a great friendship and I'm glad we could help each other through tough times. Good luck if you are mad enough to do this again.

Everyone at HarperCollins: Thank you for this opportunity to tell my life story, it has been a lot of fun.

Neil Fairbrother: Harve, thanks for being there, mate. I know it has been tough at times but without your guidance, experience and voice on the other end of the phone it would have been a lot harder.

Richard Bevan: During my time with England your work with the lads was first class but the way you sorted things for me when I needed it most made me feel proud to be part of a great team at the PCA.

For all the professional help I have received from the people at Performance Healthcare (you know who you are): I thank you.

To all the coaches who have passed on their knowledge and advice to me: thanks for helping me achieve my potential and reaching my dream.

Thanks to all the lads I played international cricket with; thanks for some good memories and cracking nights out drinking winners' beer.

To all who have been involved at Somerset CCC; I have been a professional for 16 years but I will be a fan forever. Thanks for all the sausages.

To all the fans and cricket supporters who have cheered for me and sent me letters of support, thank you.

Everyone at Keynsham CC: Thanks for all your support over the years. I have always enjoyed popping in from time to time; always being greeted with smiling faces and a boat load of piss-taking makes me very happy.

Pete Sanderson: Sanders, mate, what can I say, your endless energy and time you have given me has made me want to keep getting better. I said to you before you were a big part of me doing well in the Ashes 2005. I just hope you're ready for the next seven years.

To my close friends Steff, Alex, Jase, Donna, Tux, Dewsy, Greg, Emma: you make my and Hayley's life so much fun. Here's looking forward to when we can all dine out together again and get our children to taxi us home.

Last and most important, to Hayley's parents Sue and Grampy John thanks for having them for us. your endless hours of help have been so valuable and I do not know how we would have coped without you. Me, Hayley, Ellie and Millie love you both very much.

Marcus Trescothick
March 2009

* * *

Thanks to all those who helped us tell Marcus's story: to England players past and present, Mike Atherton, Neil Fairbrother, Andrew Flintoff, Angus Fraser, Ashley Giles, David Gower, Nasser Hussain, Steve James, David Lloyd, Alec Stewart, Andrew Strauss and Graham Thorpe; to Peter Anderson, Richard Gould, Andy Hurry, Vic Marks, Peter Robinson, Brian Rose, Gerry Stickley and all the staff at Somerset County Cricket Club; to my colleagues in the media, especially Jon Agnew, Simon Briggs, Mike Dickson, John Etheridge, Iain Fletcher, David Foot, Barney Francis, Richard Latham, Alison Mitchell, Adam Mountford, David Norrie, Scotland's greatest warrior poet, Derek Pringle, Mike Walters and Richard Walsh; to Richard Bevan of the Professional Cricketers' Association; to Andrew Walpole of the England and Wales Cricket Board; to Kirk Russell; to Gerrard Tyrell; and to 'Chris'.

Thanks to Alison Sieff and to Tom Whiting at HarperCollins.

To Sally Davies, Mary Reid, Philip Hayter and Bunty Salisbury, to the late Ann Hamlyn, to Nick Swift and Mary Bunting, and to Reg and Lucy Hayter, as always. Thanks to Mary Hayter, for more than you know, and to Max and Sophie Hayter for putting up with a grumpy old dad.

Thanks to Hayley Trescothick and to Linda and Martyn Trescothick. And finally, to Marcus; mate, we're getting there.

Peter Hayter
March 2009

Chapter 1

THE END

*'That sadness swept over me. The thing
I had feared most was happening and,
if my previous experiences were anything to
go by, the process was as unstoppable
as a domino chain.'*

In the good times, the times before the long days and longer nights when depressive illness turned stretches of my life into a slow death, I had occasionally caught a glimpse of the perfect end to my career as an England cricketer; at The Oval, pausing on my way back to the dressing-room to acknowledge the applause celebrating the Test century with which I had just secured our latest Ashes victory.

That was what I saw in my sunlit daydreams. That was how it was supposed to happen.

The reality? Hunched-up, sobbing, distraught, slumped in a corner of Dixon's electrical store at Heathrow's Terminal 3, unable to board the 9 p.m. Virgin Airways Flight VS400 to Dubai for which I had checked in alongside my Somerset CCC team-mates on the evening of Friday 14 March 2008; but which I was now in no physical, mental or earthly state to take, hanging on for the pain and terror with which I had become so familiar during the previous two years to subside, and let me breathe.

I almost made it. I got almost as far as it is possible to get without actually walking through the door onto the plane and I had wanted to so much. Until the very eve of our departure, in the weeks leading up to it, I never seriously thought that I would have a problem going on the 12-day pre-2008-season tournament also featuring Lancashire, Sussex and Essex. I was well in myself and I was cautiously optimistic about what getting through the trip might mean in terms of my hopes of a future with England, even though my last appearance for them was now 18 months behind me. England's players, selectors, management, coaches and captains had all stated that, while they had no desire to put me under undue pressure to return, when I felt I was ready, so would they be. This was a real chance to find out if I was. The tournament was to be pretty low-key though Andrew Flintoff would be there to continue his recovery programme following his latest ankle operation back at home, with relatively little of the intense media coverage I had always found so discomforting.

All things considered I was looking forward to the test and what a successful outcome might mean, even though I knew failure would end all hope and all argument. After two aborted overseas tours with England, to India in 2006 and Australia the same winter, I knew it would be strike three – you're out.

I had spoken to my wife Hayley, who had given birth to our second child, Millie, a sister to two-year-old Ellie, on 19 January, and, mindful that separation from family, friends and the familiar had been at the root of my problems, she had said all the right things: 'Twelve days? You'll be fine.'

The day before I left I talked with the Somerset coach Andy 'Sarge' Hurry, a former marine turned PT instructor, about what might lay in store. He had asked, 'What can we do to make this easier for you?' and had already arranged with the rest of the staff and players that, once I got to Dubai, I was going to be kept fully occupied. With no time to wander, my mind might just be able to stay away from the thoughts that had, on occasions, made existence seem unbearable and that way, perhaps, the illness could be kept at bay. Busy days playing, training and practising would have been followed by lengthy team planning and selection meetings and I was never, ever, to be allowed to dine on my own unless it was my choice. Not that they were going to ask me for my belt and shoelaces, just that they wanted to create a comfortable environment in which I could relax and remain calm.

I had told Andy: 'Look, I really think I'm going to be fine ...' then added, 'as long as nothing out-of-the-ordinary happens.'

After six weeks of disturbed sleep following Millie's arrival, a part of me was also looking forward to the shut-eye I was going to be enjoying in Dubai.

Maybe I should have taken more notice of the slight twinge of anxiety I had felt that day, but I had known all along that this was not going to be straightforward. In any case the feeling was nothing like as intense as that warning sign which usually preceded a full-blown crisis; some people might describe it as a shiver down the spine, for me it was more like a progressive freezing, vertebra by vertebra from top to bottom.

And I wasn't too alarmed because, in general, I had been feeling fine for a while now and the medication which had helped to stabilize me through the darkest times was, I was pretty convinced, something to turn to only in dire emergency.

True, I had hit a snag the previous summer, when I first made myself available for England's World Twenty20 squad, then pulled out after a lengthy telephone conversation with the coach Peter Moores. While never presenting me with an ultimatum as such, he made it clear he wanted me to make myself available not just for the World Twenty20 in South Africa, a tournament I firmly believed at that stage I could manage, but also the one-day series in Sri Lanka that followed, something which, at that stage, I could not in all conscience commit to.

Nevertheless, again freed at least temporarily from having to consider the question of my future with England, I finished the 2007 domestic season with Somerset on a series of huge highs, topping Division Two of the Championship, winning promotion to Division One of the Pro 40, with my personal contribution being stacks of runs, including my career-best 284 at Northampton. And the celebration ale tasted sensational.

During the winter I had deliberately refrained from making any statements to the media or doing any significant interviews about my future plans. And I loved the anonymity of that. I had made one public appearance, as part of my benefit year, at a Question & Answer session in the Herefordshire town of Leominster, conducted by a journalist friend of mine, Peter Hayter of the *Mail on Sunday*, who lives locally. Brian Viner, of the *Independent*, another locally-based newspaper columnist wrote: 'Trescothick talked about the emotional illness that appears to have scuppered his England career with engaging candour.' And even I was quite surprised how much I enjoyed the experience and how easy I found it to talk openly in front of strangers, as indicated by the following exchanges:

PH: I think even now people are still somewhat confused about what happened to you and what you were suffering from, your illness and the effects of it. Can you explain what the past 18 months have been like for you, what you've gone through?

MT: At different stages I have had totally different feelings really. Over the last, say, now nearly a year, I would say it's been pretty good, just being away from the environment of the England setup and the pressure that comes with playing for England and the media attention that you have to deal with. Yeah, I'm moving along very nicely. The question's obviously always going to arise about what happens next and at this stage I'm not too sure, I want to drive it on from hereon in, but looking back to India, the first time, it was a really tough place and a tough situation to go through because I literally didn't know what was happening. I genuinely thought I had an illness that was going to see me off and, not knowing, at that point what to do. After I came back it got worse for a while, then it got better, then it got worse again. You're being followed by media people around your home town and they were waiting on your doorstep when you walk out the house. There were articles in papers, complete and utter rubbish, it's just like where do you go? There was no hiding place for me and for two or three months when I came back then it was real hard work and something I never want to have to experience again because it was a real tough place to be and I didn't really know what to do at that point, just taking advice really from people and colleagues and obviously counsellors to help get me through the situation. And it was really tough, you know. I'm such a better person for it, though. I've come through the other side. I'm sure I'll never be clear of the whole process ... at some point throughout my life at different stages, it may hit me again. Even now, I have the odd day when I relive memories and things and feelings that come back after a while, but I'm better equipped now to deal with situations and understand the beast that lives inside, and understand he's going to come back and come knocking on your door again. You've just got to deal with that process and just keep riding the journey until eventually it dies down and you carry on living your life as normal. You know, I'm a better person, as I've said, and I've learned so much from the whole situation.

PH: In your heart of hearts, do you think you'll play for England again?

MT: I can't honestly answer that question. All I know is that I'd love to have another go and I'm going to give myself every opportunity to have another crack at it. I think it's going to take a lot more hard work the longer it goes, of course. The team has changed totally. You've got Peter Moores in charge. The lads in the team are totally different. In my heart I still want to have aspirations to have another go. I haven't actually got to the point where I've admitted to myself that I can't do it any more. So until I get to that stage I'll keep trying.

A couple of weeks later, Peter rang me for a brief interview for his paper concerning the trip to Dubai. It is worth revisiting my response. 'I won't deny I am a little nervous about the prospect,' I told him. 'I don't want to pre-empt anything, but I know the signs and how to work through them. I'm feeling well at the moment and things are pretty good, so I'm 95 per cent certain that the trip will be all right. It is a big step and I'm not taking anything for granted. It will be interesting to see what happens.'

Ninety-five per cent certain?

Yet, I actually felt strong enough to offer my help to the Australian fast bowler Shaun Tait, who had recently announced he was quitting all cricket indefinitely, citing physical and emotional exhaustion, and, overall, my level of contentment could be gauged by the fact that I had only met with my personal counsellor, with whom I had been in regular contact since I returned home in crisis from England's 2006 tour to India, on two occasions since the previous July.

First, on 27 December 2007 we had reflected on the summer I had enjoyed with Somerset, discussed my future plans and a possible return to international cricket, the impending addition to my family and my benefit season. At the end of the meeting it was left up to me to make contact if I felt I needed to, and apart from the occasional text message of reassurance that I was doing okay, I hadn't. Closer to the time when I was due to leave for Dubai I rang him to say we must chat about this before I went and we did, at Somerset's home ground in Taunton, where I told him: 'It looks good. I'm looking forward to it. It's fine.' We arranged that I would ring him early on the day of departure, for a final check on how I was.

That morning I went over the plan one more time; first I would pack for the journey, then I would ring my counsellor. Next I would take Hayley and the girls out for lunch before they dropped me off at the ground in time for me to catch the bus along with the other lads, ready for a 3 p.m. departure to Heathrow.

Prior to my troubles, one of the aspects of touring I had enjoyed most had been packing. Ever since I can remember I had been a 'kit bully'. As a kid, growing up in a cricket-mad household, with a playing dad, Martyn, who represented Somerset 2nd XI, and a tea-making mum, Linda, I had loved poring over the magazines advertising cricket equipment. I had loved the physical sensation of unwrapping and trying on new pads, gloves, sweaters, boots, anything to do with the game of cricket. And bats. I just loved bats. This time I had laid out my kit, meticulously, and the act of placing it in my 'coffin', all in the correct order, was almost meditative.

After lunch, we set off for the ground and it was there, around 2 p.m., out of a clear blue spring sky, it all started to go wrong again.

Hayley had driven to the ground with the kids in the back of the car. When the time came, I kissed them all goodbye and as the car pulled away, I was suddenly, acutely and terrifyingly aware of the *shiver*. Straight away, I understood. If it hadn't meant so much to me to at least try, I might even have told the lads there and then that they had better go without me.

'Oh, no.' I said to myself. 'Oh, no.' Then, before I could close my mind to it, an image appeared of Ellie, back at home, asking

Hayley 'where's daddy?' and the look of sadness as she understood I wasn't there. That sadness swept over me. The thing I had
feared most was happening and, if my previous experiences were
anything to go by, the process was as unstoppable as a domino
chain.

I still hoped I might be able to stop it taking over completely, as
it had done so many times before. I started to try and fight it and
the feeling subsided as the usual cricketing banter began. 'Maybe
this time, maybe this time I'll beat it.'

I boarded the bus and started to calm down and, as we set off,
I realized something had slipped my mind, namely the pre-
arranged morning phone call to my counsellor and that realization
temporarily buoyed my spirits. I started thinking to myself that the
fact I had forgotten to make the call was a great sign. I rang him
on my mobile and told him: 'I forgot to call you. We're on the
coach. On our way to Heathrow.' I sat there afterwards, attempting
to persuade myself that if I hadn't been worried enough about the
trip to have made the call to my counsellor, I must actually be okay
to go. Except that, for the rest of the coach journey I was wavering
between that hope and a growing sense of unease.

I don't know whether any of the other guys could sense what
was happening. James Hildreth certainly can't have done. Somewhere around 500 yards away from and in sight of the terminal he
started taking the mickey big-time. 'Getting nervous, Bang?',
'Excuse me, driver, this is as far as Mr Trescothick is going,' etc. I
was used to it. I got heaps of that sort of stuff anyway from guys
like Andy Caddick, my former England colleague, Steffan Jones
and Jason Kerr, the two best men at my wedding to Hayley in
January 2004 – normal stuff that I had been more than happy to
take inside the dressing-room at Somerset for some time. Madfish,
they used to call me, after Madfish Willie, a character in the gangster film *Snatch*. And I never minded the name-calling for a

second because to me if people felt okay about taking the mick out of me, they must have reckoned I was okay enough to have it taken. Unfortunately, however, by now I was struggling badly, though they had no way of knowing as the illness had made me an expert at hiding my true feelings.

By the time we checked in for the flight at around 7.30 p.m., I was clinging on and clinging to the idea I might just be able to get on the plane and once aboard, maybe the feelings would go. Take-off time was about 90 minutes away. I had the length of a football match to try and hold myself together. We went through to the departure lounge and I made my way with Steffan and Jason to the nearest coffee bar. I ordered a bacon and egg sandwich and as I finished the last bite, time stopped for a millisecond. In that blink of the mind I was cooked and I knew it. Sensing I could go at any second, I was desperate to get up from the table and get away from the other two lads because I never liked breaking down in front of other people. I managed to make it as far as Dixon's. 'Oh, God.'

I rang Sarge, and asked him to come and meet me straight away, though I didn't tell him why. He said later that he thought I wanted some clarification over what speakers I should get for my iPod or some such. When he finally arrived he could see the state I was in. This isn't intended to earn me a badge, but this is a guy who had seen active service and he was clearly taken aback by what he saw. Later, he told me: 'To see a grown man in this state was quite tough.'

At first he tried to talk me round. 'Marcus,' he said. 'You've got to fight it. You've got to get yourself over this wall.'

I understood what he was saying. And I would have loved to have been able to say 'Sarge, you're right. That's what I've got to do and I'm going to do it.'

The fact was I couldn't. In between the sobs and tears, I told him: 'Andy, I'd love to be able to but I'm not sure I can. I don't want to get over to Dubai and f**k it up and have to come home again. That is the last thing I want to do. I'd rather walk away from it now than go over there, then have to get a flight home again, because I've done that twice before and it causes me so much pain.'

Andy and I walked out of Dixon's and found a little corridor which was a bit more private. Jason had joined us but by now Andy had realized that his original approach was doomed. Now they were just listening, sympathetically but clearly conscious of the significance of the moment.

I told them: 'I just can't keep putting myself through this. It's too painful. I can't keep doing it. I don't want to do it to myself any more. I don't want to do it to Hayley. That's enough.' Someone said: 'Okay. We'll get your bags off. You're going home', and I said, 'Yeah, sorry. That's it.'

It's hard to say how long it took for the symptoms of my illness to subside long enough to allow me some clear air to think about something, anything, other than how awful I was feeling. But when that moment came, so did certain truths and the most hurtful one was this: I could never again contemplate the possibility of playing cricket for my country, the love of my professional life.

I knew, finally and without a shadow of doubt, that my days as an international cricketer were over. I'd run out of road.

Transport was arranged for the trip home. It was a long journey. Whereas, after my two previous breakdowns, the overwhelming reaction to coming home had been relief, this was different. The implications of my inability to go on a gentle pre-season trip with my county were obvious and they hurt because I had so loved playing for my country. Not only did I feel dejected, but also, and, for the first time, I felt guilty because I had let down not only myself but everyone else who had tried so hard to help me get better; people at the club, my family and my counsellor, who had given so much to try and make it happen for me. I had assured them I was going to be all right and I truly believed I would be. Now I knew there was no going back.

I rang Hayley and told her what had happened and that I was coming home. I rang my parents and I rang Brian Rose, the club's Director of Cricket, who, along with everyone at Somerset had been so incredibly supportive of me throughout my troubles. And we agreed to issue a statement the next day. Then someone at the club realized the news had to be put out immediately because Sky TV were due to meet the plane in Dubai. Imagine what kind of story would have emerged if the TV pictures had shown all the Somerset boys arriving, except me.

So Richard Gould, the club's Chief Executive, put out the following holding statement at 10.22 p.m. that night:

'Marcus Trescothick has withdrawn from Somerset's pre-season tour to the United Arab Emirates.

'The decision was taken last night (14 March) shortly before the other players boarded a plane for the 12-day trip.

'Marcus's absence is due to a recurrence of the stress illness which caused him to quit two England tours.'

As soon as I got home, I went straight to bed. The emotional strain of the day had left me shattered. And I didn't feel a great deal better when I woke up the next morning because I knew what was facing me. In the meantime, another statement was issued by the club at 9.54 that morning, saying:

'Brian Rose has assured Somerset supporters that Marcus Trescothick will be fit to play a full part in the coming county season. Brian said: "I spoke to Marcus last night and, while it is unfortunate that he has suffered a recurrence of his stress problems, I am certain he will be available to start the season for Somerset.

"I don't see the setback as a major problem. Marcus did a tremendous job for us last season and will be a key player again this summer.

"His cricketing life is with Somerset and I am sure he will continue to enjoy playing for the club as he has done for many years".'

It was about now that my counsellor switched on his television at home, called up Teletext and learned for the first time that I hadn't boarded the flight. He told me later that the news had come as a complete surprise, so sure had he been from our meetings and phone calls that I would be able to make the trip.

I knew the first thing I had to do was get to the ground as soon as possible. I said to myself: 'I'm going to go out and face people now. There's no point p***ing about with it. I've got to face them at some point, let's just do it today.' And I walked into the club shop and bumped into an ex-colleague of mine, Mike Burns, and something lifted. I had a laugh and a joke with him, then I realized I still had my plane ticket in my pocket. 'Burnsy,' I said. 'I've got a ticket here to go to Dubai. If you fancy a trip … the lads find themselves unexpectedly a man short.'

As far as the England situation was concerned there was only one thing left to do. Already, and not unnaturally, some of the Sunday papers, whose cricket correspondents were down in New Zealand covering the England Test tour, had speculated that my international career was now almost certainly over. I knew we had to put something out as soon as possible confirming my intention to retire immediately, but, and even though it was a slim possibility it would, I didn't want the news to cause a distraction for anyone in the camp 11,000 miles away. Even on the day I had failed to get on the plane to Dubai, Paul Collingwood had been asked at a press conference, at the end of day one of the second Test in Wellington, for his reaction to my news; the guys certainly didn't need to have to answer any more questions about me when they had other things on their mind, like trying to come back from 1–0 down against the Kiwis.

I met with Richard Gould and Brian Rose. We discussed the pros and cons with the club chairman Andy Nash and we all agreed the best thing would be to prepare a statement for release after the end of the third and final Test match in Napier, with a press conference at Taunton on Thursday 27 March.

Unfortunately our plans had to change when, on the morning of Saturday 22 March, the first day of the third Test, sitting at home in my dressing-gown with Hayley Trescothick, I took a phone call from Richard Gould.

'Morning, Marcus,' Richard said. 'There's a bit of an issue.'

My heart sank.

'The BBC radio *Test Match Special* guys have been on to Andrew Walpole [the England Media relations general manager, in New Zealand with the team] enquiring whether it is true that you are about to announce your retirement from international cricket.'

Not again, I thought. This was the fourth time since my troubles began that confidential information about me had been passed on to the media – first, to the *Sun* regarding the possibility that I might be flying home from the 2005 tour to Pakistan to comfort Hayley following her father's serious accident; next, to the *News of the World*, concerning the background to the infamous interview I gave to Sky TV on my return from India in early 2006; later, to the *Sun* again, about me making myself unavailable for the 2006 Champions Trophy in India in September the same year; and now this. I found all four incidents disturbing and the middle two quite damaging. But now I was simply saddened that my efforts to announce my retirement on my own terms had been spoiled by careless talk.

The release of the statement was duly brought forward to the morning of Saturday 22 March. It read:

'*Marcus Trescothick today announced his retirement from international cricket.*

'The 32 year old Somerset batsman's decision follows his recent withdrawal from the county's pre-season tour to Dubai with a recurrence of the health problems which caused him to quit two England tours.

'Trescothick said: "I have tried on numerous occasions to make it back to the international stage and it has proved a lot more difficult than I expected. I want to extend my playing career for as long as possible and I no longer want to put myself through the questions and demands that go with trying to return to the England team.

"I have thoroughly enjoyed my time playing for England and I am very proud of having been selected for 76 Test matches and over 120 One-day Internationals. It has been a great privilege to represent my country and I am grateful to the game of cricket for giving me the opportunity to excel at a sport that I enjoy so much.

"My desire to play cricket is as strong as it ever was. But, due to the problems that I have experienced, travelling abroad has become extremely stressful for me. I now think that it is in the best interests of all concerned that the issue is put to rest so that the England team can concentrate on moving forward and I can concentrate all my efforts on playing well for Somerset."

'England managing Director Hugh Morris paid tribute to Marcus from New Zealand: "I would like to place on record my thanks to Marcus for the enormous contribution he had made to the England team in both Test and One-day International cricket. I fully respect and understand his decision to retire from international cricket and wish him every success in his future career with Somerset."'

I was particularly touched by the response I received from the public. Down in New Zealand, the BBC's Alison Mitchell neatly captured what I felt in her *Test Match Special* internet blog: 'Far from succumbing to the strains of his illness, Trescothick is taking charge of his life,' she wrote. Her comments had encouraged a number of replies from fellow sufferers, perhaps the most poignant from one named 'Owls Fan', who wrote: 'I have every sympathy. Depression and stress over several years nearly cost me my home, my family and my life. Nothing's more important than removing the causes and getting on the road to recovery. If it feels right, it is right.' The website received 117 other such responses before it was closed to new comments.

I made sure the day's play in the Test was over and done with before texting four or five of the team; Andrew Strauss, who, with his wife Ruth and young son had visited us the previous winter, Kevin Pietersen, Michael Vaughan, Paul Collingwood and Steve Harmison, my colleagues from our Ashes victory of 2005, just saying thanks.

The next time I sent a message to Vaughan he probably wished I hadn't bothered. Prior to the final Test in Hamilton, the skipper was coming under growing pressure not just because the team had failed to dominate supposedly weaker opposition, but also because of his poor form with the bat, 7 runs in six first-class innings on the tour thus far. When I saw him scratch around for 2 in 11 balls on the first morning of the match, when England slumped to 4 for 3, with the ball zipping around, I decided the time had come to intervene. My text message was brief and to the point. 'What the hell is going on? Just go out there and whack it.' I told him. In the second innings he took my advice and, after amassing a glorious four in four balls, he made a ludicrous attempt to slap a good length ball on off stump from Chris Martin to the square leg boundary, only to feather a nick to Brendon McCullum behind the stumps. Vaughan didn't text me back, but I got the message. It was definitely time to leave England well alone and get on with the rest of my life.

There was one other bit of unfinished local business to deal with. Word had reached me that, on the night of the Heathrow incident, as soon as the other lads heard that I was not going to be getting on the plane with them, poor James Hildreth was distraught. I learned later that he had spoken to one of the other guys and said, 'I wish I hadn't said those things to Banger.' There was a suggestion that he felt responsible for what had happened because of the piss-taking as the coach approached the terminal building. Apparently he couldn't get rid of the feeling that by saying what he had said he had set in motion the chain reaction that culminated in my collapse.

When I heard that I knew I had to speak to him as soon as the guys got back from Dubai and I did. I told him: 'Listen, I have absolutely no problem with what you said. It was nothing and it had no bearing on what happened afterwards.' He seemed pretty relieved. And by then, so was I.

Chapter 2

BANGERS AND BATS

'In the kitchen, in the living room, in the garden, wherever she happened to be, I'd hand the ball to her [mum], she'd bowl it, I'd hit it, fetch it, carry it back to her and say again "bowl to me, bowl to me."'

You've heard of people who eat, drink, sleep and dream cricket. For a large part of my life, that was me.

My earliest memories are not of teddy-bears, bows and arrows, mud pies or ray-guns, but of bats and balls, and mainly bats. I can't recall when I first picked one up, but I have retained a fuzzy memory of what happened when I did. It felt great, and even better when I hit a ball with it. That feeling has never left me.

I was born into a cricket-mad family. With my dad Martyn – a stalwart, top-order batsman and brilliant slip fielder for Keynsham Cricket Club, in between Bristol and Bath, good enough to play second team cricket for Somerset and be offered a contract which he turned down – and my mum Linda, already well into her eventual 35 years of making the club teas, it was hardly surprising that I should have an interest in the game.

But an article in the local paper, recording the birth of Marcus Edward Trescothick at 9.15 a.m. on 25 December 1975, weighing a 'healthy' 9lb 4 oz, said it all. Under the headline 'On The Team For 1991?', it read:

The couple, who live at Glenwood Drive, Oldland Common, already have a three-year-old daughter Anna, aged three.

Said Martyn: 'I was secretly hoping for a boy, and he will have every encouragement to become a cricketer when he grows up.'

While that first paragraph was apparently put together by someone who had necked a glass too many of the Christmas spirit, the second one was spot on.

Mum tells me I had a little plastic bat thrust into my hands at 11 months old, only a couple of weeks after I started walking, and, from that moment, I went round hitting everything I could find. If there weren't any balls to whack I'd have a go at those square wooden alphabet bricks, an early indication of my preference for sport over academic life. When I was about two, a family friend called Roger Loader cut a small bat down to a blade of around six inches and gave it to me as a present. It had a bit more go in it than the plastic one and, by all accounts, I was absolutely lethal with it. When mum and I returned after dropping off Anna at school, we'd get back in the house and I'd plead 'bowl to me, mum, bowl to me'. In the kitchen, in the living room, in the garden, wherever she happened to be, I'd hand the ball to her, she'd bowl it, I'd hit it, fetch it, carry it back to her and say again: 'bowl to me, bowl to me.' I never got tired of this. How she didn't I'll never know. No wonder, whenever they heard me coming, our pet cats, *Cricket* and *Biscuit*, would run for their nine lives. Anna thought I was just plain daft.

When I was four, dad went on a cricket tour to Sussex and came back with my first very own new bat, a Gray-Nicholls Powerspot which I still have at home to this day, and it was carnage. In the living room there were three sets of wall lights, each with two lamps under their own shades. By the time I had finished, of the six lamps and shades only one remained intact. I'd had all the rest. And one day, I managed to put a bouncy rubber ball straight through one of the French doors, clean as a whistle. Mum and dad never seemed to mind too much. In fact I was more likely to get told off for not hitting the ball hard enough than for the latest breakage.

From my young as I can remember, if I wasn't tugging at mum's skirts pleading with her to 'bowl to me' or outside in the garden with dad, playing cricket, and by now, football as well, I was glued to the television whenever the cricket was on, so much so that mum would often find me standing in front of it, bat in hand, repeating the shots I'd just seen. She is convinced that is how I became a left-handed batsman even though I am naturally right handed. In those days, the late 70s and early 80s, the England side was dominated by right-handed batters like Graham Gooch, Geoff Boycott, Chris Tavare, Peter Willey and Ian Botham. David Gower was about the only one who batted the other way round. So, in mirroring the right-handers I was actually adopting a left-hander's stance and practising the shots left-handed. The shots played by Gooch and Beefy obviously appealed to me more than the ones played by Boycott and Tavare.

Inevitably there were scrapes. I've still got a y-shaped scar on a my left hand from when I tripped on the doorstep bringing in the milk and I very nearly became living proof of the warning passed down by parents to kids from the beginning of time: 'It's all good fun until somebody loses an eye'. I had my luckiest escape thus far when I tried to climb up the washing machine, planted both Wellington-booted feet through the open door, slipped sideways, and the door hinge made a deep cut along my eyebrow.

By the age of six, whenever people asked me what I was going to do when I grew up, I didn't just say 'play cricket', I said 'play cricket, of course.' At seven, with dad running the junior section at Keynsham, I was already playing for the club's Under-11s.

At St Anne's Primary School, I was extremely lucky that one of the teachers, a Rick McCoy, was sports-mad. He ran the cricket in summer and the football in winter, and by then I was even branching out into other sports. Aged nine, at the 1984 Warmley & District Schools Athletic Association Annual Sports Day, for instance, I was good enough to win bronze in the lst Year Boys' Sack Race and, a year later, in 1985, I took the gold, with the theme to *Chariots of Fire* playing softly inside my head.

Football was great fun. I was always a Bristol City nutter and it was pure joy when, after the Ashes of 2005, the club made me an honorary vice-president. I played alongside a lot of good mates for the St Anne's side: it was me in goal (a formidable barrier even then), Eddie Gregg in midfield, Lee Cole a striker and his brother Mark, a chunky, slow right-back. Lee and Mark's dad was a printer who worked from home and we used to get together to compile a programme for every match we played, price 5p, with the proceeds going to various charities, including Dr Barnados and Cancer & Leukaemia in Children, something we would all have cause to remember years later, around the time I was starting out on my senior England career.

There must have been a few watching because one week we raised £7. Each programme comprised eight pages of articles – Manager's Message by Rick McCoy, Captain's Corner, by Matthew Bliss, reports of previous matches and stats – results, scorers, today's teams and goalscorers and appearances, and two special features called Player Analysis and Player Profile. The issue for our match against Bridge Farm on Thursday, 28 November 1985 (kick-off 3 p.m.) is a real collector's item, as I am the Player in question.

In Player Analysis, Lee Cole writes: 'Marcus Trescothick is a very good goalkeeper and has proved to be the best St. Anne's have ever had.' Lee was known to be an excellent judge.

In Player Profile it was my turn:

Full Name: Marcus Edward Trescothick

Birth date: 25 December 1975

Favourite Food: Bread and chips

Nickname: Tres

Worst Food: Meat

Most Embarrassing Moment : Letting in eight goals

Favourite Moment: Saving a penalty

Superstitions: None

Ambition: To score a goal from a goal-kick.

I never was too sure about that rule.

In 1986, aged ten, I was first picked to play cricket for the county, Avon Schools, and had a reasonable start, top scoring with 75, and later St Anne's made it through to the regional final of the English Schools Football Association six-a-sides. Though we failed to progress to the final at Wembley, I did find time to practise my autograph all over the page in the commemorative magazine set aside for getting other people's.

Then, in 1987, three things happened that turned out to have somewhat more bearing on my later life.

First, on Sunday 21 June, aged 11, I scored the first-ever century for Avon Schools Under-11s, 124 against Devon at Exeter School. Two weeks later, against Worcestershire at the Bristol Grammar School ground at Failand, I scored 183 not out. When asked why he declared, the manager, Mike Docherty, apparently said: 'If I let him get a double-hundred at his age, what else would he have to aim for?' The innings caused quite a stir. The local BBC TV asked if they could come along and film the next match, but we weren't comfortable with that. But the *Bristol Evening Post* decided to scrap their weekly Top Man cricket award and nominated me as Top Kid instead. Nice to see that the photo of me accompanying the article has me pointing the manufacturer's label straight at the camera. My interest in schoolwork may have been minimal, but, even at this tender age, I was showing signs of sound commercial sense. Slazenger, since you ask.

Their interest suitably aroused, and Bristol being within their boundaries, Gloucestershire County Cricket Club then picked me to play for their Under-11s, and when I made a century for them in my second match, against Somerset at Frenchay CC, Somerset made enquiries, realized I was eligible to play for them because Keynsham was in their territory, and my Gloucestershire career was over. From now on I would be playing for Somerset, my dad's county, *my* county.

The other thing that happened? A school trip to Torquay.

All kids get homesick, of course. But this was different. This was more or less unbearable. It was our last year at St Anne's and they decided to take us all to Torquay for a week together before we all moved on to our senior schools. It was the first time I had been away from home in my life and I hated it. I just hated it. I cried and cried and cried. Even though I was with all my mates, and we couldn't have been more than 100 miles or a couple of hours' drive from Oldland Common, I just couldn't bear being away from home. I wasn't a bit sad, or down in the dumps. I was terrified, irrationally so, and that scared me even more. Away from mum and dad and my home and my sister and my cats and my stuff and outside of my place, all I felt was dreadful, but the moment I got home I was fine again, as if it had never happened. I told my folks I hadn't enjoyed the trip much but I didn't tell them any more. Photos of the trip showed me joining in and smiling and it can't have been all bad. But there were moments when it was, and, from then on, I never felt really comfortable being away from my home, family, friends and the familiar again. Not long afterwards, I travelled to Cheltenham College for a county coaching clinic, felt terrible the moment I arrived, made up some story about not being well and asked mum to come and collect me the same day. Cheltenham? About 45 minutes from home.

Those feelings stayed within me, on and off, throughout a 15-year career in county and international cricket. For long periods they would disappear or lie dormant, and initially, even when they came, they were completely manageable. Playing top-level cricket gave me such a buzz that I could force them to one side. As time progressed, however, and the exhausting effects of burnout weakened my resilience, the feelings grew stronger and stronger.

Years later, when I discussed the history of my illness with my counsellor that week in Torquay took on great significance.

For now, however, the only thing on my agenda was sport, and plenty of it, as from September 1987 I joined the Sir Bernard Lovell Comprehensive School, also in Oldland Common. It probably didn't take long for the teachers and staff to work out that they weren't going to win any industry prizes for their work with me. An early indication of the kind of impact I would have in the classroom can be judged by the two credit notes I received in my first term, the first for 'Full marks in the beautiful babies competition', whatever that was, the next for 'Effort in gathering a most interesting collection of personal items for display in class'. By 1988 I had graduated to 'For giving freely of your time and interest to make the New Intake Parents' Evening a success' and 'Doing a week of litter duty'. My year grades were okay, not outstanding, but okay. I didn't get into much trouble, if any. I wasn't disruptive. I just wasn't interested. The only subject with which I had more than a passing acquaintance was drama. I was brilliant as one of the T-birds in *Grease*, singing *'We'll get some overhead filters and some four barrel quads, oh yeah – Grease lightning, wo-oh grease lightning'* etc., though I quite fancied having a go at John Travolta's part, as it happens. And I was growing more and more confident that cricket would not only be my passion, it would also be my profession. So much so that when someone at school recommended I spend more time on my truly appalling French, I replied: 'The only places I'm going to go are Australia, New Zealand, India, Pakistan, Sri Lanka, South Africa, Zimbabwe and West Indies. If I start speaking French in any of those places they won't have a clue what I'm on about.'

The only thing I wanted to learn about was cricket, and not just the playing. Even at this age I was a kit bully. Unwrapping a new pair of pads or gloves, or running my hand down the blade of a new bat, was pure ecstasy for me. And, looking back, the amount of time I spent getting my gear in order and just right was down-right scary. My obsession with bats and handles and grips and the like was, well, an obsession.

The runs just kept on coming, though. Still bigger than most of the other lads, still able to smash the ball harder and farther than anyone else, and still loving that feeling, I was still piling on the scores and keeping pretty well when required, for my school, for Avon Schools, for Somerset and for West of England and I was selected as one of the top 24 in the country in my age group for a national coaching course at Lilleshall. I made my first century in senior cricket, for Keynsham in the Western League in 1989, aged 14 and in 1990, after an England Schools Cricket Association trials tournament in Oxford, when England named their first-ever Under-14 squad, selected by David Lloyd among others, I was in it, along-side Andrew Flintoff and Paul Collingwood. Fred was a big boisterous bloke who could launch it miles. Colly, at that stage was an irritating dobber who bowled gentle inswing to left-handers and I whacked the living c**p out of him. If you had said to us then that, in 15 years' time, we would be standing at The Oval drench-ing ourselves in Ashes champagne...

David Lloyd was impressed by my batting, less so by my size and shape, which by now was on the portly side of chubby. Unsurprising really, as my diet comprised all and only the wrong things; sausages were my favourite, hence the nickname 'Banger', later coined by Bob Cottam at Somerset, that has stuck with me ever since. Then, in no particular order, sausages, chips, sausages, toast, sausages, baked beans, sausages, cheese, sausages, eggs, sausages and the occasional sausage thrown in, topped off with a sprinkling of sausage. The only muscles I had in my body were around my mouth. If someone put a slice of cucumber in front of me, or any other salad item for that matter, and said 'eat that and I'll give you £100', I'd say no chance. Fruit? Forget it. Vegetables? Why?

Christmas dinner in our house was a bit strange, to say the least. While everyone else would be tucking into traditional roast turkey with all the trimmings, my festive fare consisted of tinned carrots (I didn't like the fresh ones, obviously) and a variety of potatoes, roast, boiled and mashed, which I'd stuff between slices of bread to make spud sarnies.

I cannot eat enough steak these days, but then I couldn't stand the taste and texture of meat at all. When mum used to try and feed me meat of any kind as a toddler I would just retch or spit it out. I didn't eat chicken until I was 20, when my Somerset team-mate Rob Turner persuaded me to try a McDonald's chicken-burger. I was so proud I rang my mum and told her, as I was washing it down with a million cans of fizzy-pop. I ate my first beef burger when I was 29. No, really. I'm not kidding.

Lloyd did mention to someone that perhaps the subject of my weight and general fitness might have to be addressed and I know it later cost me a place on the West of England Schools tour to the West Indies and possibly a place on the following year's England Under-15 squad, but, at 14, the fact that I could hit the ball harder than seemingly anyone else my age in the entire country covered a multitude of sins. I might not have been the sprightliest in the field or between the wickets, but when you stood behind the stumps with the gloves on, and hit the ball like I did, what did I need to run for? Dad did try and take me out jogging a few times but I could barely make it to the end of our road and he soon gave it up as a bad job.

If there had been the slightest doubt about where my young life was heading, the summer of 1991 sealed my fate.

God knows how many games of cricket I played that season – for the school, for Keynsham, for West of England Schools, for Avon Schools, and, as a 15-year-old, for Somerset Under-19s under the county coach Peter Robinson, who had already bowled a million left-arm spinners to me in the freezing cold of Peter Wight's Indoor School in Bath on Wednesday winter evenings. Sometimes I played twice in a day, a match for the club Under-17s in the morning, then an afternoon game for the 1st XI. I reckon I played more than 50 innings in all and I scored millions, including 13 hundreds and my first double. It was not enough to win selection for the England Under-15s, which hacked me right off – Phil Neville, then of Lancashire schools but later Manchester United and England, was picked ahead of me – but, by the time I began my last innings of the summer, in the last match on the last day, for Keynsham against Old Georgians, what I did know was that mum had totted up all the scores and I needed 84 runs to reach 4,000 for the season. That might be something to interest the selectors who had left me out of that England side, I reckoned.

Then the batsman's nightmare. My sister was to-ing and fro-ing at home so we arrived late for the start of the match. All I had been thinking about was getting in early enough to give myself the best chance of making the required number of runs. But, when we arrived late and I was told we had won the toss and were already batting, that meant less chance for me. And what if the openers never got out?

Eventually I went in, but time was running out. The tension built up because everyone there knew what was at stake, and, with one ball to go in our innings I still needed two runs. I got a bottom edge on a decent yorker and groaned inwardly as the keeper parried it. I set off for the other end knowing I might be able to run a single but unless something extraordinary happened there was no way I would get two. Then, something extraordinary did happen.

Their keeper threw the ball at the stumps to try and run out my partner; he was in by miles when the ball hit the stumps and ricocheted off into the covers and I was able to scramble back for the second. I remember walking off the pitch bawling my eyes out.

And 4,000 seemed to be the magic number. Soon afterwards *The Cricketer Magazine* told me I had won their award for the outstanding young cricketer of the year. I duly pitched up at Lord's to receive my award and a load of kit from Mickey Stewart, the England senior coach, Angus Fraser and Carl Hooper, who had been opponents in that summer's Test series, and the radio commentator Brian Johnston. When he watched me in the indoor school nets at Lord's that day Mickey made a point of querying why I hadn't been picked for the Under-15s, and soon afterwards he made sure I was awarded a place on the MCC School of Merit training scheme there, for which I travelled up to London once a week throughout the winter, which was a wonderful consolation.

Brian Johnston's behaviour that day was magnificently eccentric. Johnners had an absolute obsession about the Australian soap opera *Neighbours*. Wherever he was, if *Neighbours* was on the telly he had to watch it. Everything stopped for Ramsay Street. And there and then, as we were settling down to a buffet reception after the awards had been completed, Johnners set up a portable TV in the corner of the room and switched it on for his daily dose of Kylie, Jason and Madge.

After all that, then scoring heavily for Somerset Under-19s, including an unbeaten 158 against Warwickshire, followed by a 2nd XI appearance, sitting my GCSEs in the summer of 1992 seemed somewhat beside the point. Bob Cottam, the Director of Cricket at Somerset, and Peter Robinson, the coach had already indicated they would be interested in signing me. The headmaster at Sir Bernard Lovell recommended I should turn them down and go back for A-levels, but, as I'd managed the sum total of one pass in my GCSEs, a 'B', in Drama, I can only think he must have spotted something in me no one else had done thus far. I told him, politely, that I could get an education at any age but I would only get one chance at cricket. There was talk of me enrolling at Bath Technical College to do a sports training course or some such, but when it became clear the only thing I wanted to do for a living was play cricket, mum sat me down and said: 'Right, well, if you're going to play cricket, do it properly. That means you've got to knuckle down and train and do everything you have to.'

Just before the end of my academic career I received news that I had been selected for the England Under-17s, to play three Tests against South Africa in July and August, and, only a few days after I left school, aged 16 and a half, dad received a hand-written letter from the Somerset secretary Peter Anderson, confirming that they wanted me to join them, as of 17 August, on a contract that would see me through until 1994.

'The salary level is in line with that of other junior players,' he wrote.

'There is a minimum wage agreement but that does not come into force until a player has two years' service. I think that with accommodation paid for plus allowances on match days, it is not too bad for youngsters. However, should you wish to discuss this or any other matter, please give me a ring.

'We are very happy that Marcus wishes to join us. He will have a lot to do and learn, of course, but at least he now has a chance to realize his ambition.'

I can't actually remember how much they offered me to start off with. I've got a vague recollection of £100 per week plus accommodation. Then £3,000 for 1993 and £3,300 for '94. It sounded and felt like a king's ransom.

In any case, I would have paid them.

Chapter 3

A JAMMY BASTARD

*'It absolutely confirmed that this was the life I
wanted to live, to play and bat against men, not
boys. And it showed those around me in the
dressing-room that, if nothing else, I wasn't
easily intimidated ...'*

I was 16 years old when I became a Somerset player. I was 24 when
I became an England player, and the eight-summer journey was
long and anything but straightforward.

I encountered a few spectacularly massive highs and some
pretty low lows along the way. Many times I doubted whether I
would ever fulfil my potential and a number of county bowlers
were kind enough to suggest I might be right.

In my first full year, 1994, aged 18, I scored more than 2,500 runs
in all forms of cricket – first-class, domestic one-day and England
Under-19 Test and ODIs. Most important from my point of view
was that I made 924 championship runs at 48.63 with a top score
of 121 and almost certainly would have become the youngest
Somerset batsman to score 1,000 runs in a season had England
not insisted I miss three county matches to play for the Under-19s
against India. Within three years however, I was not far short of

being convinced that I was finished, undone by a technical flaw I could not seem to eradicate no matter how hard I tried. By the time my career kick-started again in July 1997, a measure of how desperate my situation had become was that the innings that did it, a marathon 322 against Warwickshire at Taunton came in the 2nd XI, for whom my previous best that season had been 55. I was batting at number five, in the process of being converted by our coach Dermot Reeve, into an all-rounder and wondering where all this was going to end. And it took not one winter in Australia, but two, to help me find the tools I needed to rebuild my hopes and forge my future as an international cricketer.

I had mixed feelings when, as arranged, I walked through the gates at the County Ground in Taunton on 17 August 1992, to embark on a career being paid to play cricket. England's three-Test Under-17 series against a South African side starring their 'gun' player Jacques Kallis had gone well, particularly the second at Oundle school where I made 158 and 79 in a high-scoring draw, so I was not short of confidence in my own ability. I was extremely uncomfortable about leaving home, however, and the first week or so was pretty tough. But gradually, after forcing myself to get involved and do the stuff that I had to do, I was able to push the feelings of homesickness into the background.

It helped that we were into playing cricket almost straight away and that I had already turned out for the seconds that summer and scored some decent runs. It was also greatly in my favour that in one of my early matches, against a Surrey side containing Adam Hollioake and Mark Butcher, I had withstood a rather tasty spell from the South African paceman Rudi Bryson. This is what it's all about, I thought, as I prepared to face Bryson for the first time, with a score to make and a total to reach for victory on the last day. This is what all those hours in the nets, all that batting, all that practice had been for. Bring it on.

Bryson spent the next two hours bowling four or five bumpers an over at my head. I had never seen a ball travel so fast or rather, initially, not seen it.

For what seemed like ages, I just kept ducking it and ducking it, trying desperately to show no outward signs of the truth that I was, in fact, inwardly screaming: 'JESUS CHRIST, DON'T LET HIM KILL ME. DEAR JESUS CHRIST, JUST DON'T LET HIM KILL ME'.

Somehow, I got through it, managed first to survive then make solid enough contact to score 34 not out to finish off the game. It was the most exhilarating experience of my cricketing life. On the one hand I was asking myself: 'How the hell could anyone bowl so fast?' And on the other I was thinking: 'No matter how fast he bowled, I won.'

The experience did two things for me. It absolutely confirmed that this was the life I wanted to live, to play and bat against men, not boys. And it showed those around me in the dressing-room that, if nothing else, I wasn't easily intimidated, though some might have ascribed that characteristic to the old adage about no sense, no feeling.

I made my second significant contribution to team morale in my first match as a 'contracted' player, against Sussex at Eastbourne. We stayed at a rather tired-looking seaside hotel and I was rooming with Iain Fletcher, one of a number of slightly older young players trying to make the grade at the club. When we went down to breakfast on the morning of the match I couldn't work out why he was having quite so such trouble containing his mirth, until he announced to the assembled assortment of old stagers and young shavers that he had just witnessed me making my own bed. Mum would have been proud of me. The other lads thought it pretty hilarious that I had no idea hotels employed people to do that kind of thing for you.

That winter I was off abroad again, this time with the Under-18 schools in a very short four-nation tournament in South Africa, at Stellenbosch University near Cape Town.

When I turned up at pre-season training in 1993 I was ready in my own mind to take the next step, hoping that my chance would come soon and confident I would be big enough to take it.

And the kit. Oh Lord, the kit. If ever someone asked me to go on Desert Island Discs, if I managed to get past the title of the programme, as well as the complete works of Eminem to listen to there would be no question of my luxury item. It would be a spanking new kit catalogue stuffed page after beautiful page full of brand new kit. From a very young age my idea of paradise on earth on a rainy day was to pore over the pages of the latest catalogues revealing all the joys of this year's new kit; bats, pads, gloves, inners, boots, sweaters, shirts, boxes, arm-guards, thigh-pads; I adored them all, especially anything worn by Graeme Hick, whose batting I found inspirational to watch.

I was already obsessed by bats, to the extent that if anyone in the dressing-room wanted a couple of millimetres shaved off the bottom, or a new rubber grip put on the handle, I took it upon myself to do the job. And even if they didn't want me to, I'd do it anyway. Anything to do with bats and bat care, I was the expert, and that has never changed. Call me Doctor Blade. Even at this age I told Iain Fletcher that when I retired from playing I wanted to be a bat-maker and I still might, at that. Fletcher reckons my behaviour was something between dedicated and obsessive compulsive; which, incidentally would explain a lot of other things like my sausage-only diet and later, when it was time to try and get myself fit for England, the fact that you would have to blindfold, cuff and gag me to get me away from the gym.

For now, when I turned up at Taunton as winter was giving way to spring that year and saw wave after wave of new kit coming in, all this brand new stuff to ponce around in was bliss. The idea that I was going to be given it for free, rather than have to pay, as I had done until this point – quite frankly I couldn't think of anything more wonderful on God's green earth.

Then there was the money. Three thousand pounds of real actual money for the summer, just for playing cricket. At 17, with mum and dad still supporting me, no car yet, lodgings supplied and only maybe a bit of food and drink to have to fork out for, how the hell was I going to spend all that loot? I'd been paid for odd jobs around the house before, and we were always doing little earners like the paper round for three quid a week. And suddenly three thousand pounds was coming my way. The figure was quite fantastic.

My accommodation was less so, however. It was only a stone's throw from the ground at Taunton, as you could tell by the number of broken windows. Four of us young lads shared what was notionally a two-bedroom house, me and a guy called Paul Clifford in a tiny box room and Andy Payne and Jason Kerr in another slightly bigger box room. It was a disgrace. Apart from the fact that I could touch all four walls of my bedroom from the middle of it, the other notable aspect of the house was that it smelled of cat's urine – all the time. No matter what we tried, air fresheners, keeping the windows open, everything, the place stunk of cat urine 24 hours a day and it was worst first thing in the morning. We reckoned they used to wait until the house was quiet, come in for a few bevvies and a game of cards and then get down to some serious urinating before wandering off for another day on the tiles.

Payne was a menace as well, a complete psycho whose most prized possession was the air rifle with which he spent most of his spare time shooting me. He'd stuff these little white plastic pellets down the barrel, aim and fire. Day or night, watching TV or reading the paper – *whack!* – suddenly, out of nowhere, I'd take one in the side of the head. To this day I still carry a slight scar on my left cheek as a result of one of his numerous attempts on my life. It was like living with Lee Harvey Oswald.

It was great fun, all of it, and, with regular mercy dashes home to stock up on mum's cheese flans, it made being away from home better than bearable.

I'd like to say that when the call finally came, on 12 May 1993, informing me I would be playing in the 1st XI against Lancashire the very next day, I was up for it and ready for anything.

I'd like to say it, but actually I was anything but. My feelings on that first morning were jumbled. I was incredibly excited to be sharing a dressing-room with players like Andy Caddick, just about to make his Test debut; our captain Chris Tavare, one of the 1981 Ashes heroes I had copied as a child in front of my living room telly; Mark Lathwell, who, that season, at 22, scored two 20s and a 30 against the rampant touring Australians and was promptly discarded but whose talent sometimes left you speechless; and Mushtaq Ahmed, the Pakistan leg-spinner who was one of the most feared bowlers in the world, making his championship debut.

But one look over at their dressing-room balcony also made me very nervous. No one said it was meant to be easy, but my early season form with the seconds had been pretty poor – I had just made a big fat nought in a 2nd XI match at Edgbaston. The pitch that morning at Taunton was the colour of Robin Hood's tights and Lancashire's opening pair were Phil DeFreitas, on his day one of England's best swing bowlers, and Wasim Akram, the Pakistan Test star who was almost certainly the best fast left-arm swing and seam bowler ever to draw breath. I'm not ashamed to admit it, but I *was* actually a bit scared of the idea of Wasim's pace. At the same time, however, as with all really quick bowling throughout my career, that tingle of fear was like an energy charge. Even though I had some success against 'Was' later with England, including my first Test hundred in this country in 2001, facing him was always an intoxicating mix of fear and anticipation.

In the end I was proud to be part of an epic victory, gained by 15 runs at 5.30 p.m. on the second day and watched by mum and dad. Some say it was the bowling of Mushy and Caddick, who took 12 wickets in the match and his career-best 9 for 32 in 11.2 overs in their second innings of 72 all out, which tilted the balance our way. I'd like to think my four runs (1 and 3, out to DeFreitas lbw and caught behind) also helped, a notion Mike Atherton found strangely difficult to comprehend when I shared an England dressing-room with him years later. All I remember, in actual fact, was just not being able to hit the ball, apart from two edges through the vacant slip area to third man that brought me the single and the three.

My education was advanced in one other way, though. I was sledged for the first time and not in the general, genial, jokey way that I had been brought up to believe was all part of the camaraderie of the game, but nastily and unnecessarily. Looking back now it was probably just a throwaway line long forgotten by the bloke who said it, the Lancashire batsman Nick Speak, but, at the time it left a sour taste. After Warren Hegg had caught me off 'Daffy' in the second innings, Speak walked up to Wasim within my earshot and said: 'This bloke is sh**.' I'll never forget it because it annoyed me so much. It wasn't the worst thing he could have said and I could handle myself all right, but I was a 17-year-old kid trying to find my way in the game and to me what he said just amounted to an attempt to bully me, no more no less. I used to get a lot of that stuff. To me, it wasn't really sledging, or trying to get under someone's skin or put them off their stroke. It was bullying, pure and simple. And I have always hated bullies. In years to come, whenever dressing-room banter crossed the line I made it my business to keep an eye on things.

I was due to get another go in the next match, against Worcestershire at New Road, but I then managed to make myself fairly unpopular with the club by turning out to play for Keynsham the next day without telling them, diving on the boundary to stop a four and knackering my knee. The county's mood with me barely improved for the rest of the season. At least I was consistent. At the beginning of July I followed up my 1 and 3 with 6 and 0 against Sussex at Thornton and rounded things off nicely with 4 and 0 against Leicestershire at Weston Super Mare in mid-August. No wonder they never bothered taking me on any away trips. Fourteen runs at 2.33, with allowances, expenses and, remarkably, two win bonuses from my three matches, I was working out at around £250 a run.

But Peter Robinson, our coach, kept faith. I had wondered when I joined whether the coaching staff might try and get me to change or adapt my batting style, but they didn't, even though I was clearly struggling to cope with the demands of playing at this level. My game was basically the same then as it is today, with a few adjustments. For my big scoring shots, on the offside and straight I would cut and drive, sweep or slog-sweep the spinners and pull or whip the quicks off my legs hard and, if safe, in the air. There was always talk about my footwork, or lack of it, but my game was based on my knowing exactly where my off stump was, and playing with my head and body still, straight and facing wicket to wicket. Robbo kept telling me to stick to what I was good at, encouraged me to express myself and I was still scoring good runs in the seconds, including my first 2nd XI century against Kent, for whom a lad called Duncan Spencer was making waves as a tearaway paceman. Whatever questions were already being asked about my technique, at least I was able to show my courage against the fast stuff was never going to be in question. It wasn't much use on my first England Under-19 tour that winter, however, under skipper Michael Vaughan, against the Sri Lankan spinners.

*   *   *

Luck. However you dress up a person's life or career, whatever talent a person has or whatever opportunities arise, somewhere along the line everyone needs luck in order to succeed.

I had mine when I needed it most, soon after the start of the 1994 season, just around the time when some at Somerset might have been starting to have second thoughts about me. Though Robinson and Bob Cottam insisted they would carry on backing me, others at the club might not have been so sure after my wholly unimpressive baptism in championship cricket. Prior to the start of the season, Bob called me in and told me that, at some stage, they were going to give me a run of at least three championship matches to see how I was progressing. He didn't spell out what might happen if I failed, but my two-year contract would be up at the end of the season and a decision on whether I was worth persevering with would have to be made one way or the other before then.

I started brilliantly, scoring 0 and 7, again versus Lancashire, batting down the order at Southport at the end of May. So promoting me to open in the next match against Hampshire at Taunton at the start of June was either a tactical masterstroke or one of the last few remaining rolls of the dice. It looked very much like the latter when, on two, the West Indies paceman Winston Benjamin sent down another very quick ball, I fended it off and waited for Tony Middleton, under the lid at short leg, to bring this latest epic innings to a close.

They say your whole life flashes in front of you in the instant before you buy the farm; even as the ball was travelling towards Middleton, ready and waiting no more than three yards away on my left-hand side, with the roar of celebration beginning to gurgle up from the pit of Benjamin's stomach, I had more than enough time to work out the following equations: $1+3+6+0+4+0+0+7+2 = 23$, and 23 divided by nine = not enough (2.55 recurring, in fact).

And then Tony Middleton dropped the ball. I could have kissed him. Eight runs later I had, as *Wisden* recorded, 'escaped single figures for the first time' in my ninth first-class innings, and I went on to make 81, an innings I must have played in a trance because I remember absolutely nothing whatsoever about it. After two days of rain, our declaration and a double forfeiture of innings meant they were chasing 333 to win on the last day and we prevailed thanks mainly to the 90mph bowling of Andre Van Troost, our Flying Dutchman who remains the fastest bowler ever to come out of the Netherlands, and, swearing his head off in a unique twisted mixture of English and Dutch, the most unintentionally hilarious when angry as well.

I was away. Opening with Lathwell for almost all of the remainder of the season, I followed up my maiden first-class 50 with another, in my very next innings against Yorkshire at Headingley and then, at Bath a week later, my first hundred, against Surrey. Lathwell kicked off with a double in our first innings, Somerset's first-ever on this ground, then I scored 121 in our second as we declared on 329 for six, setting them 470 to win and had them 48 for three at the close on the Saturday.

I was ecstatic and spent the rest of the evening down the road at Keynsham with Eddie Gregg, Lee Cole and the rest of the lads, playing silly drinking games, like spoof and piling up beer mats on the edge of a table, flicking them up with your hand from underneath and seeing how many you could catch. Once a club cricketer, always a club cricketer. Utterly bladdered by the end of all this, I crashed out that night wondering if life could ever get any better. And the runs kept flowing like Taunton scrumpy.

The day after we had finished off Surrey by 317 runs, I made 116 against Oxfordshire in my NatWest debut, then four 50s in the next six championship innings, and, at the end of July, another century, against Sussex at Hove. At that stage, from and including the innings when Tony Middleton gave me a second chance against Hampshire back in May, my run of scores in the championship read 81, 54, 26, 121, 55, 0, 53, 59, 8, 87, 0 and 115. Forget 23 in my first nine innings, I had made 659 in the next ten, including six fifties and two hundreds.

Now, up to this point I'd never exactly been thought of as the next Che Guevara; even at school I was more of a hopeless case than a rebel with, or without, a cause, but what happened next took me about as close to challenging authority as I had ever been before. In the middle of this unbelievable about-turn and run of form against some of the best bowlers in the country I had to stop playing for Somerset and start playing for the England Under-19s.

At the beginning of August, instead of playing two championship matches against Durham at Taunton and Middlesex at Lord's, I had to play in two Under-19 one-day internationals against India and the first of three Tests, again under Michael Vaughan and, unbelievably irritatingly, at Taunton. There was just no comparison in the standard of cricket, and while it was, of course, always an honour to represent my country at this level, I felt it was also a complete waste of my time. My heart wasn't in it. I wasn't being arrogant or getting too big for my bangers, it was just that I knew I would learn so much more playing for my county than England Under-19s at this stage; I was on a roll and I had my eyes well and truly fixed on making 1,000 runs for the season and a possible England A tour place at the end of it. And I told them so.

When Micky Stewart, who had just stood down as senior England coach to be succeeded by Keith Fletcher but was still heavily involved in the set-up, came down to Taunton to discuss the issue and asked if any of those present in the room among the Under-19s squad would rather be playing for their clubs, of the nine in our squad who had played first-class cricket, I was the only one in the room who said yes and why. 'I just think I'll learn more playing senior cricket than against players my own age,' I said.

It didn't work. After making 15 and 92 on my return to county cricket against Essex, it was off to the second Under-19 Test where I hit 140 in our second innings, and with another 64 runs under my belt against Northants, on 8 and 9 September, in the third and final Under-19 Test at Edgbaston, I took out my frustration at having to miss a third championship match, against Kent at Canterbury, on the Indian attack. After a rain delayed start we slumped to 27 for five at the end of the first day, of which I had made 11 not out. The next day we finished up 381 all out, with me making 206 from 233 deliveries.

Starting the final championship match of the season, against Derbyshire at Taunton I needed 127 runs to reach the magic 1,000.

Rain washed out play until after lunch on the third day so, realistically, I had to make them all in one go. I scored 51 in our first innings, edging to 924, only 76 away, and spent the rest of the rain-ruined match cursing the fact that playing for England Under-19s had cost me a probable six innings in which I would only have had to average 15.81 to become, at 18 and a half, the youngest Somerset player ever to make 1,000 runs in a season.

Not that I'm bitter but, to cap it all, England then picked Vaughany ahead of me for the A tour to India and Bangladesh, while they gave me the runners-up prize, captaining the Under-19s in West Indies that winter. On second thoughts…

I consoled myself by passing my driving test, at the second attempt, not before nearly wiping myself out in a scene reminiscent of the final moments of the original *Italian Job*, starring Michael Caine, when their getaway coach is teetering on the edge of a 1,000 foot drop on an Alpine road. Practising my reversing and three-point turns in a private road running left-to-right halfway up a hill and parallel to the ground, I attempted to reverse uphill into a driveway, got my left and right hands confused, reversed down the hill, and back wheels first, over a four foot sheer drop and smashed the rear of the car into a concrete post. There I was sitting in the driver's seat of my Ford Sierra staring straight ahead at the sky above me. I jumped out, took one look at the car and realized that if the post hadn't stopped the car dead it would almost certainly have rolled backwards all the way down the hill and quite probably into the stream at the bottom. The RAC had to come and rescue the car. The undercarriage was totally wrecked. I was lucky I wasn't.

I duly skippered the Under-19s in the Caribbean, with David Lloyd as coach and Freddie as all-rounder. Alex Morris of Yorkshire and later Hampshire provided the musical talent – his dad Chris had had a couple of UK hits in the 1960s under the name Lance Fortune, the best-known being 'When Will You Be Mine' which became our unofficial tour anthem, though nobody ever sang it or knew any of the words, not even 'Almo'. The name Lance Fortune had been dreamed up by his manager, Larry Parnes, who liked it so much that when Fortune's fame dried up, Parnes simply recycled it, giving it to another act he managed, a bloke called Clive Powell, who later became the sixties pop icon Georgie Fame. Despite my disappointment at being overlooked for the A tour, and after the usual early tour shakes, I had an incredible time as one of 15 young blokes playing cricket in the Caribbean, all expenses paid. I made a century in the first Test in mid-January, 106 not out, out of 199 for four declared to set West Indies a target, and batted quite well throughout. At the end of it I organized a bumper end of tour dinner in Port of Spain, Trinidad at which I ate only bangers, of course, washed down with litres of fizzy soft drinks. It really is a wonder I have any of my own teeth left.

When I came back to Somerset I negotiated a pay rise to £12,000 per year from 1995 and that was about as good as it got for quite some time. What happened next? I flat-lined.

Everyone's heard about second season syndrome; what happens when the county bowling fraternity have absorbed the lessons of bowling to a new batsman, identify a weakness to attack and pile on the pressure in his second season. My second season ~~~~~~~~~ seemed to last longer than usual – about four seasons in total.

I had my good moments. I made a third championship ton in 1995, against Northants, but scored only 373 runs in total and though I cashed in against South Africa Under-19s, featuring Kallis again alongside Makhaya Ntini, Boeta Dippenaar and Mark Boucher, by now I was well aware that the pros had worked me out. They knew exactly where to bowl to me, just short of a length and just outside off stump and I couldn't help myself. I went after them time after time, I couldn't bring myself to leave the ball and consequently I just couldn't stop getting out caught behind, in the slips or the covers, or just playing and missing. Some days I didn't look as if I could bat to save my life.

Same again in 1996, though with all the upheavals going on at the club that season I'm not sure too many people actually noticed. Our form was unsatisfactory all round and, as time went on, the captain Andy Hayhurst appeared to let his own poor form affect his captaincy and the burden of captaincy affect his form. There were rumours that Caddick was looking to move on, that the committee weren't happy with the way things were being run on and off the field and that Peter Bowler, the experienced Australian who had joined us from Derbyshire, was keen to take over the reins. Brian Rose, a club stalwart, England batsman and supporting act in the side that included Ian Botham, Viv Richards, Joel Garner, Peter Roebuck and Vic Marks which filled the previously empty trophy cabinet in the 1980s, was brought back to the club as chairman of the cricket committee, though he carried on his full-time job in the paper industry.

On 1 August, an hour before our championship match with Hampshire was due to start, a funny thing happened on the way to the scrapheap.

I had struggled all season with the same technical problem that had scuppered me in '95. But Rose had decided that the way things were going the best way forward for the club was to back the young players through thick and thin. When Rose rang Peter Anderson at 10 a.m. that day from his office in Watchet, and the club secretary read out the team Andy Hayhurst had selected to take with him into battle, with me not in it, Rose's response was swift and decisive and, to some, quite barmy.

'Sorry, Brian,' Anderson said. 'I'm not sure I quite got that. You want me to do what?'

'Peter, let me say it again,' Rose replied. 'I want you to go into the dressing-room and tell Hayhurst he's dropped, bring in Marcus Trescothick in his place and ask Peter Bowler to take over the captaincy.'

'You've got to be joking,' Anderson said. 'Tell the captain he's dropped? He won't be happy with that. Why can't you do it?'

'Because I'm stuck at work and won't be able to get there until lunch.'

'You're sure this is what you want me to do. If this goes wrong the press will have a field day.'

'Sod the press. I'm chairman of the cricket committee. It's my decision. I'll take full responsibility.'

Peter Anderson tells the story that by the time this conversation ended Andy Hayhurst had not only made it to the middle to toss up with the Hampshire skipper John Stephenson, but that the coin was already in the air.

Even allowing for Anderson's poetic licence, Hayhurst was obviously rather taken aback to receive the news that he had been effectively sacked as captain by the chairman of the cricket committee. As for me, instead of heading off for a 2nd XI match, I was back in the 1sts.

Rose arrived at the ground at lunchtime, preparing to face the local press and talk his way out of a tricky situation. Andy was a top bloke and very popular in these parts, and what had happened and how and when it had happened would take some explaining. Anderson saw Rose's car pull into the car park and ran out to try and head him off.

'What's happened, Pete?' Rose asked. 'Is it bad?'

'Well, Brian, you might say your actions have caused quite a stir. Andy didn't take it too well, as you can imagine, and, er, Peter Bowler got nought.'

'Oh Christ!' said Rose, and then he noticed a smile creep across Anderson's face.

'You jammy bastard,' Anderson said. 'Marcus is 100 not out. He's been bashing it everywhere.'

I finished with 178, my highest score to date.

Chapter 4

THANKS, GUS

*'Is this the same bloke who got all those runs
as a kid?' he asked. "kin 'ell, what happened
to you, then? I thought you were going to
be a player. Any chance of you fulfilling
your potential? Ever?'*

I was sorry to see Andy Hayhurst go when he left at the end of the 1996 season, and just as sad when Bob Cottam was also released. But all of us at Somerset were enthused by the arrival of the man to replace him, the incredibly successful captain of Warwickshire, the recently retired Dermot Reeve.

Dermot was a radical thinker, a livewire who was always questioning and challenging conventional cricketing wisdom. He held certain things as given; firstly, whatever your talent, you had a better chance of employing it effectively if you were super-fit for the purpose. And that meant me. Secondly, very much like Duncan Fletcher later, he wanted players to have more than one string to their bow. And that also meant me. During the time he was in charge he got me fitter and he got me bowling, pretty successfully. The downside was that, at least initially, my batting stalled. I didn't exactly go backwards but I definitely failed to make any significant progress until my second winter in Australia, in 1998–99.

For various reasons, another young batsman was also starting a difficult period, but in the case of Mark Lathwell it was to end eventually in his premature retirement.

I cannot overstate how brilliant Lathwell was. Sure, he found the experience of playing for England unnerving. The rumour goon that when Graham Gooch rang him up to tell him he was being left out after two Tests against Australia in '93, he mumbled something along the lines of 'Thank God for that.' But what a talent – a little bit of genius. Sometimes, watching him from the other end, he would amaze you by doing things you would never have seen coming, like shape to leave a ball outside the off-stump, then, with hands quick as a cobra's strike, blast it through mid-wicket for four. There were occasions when people just could not bowl to him. I know he didn't really enjoy being under the spotlight with England but he loved playing for Somerset. Why Dermot felt he had to try and change his technique I'll never know, but attempting to persuade this utterly unconventional batsman to play in a more conventional fashion was the beginning of the end for Lathwell. He eventually lost his love of the game, then after suffering severe injury, when he tried a comeback he realized his heart was no longer in it, which was a tragedy for him and for English cricket.

One good thing did come out of the 1996 season. I met and started going out with a local girl called Hayley Rowse, who had a lovely smile, lovely eyes and a down-to-earth personality that ideally suited my own. I'd glimpsed her a few times, working in the Tony Price sports shop in town and I knew she was interested in cricket. But the first time I tried to talk to her socially, one night in Dellers nightclub, it was pretty clear she wasn't interested in me at all. I kept trying to catch her eye and pluck up the courage to talk to her, but every time I did she ducked, dived or hid behind one of her mates. I persisted, though, eventually wearing down her resistance and that was the start of a partnership that has since produced two lovely girls and lots of wonderful memories. In later years we shared fantastic times, like the celebrations at The Oval in 2005 and, when the dark times came, I'm not certain I would have survived without her.

Any notion of future success appeared a long way off as I struggled to come to terms with Dermot's idea of turning me into an all-rounder. I could bowl all right, but only medium-pace semi-filth at best. Even though I had managed to take a hat-trick against Young Australia at Taunton the previous summer, and the first of the three was Adam Gilchrist, *Wisden* correctly described the move to employ me thus: 'Trescothick, brought on in desperation to bowl his innocuous seamers ...', a view supported when you consider the identity of my other two Aussie rabbits, Jo Angel and Peter McIntyre.

As for my batting, even accounting for my 178 against Hampshire following the intervention of Brian Rose, I finished the season with 628 runs at 28.54 and at the start of '97 I couldn't get going at all. I opened up with scores of 10, 1, 4, 16 and 4 in the championship, and was quietly taken out of the firing line to play for the seconds for the next six weeks, through June and the start of July.

For all the world it looked as though my decline might be terminal. I was 21 and a half now, the age when, if I'd had what it took, I should have been ready to kick on to the next level. The reality was that I was a second-team cricketer, still seemingly unable to correct a major technical flaw in my batting that had brought my progress to a grinding halt, and being encouraged instead to see myself as a 'bits-and-pieces' all-rounder, bowling medium-pacers and bashing it about a bit down the order.

It would take something pretty special to blow me out of the doldrums, to remind myself and everyone else that my talent was worth renewed attention and support – and then, in a four-day game against Warwickshire 2nd XI at the County Ground, it happened.

I'd taken four wickets in their first innings of 296, but when we were bowled out for 176, me for 21 by the Aussie-bred all-rounder Mike Edmond, their second innings 491 for six declared (Edmond 135) meant we were set a mere 612 to win in a day and a half. What made the idea of winning even more fanciful was that Andy Cottam, a batsman and left-arm spinner and the son of Bob Cottam, had had his right knuckle broken in our first innings and would be unable to hold a bat, let alone use it the second time round.

Even when we finished the third day on 241 for two, with me not out 91 and Mike Burns not out 50, everyone believed the final day would be all about surviving for the draw.

I don't quite know what came over me, to be honest, but from the first ball of the next morning I just launched myself at the bowling. Whatever they bowled and wherever they bowled it, I smashed it.

After an hour or so, my stand of 154 for the third wicket with Burns ended, and it was about this time that someone noticed that there were only ten of us present. Unbeknown to all but a couple of us, Andy Cottam had headed off home to Seaton, about a 45-minute drive away, to drown his sorrows at the fact that he would probably be out for the rest of the season. It had never occurred to him, or anyone else, that he might actually be needed on the field.

Then, as the afternoon session progressed and I put on 144 for the fifth wicket with Luke Sutton, of which he made 34, somebody jokingly said 'We'd better get Peter Anderson to go find Andy ...' and someone else, reading a scoreboard of around 480 for five said: 'Christ, we better had, at that.'

So Anderson was duly dispatched to Seaton to try and track down Andy, tell him what was going on and get him back to the ground just in case. The club secretary had a shrewd idea Andy would be in the pub. His problem was, which one?

There were 16 pubs in Seaton, a popular holiday destination in North Somerset, and Anderson tried most of them. By the time we reached 500 he had looked for Andy in The Fountain Head Inn, The Ship Inn and The Dolphin Long Bar. By the time we scored 520, Anderson had scoured The Barrel of Beer, The Masons Arms, The Harbour Inn and the The Hook & Parrot. No sign of Andy either at The Gerrard Arms, The Kingfisher or The Eyre Court Hotel. Finally, with us now on 550 for five, Anderson found his man, somewhat the worse for a few pints, dragged him into his car and sped off back to Taunton.

Anderson's foot never left the accelerator, while Andy Cottam spent the entire journey with his window open trying desperately to blow away a certain fuzziness.

Back at Taunton, Edmond was in full swing again, and three wickets in quick time left us seemingly stranded at 595 for nine. 'Well tried, Banger,' some of the Warwicks lads congratulated me, as we all prepared to walk off, before the sight of Andy Cottam making his way somewhat unsteadily towards us stopped everyone in their tracks.

'I'm coming, Banger.' he called out to me. 'I'm coming out to bat.'

No one was quite sure if this was supposed to be some kind of gag. But Andy, his hand wrapped in bandages and hanging limply from his side, kept on coming, the match was still on and we needed 17 to win.

'Right, Banger,' Andy breathed all over me. 'You get the runs and I'll just run.' And that is what we did, up to 604 with just eight to get, when I turned a ball from Edmond behind square on the leg-side and Andy called out 'YEESSS ... !!.'

The problem was Andy's judgement was still somewhat impaired, so much so, in fact, that he hadn't noticed the fielder coming round to try and restrict us to the single that would mean he must face the bowling.

'Run two!' I shouted as we crossed, knowing I had to protect Andy from the bowling at all costs. I nearly made it too, but a direct hit from Mike Powell beat me by a foot, run out for 322, my highest ever score in any form of cricket, made from 417 balls, with 53 fours and three sixes.

As a result I was soon back in the 1st XI and the club decided to persevere with me for a couple more seasons at least, and set about finding ways to help me over the hurdles I kept bumping into.

It took another season at home and two winters away for me to finally crack it.

Their first idea was to send me to Australia to get fit and, playing for Melville in Perth alongside Andre Van Troost and Jason Kerr, I did, swimming in the sea, playing golf with my mates and good standard grade cricket against players like Justin Langer and Damien Martyn. The whole experience of fending for myself definitely helped me grow up fast, even though I suffered occasional moments of homesickness and realized I was missing Hayley a lot, especially as the house we all shared in Cottesloe was worse than my first lodgings in Taunton. The thought of sleeping under the stars might appeal to romantics but this was different. I was gazing up at the stars through the holes in my bedroom ceiling and any piece of food that wasn't nailed down was pinched by rats the size of bears.

But I was determined to get through it and the regime instigated by a coach called Peter Wishart made sure we were kept busy. Up at 7 a.m. to do yoga and stretches, breakfast at 8 a.m., then either play or train in the morning, have lunch, train some more in the afternoon and finish off with a race against the great whites in the evening. The day we arrived in Perth we read reports of a shark attack so that kept you on your fins.

While I had some success with the bat, it was only when I returned to Perth the following year to work with Peter Carlstein, the world-renowned batting coach from South Africa whom English counties enlisted every winter to help out their young players, that I was finally able to make the breakthrough.

Peter took a thorough look at my game and confirmed what we already knew, that my strength outside off-stump was also my biggest weakness. The fact was when bowlers put the ball in that area, I never knew when to leave well alone and ended up chasing everything.

Of course, with the power and eye and timing I possessed, if it was my day I would still be able to score plenty. But when it wasn't, or the ball deviated slightly off the seam I was dead in the water. For three years, any one of a number of seasoned county and sometimes Test bowlers would line up to bowl just around or outside off stump with a full array of slips and gulley and just wait for me to play one shot too many. My worst and most humiliating experience came when I batted against the canny Indian pace bowler Javagal Srinath in a Benson & Hedges match. He bowled at me for about six overs and I reckon on average I must have played and missed about four times an over. And by now my feeling of win some/lose some had been replaced by the horrible fear that if I didn't come up with an answer soon I would be finished for good.

Peter and I discussed the issue and he devised a new plan. Instead of saying that's my game, that's what got me this far and if it's risky, so be it, we set about overcoming my instincts and re-training my brain.

Instead of playing the game the bowlers wanted me to play I would say to them: 'No. If you want to bowl out there, that's fine by me. Bowl there as long as you want to but I'm not playing your game anymore.'

One aspect of Peter's training was utterly ruthless, and its roots lay on the beaches of the Caribbean. They say that one of the reasons the great West Indies batsmen of the past were not only fantastic, exuberant strokeplayers but also able to occupy the crease for long periods, was the first law of beach cricket; when you're out, you're out. In those days most of these guys learned their cricket playing on sand flattened and hardened by the sea and when it was your turn to bat you made sure you made the most of it because when you were out you wouldn't get another go until it came round to being your turn again, and with so many kids wanting to play, that might be days.

Peter employed the same principle with the group of us he was coaching now. He would set a maximum time for you to bat in your session, with the bowling machine cranked up to speeds in excess of 90mph, but no minimum. It wasn't 'half an hour each, lads – enjoy yourself' net practice. As soon as you were out against the bowling machine, whether it was first ball or the 1,000th, that was that. Any loose or flabby off-side shot and I would be sitting on my backside waiting for as long as it took for all the other guys in the group to get out as well and for my turn to bat to come round again, and that could take ages. It didn't half concentrate the mind.

A golfer will tell you it takes about 3,000 reps to change a golf swing. It took me about 3,000 balls from bowlers and bowling machines to get me to the point where I could actually make my own conscious decision about whether to play at the ball or not, rather than just see it and try and hit it.

And then, finally, one bright clear, hot Perth day, in the middle of making 180 for Melville against Gosnell, one ball in particular told me I was going to be all right.

I saw it leave the bowler's hand, and I recall watching it so closely that the rest of what followed happened in super slow-motion, even though the ball was travelling around mid-80s mph. I saw it pitch about two yards in front of me and slightly to my off-side and realized I had all the time in the world to make a clear choice whether to play it or not. And in the instant I made my decision to leave it, a small happy bomb went off inside my head. I'd got it. By George, I'd got it.

* * *

In 1999, cricket in England was at a pretty low ebb. England's 1998–99 Ashes trip had ended in a 3–1 defeat. David Lloyd, the coach, had been on a final warning from Lord's after his comments about the bowling action of Muttiah Muralitharan the summer before and, soon after returning from Australia, 'Bumble' announced he would be stepping down at the end of England's involvement in the forthcoming World Cup. The main contenders for his job were Bob Woolmer, the former England Test batsman currently coaching South Africa, Dav Whatmore, Sri Lanka's coach and Duncan Fletcher, the Zimbabwean who had gained a big rep- utation for his work with Western Province in South Africa and later Glamorgan, but not big enough for Simon Pack, the ECB official interviewing him for the job, who greeted him with the words: 'Hello, Dav.'

It was England's turn to stage the World Cup that summer, and that gave me the chance to face Glenn McGrath and Shane Warne for the first time, though I'm fairly certain that, for them, the event did not go down as one to tell the grandchildren. Australia, with Glenn, Shane, Mark and Steve Waugh, Michael Bevan and Shane Lee far and away the best team in the world, came to Taunton for a warm-up match, the highlight of which was when I pulled the best pace bowler of his generation for four. 'Not bad,' I thought to myself. 'Not bad at all.' I looked towards him to see if I might have earned a reaction, a 'good shot, mate', a wink, a growl, anything would have done. Nothing. Not a glimmer.

From the host nation's point of view, the great global celebration of world one-day cricket was a complete cock-up from start to finish. The ICC marketing department decided to hire Dave Stewart from the pop band Eurythmics to write and perform the official tournament song and, when he launched it at Lord's on the eve of the first match between England and Sri Lanka, on 14 May, the effect on the assembled media was profound.

The song, entitled 'Life Is A Carnival', had a passably catchy tune, but the lyrics were something else. At no point was any mention made of anything to do with cricket and the accompanying video, which appeared to be a jumpy-camera home-movie remake of the film *One Flew Over The Cuckoo's Nest*, was unintentionally hilarious. In it, a group of patients from a mental institution dressed in white tunics 'escape' from the medical staff supposed to be looking after them and run off to play a game of cricket. Quite what message Stewart was attempting to convey was beyond everyone. The song and video were met with stunned silence in the press conference, except for a few record company stooges hooting: *'Whoh, whoh, whoh'* at the back of the room. And the fact that England were knocked out of the competition at the end of the group stage, the day before the song was released, somehow said it all.

'Let's get things fully in proportion,' wrote John Etheridge in the *Sun*: 'This was only the most catastrophic day ever for English cricket.' Alec Stewart, who had led England to a Test series victory over South Africa the summer before, was sacked as captain and replaced by Nasser Hussain for the upcoming series with New Zealand. Tim Lamb, the Chief Executive of the Test and County Cricket Board, tried his best. 'The carnival lives on,' he suggested.

There was a modicum of interest in the remainder of the tournament. Bangladesh, still not playing Test cricket, beat the mighty Pakistan in a meaningless match, but it was not until much later that the 33–1 odds against them doing it assumed any significance in the eyes of the wider cricketing public. And after a last ball semi-final between Australia and South Africa, when Allan Donald's run-out prompted accusations of choking, the Aussies duly thrashed Pakistan in a damp squib final at Lord's after Pakistan almost inexplicably elected to bat first in overcast conditions and were skittled out for 132 and lost by eight wickets.

Duncan Fletcher had duly been appointed to take over as coach, but he insisted England would have to do without him for the Test series against New Zealand, as he was committed to finishing the season with Glamorgan. And that is why he was at Taunton at the start of September coaching them against us.

Even though I felt I had made that crucial technical breakthrough in Perth the previous winter, my early season form had been inconsistent again and I went back to the nets for more repetitions. And I have the great England and Middlesex workhorse Angus Fraser to thank for getting me going again, when I batted against him in a championship match followed by a National League 45-over match, from 21–25 July.

Years earlier, Gus had been one of the presentation panel handing over *The Cricketer Magazine* award for the outstanding young cricketer of 1991, after my 4,000-run season. I'd played against him a few times since then and, while you could normally rely on Gus not to have a good word to say about anything or anyone, he'd barely opened his gob.

This time was different and the result was dramatic. His celebrations were fairly low-key when he got me out for eight in the first innings, probably because he thought I was not worth wasting his breath over. But he was in an absolutely foul mood by the time he bowled at me second time round after a 320-mile wild goose chase to London and back. He had been batting as night-watchman at the end of the first day when he received an SOS call from England to get to Lord's asap to be on standby for the second Test.

Almost as soon as he arrived he was told he was no longer required, so he was steaming when he got back to Taunton to resume the match, and when I played and missed a few against him early in my second dig, he was ready to burst.

'Is this the same bloke who got all those runs as a kid?' he asked. ''kin 'ell, what happened to you, then? I thought you were going to be a player. Any chance of you fulfilling your potential? Ever?'

There's only one way I'm going to shut him up, I thought to myself. So I smashed him and his mates all round the park for the next six hours. I finished with 190, my career best, and was only dismissed when run out by a deflection at the non-striker's end. Gus never stopped. 'Come on child prodigy, you know where the edges are, now try using the middle,' and 'Turn the bat over, mate. The instructions are on the other side,' and he grew steadily more purple by the over. Gus was a great bowler for England who defied early injury to become an indispensable line and length merchant. But even in his hey-day it all looked so bloody hard and by this stage of his career he fully lived up to the description by Martin Johnson of the *Daily Telegraph* of running in to bowl 'looking like he'd caught his braces on the sightscreen'. And this day the harder he tried the more knackered he looked and the worse his outlook on life became until it got to the point when even his team-mates were trying to avoid eye contact in case he had a go at them. It was a hot day and the pitch had died and gone to batter's heaven and they all knew it was only a matter of time. Finally, when Paul Weekes let one past him like a matador shepherding a raging bull, then retrieved it from the boundary with a slight smirk on his face, Gus kicked the turf, confronted Weekes with his best double-teapot and asked him 'And what do *you* think is so f***ing funny, you gutless tw*t', and everyone fell about. Gus finished with figures of none for 106 and, after I scored 110 in 97 balls in the one-day match that followed, my undying thanks for helping get me in nick for what turned out to be the turning point of my career.

I'd never met or spoken with Duncan Fletcher before the fateful match between Somerset and Glamorgan at the County Ground, at the start of September. I didn't speak to him during it either. The fact is I never exchanged a single word with England's new coach until April the following year and we've never ever discussed the events of the second day's play to this day.

In later years, when talking in the media and in his autobiography about how I came to be selected, first for England A that winter in Bangladesh and New Zealand, then for the senior one-day and Test sides in the summer of 2000, Duncan always referred to the innings I played that day as the moment he recognized my potential to play at the highest level.

As a team and a club we were experiencing a wide range of emotions. First, on 29 August, we suffered the disappointment of losing the NatWest final, to our local rivals Gloucestershire, who won an unmemorable contest by 50 runs at Lord's. Two days later, we secured promotion to Division One of the CGU National League by beating Glamorgan under floodlights and in front of a full house at Taunton. We made 257 for nine, to which I contributed nought and Rob Turner 50. And some of our supporters took the opportunity of Duncan's first visit after being appointed England coach-in-waiting by reminding him what they thought of Rob. One banner read simply: 'The best wicket-keeper in the country is here.' And he took three smart catches as we bowled them out for 222 to win by 35 runs.

Forty-eight hours later, on 2 September, 20 wickets fell on the first day on a juicy track. Glamorgan bowled us out for 203, we then bowled them out for 113 and then I went out and played if not the best innings of my career so far, without a shadow of doubt the most important, 167 with 25 fours and five sixes, one of which, apparently, damaged a tombstone in St James's churchyard.

I can honestly say the thought that I was on trial in front of the new England coach never entered my head for a moment. And if you believe that, you probably also believe spaghetti grows on trees. But as Duncan later made plain it wasn't just the number of runs I scored that day that impressed him, it was the fact that one of the bowlers I scored them off was the South African all-rounder Jacques Kallis, who I had faced all those years ago in age-group cricket, whom Fletcher coached as a boy at Western Province and who he now rated as probably the best all-round cricketer in the world.

For some reason, whether it was Duncan's pre-conceived plan, or just Kallis's idea to try and shut me down on a still lively pitch, but, running in at a very respectable pace from the old pavilion end, and with Duncan watching every ball from above third man on the new pavilion balcony, he kept trying to bump me and, at that time of my life still being pretty much a compulsive hooker, I hardly left a ball. Instead, I just kept smacking him for four over square leg, with the odd six thrown in.

At the end of a dismal summer for England, when they followed up their poor showing in the World Cup by losing 2–1 to New Zealand even though they took the first Test at Edgbaston, the *Sun* printed a photograph of a burning set of stumps and bails underneath the headline 'English Cricket RIP', and the Board, driven by Brian Bolus, the chairman of the International Teams Group, duly instructed the chairman of selectors David Graveney, new coach Fletcher and the newish captain, Nasser, that the time had come for a clear-out and the introduction of some new faces, starting with the squad for the winter tour to South Africa.

The first time Nasser had ever met Duncan was when they came together in the autumn to begin planning the squad, and Nasser told me later that one of the first names Duncan raised was mine. Nasser said that had he done so a year later he would immediately have gone with Duncan's judgement and picked me, but this time decided against it because he himself hadn't seen enough of my batting nor known enough of Duncan to understand that when he said he had seen something in a player it was almost always something worth seeing.

'Let's keep an eye on him, anyway,' they agreed. So while Michael Vaughan, Chris Adams, Darren Maddy and Gavin Hamilton were taken on the senior tour to South Africa, I was selected for the A team tour to Bangladesh and New Zealand, alongside Rob Turner, who Chris Read pipped for the role of Alec Stewart's understudy in South Africa but who still had many backers to eventually take over as No. 1.

Of the four new bugs in South Africa, Vaughan made the biggest impact, walking out to bat on his debut in Johannesburg with England on 2 for two, which became 2 for four before he got off the mark. He kept his head to make 33 then, after a couple more useful scores, was made man-of-the-match for his 69 in England's successful run-chase in the rain-affected final Test at Centurion Park; the South African captain Hansie Cronje had offered England a target, for reasons that remained his own until the match-fixing scandal broke and the truth of his deal with a bookmaker to ensure any result except a draw finally emerged.

I didn't exactly set Bangladesh or New Zealand on fire, but the memory of events the previous summer in Taunton obviously stayed with Duncan because he insisted I should come back early from Somerset's pre-season training in Cape Town in the spring of

2000 to attend an England training camp at Mottram Hall, Cheshire. Duncan also monitored my early season form, including a painstaking (i.e. long and boring) 105 out of 262 against Leicestershire in May – from 138 for seven Ian Blackwell and I put on 100 for the eighth wicket. All that I needed now was a chance and in late June, it came.

Nick Knight cracked a finger batting in the second Tont against West Indies at Lord's, which Hussain had already missed with a broken thumb, and England needed batting cover for the upcoming NatWest triangular one-day series with Zimbabwe and West Indies. On 2 July 2000 David Graveney dialled my number for the first time and changed my life.

Somerset had been on the road down in Maidstone, playing a four-day championship match against Kent, followed by a 45-over match on the Sunday. I was dog-tired and settled down in the back of Rob Turner's car for the journey back to Taunton with a bag of sweets, ready for some kip, but decided I should probably switch on my phone for the first time that day to check my messages.

'Hello, Tres,' this one began. 'It's Grav. Can you give me a ring, please? Nick Knight's broken a finger. We want to bring you in as cover for a couple of games and see what happens. Can you call me back as soon as you get this?'

Blimey, I thought. And then I thought again. First I wanted to check it wasn't a crank call and second, if it was true, I needed to tread carefully. I knew how desperate Rob was to get a chance himself. I didn't want to start punching the air and going off on one because I knew how disappointed he might feel at being overlooked again.

'Hello, Grav.' I said, as quietly as I could, without whispering. 'It's Marcus here.'

The rest of the conversation was pretty much a blur and afterwards, my first reaction was to ring the world, mum, dad, Hayley,

Eddie Gregg and my mates at Keynsham, everyone. Yet at the same time I didn't want to trample all over Rob's feelings.

I needn't have worried, of course. When I did tell him, Rob was thrilled for me. So I hit the phone big-time and, of course, everyone was massively excited. And all pretence at remaining cool, calm and collected went out the car window. Inside I was jumping up and down that I was going to be given a chance to do what I had dreamed of doing ever since I stood in front of the telly at home copying those far-away figures in white.

Chapter 5

'ISN'T THIS GREAT?'

*'Wow. Bloody brilliant. Knackered. Run to a
standstill, but 79, SEVENTY-NINE, for England!
I loved that drug.'*

'Marcus, can I have a word?' I knew the tone of Duncan Fletcher's voice by now. I had been with the England squad for 48 hours, training and netting, initially at Lord's, then at The Oval, where the first of the matches in the triangular NatWest series with West Indies and Zimbabwe was to be played the next day, 8 July 2000, against Zimbabwe. My first-ever team meeting had come and gone, without the XI being announced, so the moment Duncan spoke I knew what he was about to tell me would either send my spirits skyward or down to my boots. I studied his face to see if I could find any clues. Nothing. On the outside Duncan was the original closed book. On the inside, until you gained his trust, the pages were blank as well.

We were standing outside the Royal Garden Hotel in Kensington, when he pulled me to one side of the group of players with whom I had just returned after dinner.

'Look,' he continued, 'you're playing tomorrow. I just want you to go out there and play your natural game. Play like you've been playing for Somerset and enjoy it.' And a funny thing happened. After all the waiting and wondering, all the uncertainty over whether I would ever hear those words and the occasional utter certainty I never would, I took what he said totally in my stride. Not in an arrogant way, nor blasé. I just thought: 'Duncan's just told me I'm playing for England tomorrow. Isn't this great?'

By the time I walked into our dressing-room at The Oval the following day, I felt somewhat different. I looked around me and, suddenly, instead of a 24-year-old with several seasons of county cricket under my belt, some better than others, I felt like a spotty school kid on *Jim'll Fix It*.

Over there was Graeme Hick, not only my early role model as a player but also my kit model as well. Alec Stewart, who seemed to have been playing for England for about 100 years and was actually about to set a new one-day international appearance record (125) and, in a few weeks' time, play in his 100th Test, was busy making sure everything was in its place; and Darren Gough and my Somerset colleague Andy Caddick were tearing into each other like an old married couple which they carried on doing for the rest of the time they played together for England. Their mainly pretend bickering had actually boiled over in the recent second Test against West Indies at Lord's when they and Dominic Cork had taken all ten wickets between them as the Windies collapsed in their second innings to 54 all out. By taking five wickets Caddick had earned the right for his name and analysis to be printed on the dressing-room honours board showing hundreds and five-wicket bowling spells in Test cricket, something Gough was desperate to achieve but had so far failed to do. Caddy had taken it too far and Duncan felt obliged to step in and pour oil on troubled bowlers, but you could tell all was well because they were back to the usual nagging and points-scoring. Graham Thorpe was there, back after having made himself unavailable for the previous winter tour to South Africa, to spend more time with his young family and suffering from burnout. 'Suffering from what?' I thought at the time. I respected Thorpe as a top batsman and great professional, who didn't? But burnout, what the hell was he on about? Still, I was impressed by the way he was operating around inside his own quiet bubble, ready to flick his switch to the 'on' position the instant he walked onto the pitch and not a moment before. Matthew Maynard was trying not to show how much he was dying for a fag and a young Andrew Flintoff was bouncing around like a 6ft 5 in, 17 and a half stone Tigger, charming and infuriating everyone in equal measure. I wasn't exactly overawed, more like brilliantly and blindingly excited by what was about to happen. But I definitely couldn't calm down so I asked Dean Conway, our one-day physio, if he would give me a head and neck massage to help me try to relax.

By the time the call came through that Alec Stewart, who was filling in as skipper for the injured Nasser, had won the toss and we were batting – or rather *I was batting* – I was trying everything I could to switch into cricket mode. But I was really cacking myself. Then, almost from the second I walked out of the dressing-room with Alec to open the innings, and the roar went up from the capacity crowd, everything felt just right.

'God, isn't this great?' I thought to myself as we walked down the steps to the pitch, our studs crunching on the concrete beneath our boots. 'Isn't this great?' I thought to myself, when we stepped onto the springy outfield for the walk to the middle and the crowd noise cranked up a notch. 'Isn't this great?' I thought to myself when Alec asked me whether I wanted to take strike and I said, 'Yes, if you like'. 'Isn't this great?' I thought to myself when I asked the umpire Ray Julian for middle-and leg guard and, when I hit my first boundary and heard the crowd burst into cheers and applause I thought to myself: 'Isn't this fantastic?'

It was like a drug. That was it. There and then. That was where I wanted to be. That was what I wanted to do.

Through the tens, with Alec, to 20, to 30, to 40 along with Hick, who made 50 and looked very much like God from where I was standing but who also, super-fit, showed everyone inside the dressing-room just how much work I had to do in that respect by running me off my feet in a stand of 106. Past 50, helmet off, arms up, bat raised. Another boundary, another roar from the crowd. More of the drug, please. More, more, more, and, finally out at 79, more, every step of the way back to the dressing-room.

Wow. Bloody brilliant. Knackered. Run to a standstill, but 79, SEVENTY-NINE, for England! I loved that drug.

Sitting in the dressing-room afterwards, the overriding feeling among the players was huge disappointment that we lost, that after we had barely made it past 200, the Zims cruised home by five wickets and that was not good enough. And there I was, struggling badly to stop myself from racing round the room punching the air and all the locker doors, chanting '79, 79, 79!'

Next day, there I was, in all the papers, my face in the photos. Me, in all the papers! And up again and straight on to play the West Indies and Brian Lara … at Lord's. More, 49 this time in the only innings of a rain-ruined match, then 29 against Zimbabwe at Old Trafford (won) and two wickets for seven runs in ten balls, and, at Chester-le-Street on 15 July, my best of the series, 87 not out with Alec Stewart 74 not out, in an unbeaten first-wicket stand of 171 to overhaul West Indies and win by ten wickets. I had made 244 runs in my first four innings and had my first close look at Lara batting. He was not at his best all summer and, later, fell to very good plans in the rest of the Test series, but what hands and what an eye. Isn't this great?

I cannot exactly recall how long Eddie Gregg, my friend from childhood and team-mate in the St Anne's kids' football team, had been ill at this stage. He had been fighting leukaemia for some time and most reports had been relatively encouraging. I had phoned him from time to time and his spirits had always been pretty high. But when I rang him in between innings at Chester-le-Street, it was obvious things were not good. He was having trouble speaking and it was quite distressing to listen to him. I told Eddie I'd call again soon. It was the last time I spoke to him.

In the final against Zimbabwe on Saturday 22 July, I enjoyed my first England victory at Lord's, by six wickets, Then, until about 2 a.m., my first skinful as an England player and, from around 6 a.m., my first belting hangover, when Hayley drove me up to Scarborough to play for Somerset in the National League 45-over match against Yorkshire the very next day. Snoring my head off in the passenger seat, we only stopped to stock up on cans of Red Bull and then my bastard team-mates took one look at me and made me bowl six overs (two for 16) as we skittled out Yorkshire for 141. How I was able to stand when it was our turn to bat, let alone score 12, is anyone's guess. I'm told we won by two wickets.

Stewart batted out of his skin in that series, finishing with 408 runs with two hundreds and 97 in the final. But after the squad was announced for the third Test against West Indies at Old Trafford, due to start on 3 August, most of the talk was about the fact that he and Mike Atherton would both be winning their 100th cap. Some of it was about me winning my first.

Unusually, the selectors had gone public ten days in advance. They had reacted to the fact that, after the first two Tests against West Indies, one lost and the second, a see-saw affair won by two wickets in near-darkness at Lord's thanks to the aforementioned exploits of Caddick, Gough and Cork and excellent second innings batting from the lattermost, England had not managed a Test fifty between them. Hicky had struggled to impose himself again as had Mark Ramprakash, who had been tried as an opener in the summer's first Test action against Zimbabwe, but in his last match, at headquarters, he made just 0 and 2; and that, along with my performances in the NatWest series persuaded Duncan and Nasser to stick with me for the Tests as well, though the first I knew of it was when I saw the announcement of the squad on Teletext.

And now I was cooking with gas. The thrill of what I had done was still buzzing inside me and now, the thought of playing Test cricket ... more, more, more ... and when, the night before the start of the match, someone read out the team and my name was in it, it was all I could do to refrain from shouting out: 'You f***in' beauty!'

Atherton, Trescothick, Hussain (captain), Thorpe, Stewart, Vaughan, White, Cork, Croft, Caddick and Gough ... The only thing still nagging at the back of my mind was when exactly Nasser was actually going to say hello.

After we bowled them out on the first day for 157, with Gough, Caddick, Cork and White never letting them get a moment's peace, I was not merely ready for my turn, I was bursting for it.

In the event, my enthusiasm to get into the battle nearly got the better of me. My only previous memory of playing with Mike Atherton, my opening partner, was in my inglorious debut for Somerset against Lancashire in 1993. I'm sure he didn't know me from a bar of soap and we never got around to discussing how our new partnership might work nor any matters of procedure, like calling, running between wickets etc.

So, when I bounded down the dressing-room steps, through the corridor out onto the pavilion concourse and down the steps towards the gate leading to the field of play, I was somewhat surprised when Athers came sprinting past me, bat first, like a bank robber running for his getaway car, nearly sending me flying into the laps of bewildered spectators.

'Blimey, Ath,' I said to him as we walked out to the middle. 'What was all that about?'

'Sorry, Tres,' he replied, amid the tumultuous applause he was getting from his home supporters celebrating his great milestone. 'I forgot to tell you. I've got this superstition. Whenever I go out to bat with someone at the start of an innings, I've got to be the first one on the pitch.'

It was somehow reassuring to think that M.A. Atherton, captain of Manchester Grammar School, Cambridge University, Lancashire and England (a record 54 times), winner of 100 Test caps, History graduate and real ale expert, was just as bonkers about the 'dark arts' of cricket as the next mug. My superstition? Never you mind.

When he was out for 1, at 1 for one, I didn't know whether to laugh or cry. But there was nothing remotely amusing about what happened next. Nasser (still no word, by the way) made just 10, six of which arrived courtesy of Courtney Walsh stepping on the boundary rope after catching him off Curtly Ambrose, which left us 17 for two; and then Thorpe, returning to the Test arena after easing his way back in the one-dayers, lost sight of a perfect slower ball from Walsh, coming out of the background of the hospitality boxes behind him, ducked and was plumb lbw for nought at 17 for three. And I looked up at the board and realized that I hadn't scored a run.

It was not that I wasn't trying to, but Ambrose and Walsh, while not as quick as in their terrifying pomp, just never gave me anything to hit. Forty-five minutes I had to wait to get off the mark in Test cricket, before I punched one down the ground for two off Franklyn Rose to a mixture of ironic cheers and appreciative applause. I wasn't worried. The absolute priority was to stay in and get a partnership going with someone. Who else, of course, in his 100th Test and on the day the nation was celebrating the Queen Mother's 100th birthday, than Alec Stewart? And what else could he possibly do other than score a century?

He batted exquisitely from start to finish, and still found time to help me concentrate on what I was supposed to be doing as well. We had both reached fifty and had taken England into the lead without losing any more wickets and we weren't far away from ending the day with a healthy advantage when I noticed how close Alec was getting to three figures. What I didn't notice, and, again my lack of experience of playing with these guys meant I had no idea about, was Alec's growing twitchiness as he approached the magic figure. Up in the dressing-room, they knew. Atherton and Hussain and Thorpe and Caddick and Gough and Cork and White, all of whom had played with Alec for all of their careers, they knew. Whenever Alec got into the 90s you had to be ready to run, sometimes at very short notice indeed and occasionally without any at all.

Alec disputes it to this day, but had Jimmy Adams, their skipper and one of the quickest fielders in the world, picked up the ball cleanly and hit the stumps with his throw, as you would have backed him to do eight times out of ten, I would have been gone, run out by a yard at least. Alec wouldn't have known anything about it, of course, so intent was he in charging down the other end for the single to bring up his hundred, but there was utter chaos going on behind him. There I was scrambling and diving to make my ground. And there was Jimmy, taking his eye off the ball, letting it clang off his hands and dribble out in front of him. No pick-up, no throw, no run out. Instead the most extraordinary and prolonged ovation anyone there could ever recall, as the capacity crowd rose to applaud and cheer Alec's win-double of 100 runs in his 100th Test, and applaud and cheer some more. The innings took three hours and the applause and the cheering about the same.

For me, a complete cricket fanatic, it was really something to be out there with Alec, sharing in his and the crowd's joy, but there was one drawback. Every time the commotion died down long enough for me to take my mark and prepare to face the next delivery, someone would start up the applause and cheering again. This happened four times before we finally got the match resumed. In all probability there are people still standing there now, still clapping and cheering, eight years on.

Eventually the noise abated long enough for us to ████ ███ ████ We made it through to the close but were both out quickly the following morning. Though we finished with a lead of 148, Lara then took control with an impeccable hundred, punctuated by a net session during the lunchtime break on day four, and that, along with the damp weather, secured the draw.

My second innings 38 not out encouraged me to tell Caddy afterwards that I was thinking of quitting Test cricket straight away.

'What the f**k for?' he asked me.

'Because I'm averaging 104, and that's better than Don Bradman.'

With ten days off before the fourth Test at Headingley, the first real break since I came into the squad, I took some time to reflect on events thus far. My overriding impression was this: at the time I arrived some of the senior players were undoubtedly feeling the pressure. I felt, particularly among the batsmen, guys like Hick, Ramprakash, Thorpe, Hussain, Stewart and Atherton, that they had become conditioned by years of inconsistency to a somewhat negative mindset. Losing to New Zealand the summer before and the absolute mauling they got in the media had obviously hurt them and by now they were so used to being hammered in print if things didn't go their way that maybe they were not prepared to be bold and take too many risks when risk-taking might have turned out to be the best policy. In short, fear of failure was preventing them from truly expressing their talent and I think they were glad to see someone like me, and other young players like Vaughan and Fred, come in from outside and perhaps take some of the focus and the pressure away from them for a while.

And then we went and absolutely smashed West Indies in the last two Tests. The fourth was crazy, over within two days, and it might have been over even quicker if I had remembered to tell Nasser Hussain something quite important a little earlier than I did.

Batting was hard work from the start. From the Rugby Stand End, the bowlers were making the ball bounce alarmingly and there was plenty of swing and seam movement as well. In West Indies' first innings, Craig White, who was now able to bowl at 90 mph regularly and was already a master of reverse swing, bowled brilliantly in tandem with Darren Gough and his swing from round the wicket into Lara made the best batsman in the world look like a novice. Craig finished with five for 57 as they struggled to 172, then Michael Vaughan made an excellent 76, and Hick, down the order at eight because Caddick had gone in as nightwatchman, a brave 59 to help us to 272 and a lead of exactly 100. When their second innings started we were determined to keep things tight because we knew chasing anything over 150 to win might be extremely tricky. But in the end we never did have to bat again. Gough got amongst them again, adding four wickets to the three he took in the first dig, then, for a while nothing much seemed to be happening. Something had been bugging me all match and suddenly I remembered what it was. 'Why don't you give Caddy a go from the Rugby Stand End?' I suggested to Nasser. 'He was unplayable from that end last time Somerset were here.'

And so he did, for the first time in the match, after tea on day two, and Caddy proceeded to bowl the over of his life. When it started West Indies were in deep trouble at 52 for five. When it ended, they were almost gone at 53 for nine. He took four wickets in six balls, one lbw and three clean bowled and, by the time he finished the innings eight balls later, he had taken five for 14 and they were all out for 61, the lowest Test score at Headingley. 'Thanks for that tip about Caddy,' Nasser said as we ran off in celebration of going 2–1 up. 'But why didn't you let me know earlier?' I'm pretty sure this was the first time he had actually said anything to me at all. And I thought: 'Isn't this great?'

＊　＊　＊

We were playing golf at Sunningdale in a sponsor's event prior to the fifth Test at The Oval when I received the phone call telling me that Eddie was dead.

One of my greatest regrets in life is that I didn't wear a black armband in that final Test match. Had Eddie Gregg died later in my career I would have done so without thinking twice, but, at the time, as the new kid in the dressing-room I felt a little embarrassed about the idea of making such a public show of my feelings. I also reasoned that if I did make this gesture I would then have to explain why and it all just seemed not quite right to me. I spoke to his dad, Alan, and told him that if I ever did manage to make a Test hundred I would dedicate it to Eddie, and, while it would not be true to say that was uppermost in my thoughts when the match began with Atherton first, then me, walking out to bat after winning the toss, it was in there somewhere.

Batting with Atherton always did help me keep focused. If ever I felt tempted to revert to instinct and try and bash the ball everywhere, one look at the bloke at the other end blocking the crap out of it soon put me back on the straight and narrow, and anyone could see how determined he was to make a big contribution here. There had already been rumours that, because of his dodgy back, he would probably retire after the following summer's Ashes series, and Athers might even have been thinking this could be his last Test here. And he had another reason to do well. It wasn't just that

England hadn't beaten West Indies in a Test series for 31 years, it was also that Ath had harrowing memories of one of those defeats in particular, when, in his first series as skipper, back in 1994, he had gone in to bat in the second innings of the Trinidad Test with his side needing 194 to win, got out for nought and watched from the dressing-room as Ambrose blew them away for 46 all out. Batting with him in this mood, relaxed but utterly determined, helped calm me down as well and we put on 159 for the first wicket, which, the way our bowlers were bowling and they were currently batting, should have gone a long way to securing a winning position. A measure of how fragile a side we still were, however, was that it took a second innings ton from him to make sure, because apart from us two, no one else managed to make fifty.

After lining up to pay tribute to Walsh and Ambrose, playing their final Tests before retirement, Caddick finished them off and we doused the place in champagne.

I was tired, but still looking forward to finishing off the season with Somerset, when Duncan told me he wanted me to stop right then. I was not convinced. After facing Ambrose and Walsh for the best part of two months I quite fancied making some runs against some less stingy bowling attacks at the County Ground. But Duncan insisted and, later that winter when I was dragging myself around Sri Lanka, I'm glad he did.

Winning the Professional Cricketers' Association Player of the Year award at the Royal Albert Hall a few weeks after the end of the season gave me my first chance to make a public tribute to Eddie, and then all my thoughts for the time being were back on the winter tours to come. First up was a 12-day trip to Nairobi for the ICC Knockout Trophy and we were duly knocked out as soon as we played a major Test playing nation, South Africa. It was pretty dismal, but one thing did stick in my mind. The following day, back at the hotel for a debriefing, Duncan gave us a good shoeing, and even went so far as to ask us to consider the subject of our commitment. Some of the more experienced pros seemed unimpressed, but Duncan just nailed any dissent in the room by citing the example of Jacques Kallis.

Duncan's point was all about just how dedicated he expected us to be while he was in charge. The day before, Kallis had been outstanding against us, taking two for 26 in his eight overs as well then just 102, then leading them to victory with the bat, making 78 not out. Yet when he got back to the hotel Duncan had seen him pounding away on the treadmill in the gym for half an hour as if he had done nothing all day, while we were all sitting around by the pool unwinding with a few beers. The point was well made and planted a seed in the minds of one or two of us.

There was very little time to do anything other than resolve to improve fitness at the very least before we were off to Pakistan for the next tour. By the time we came home, just before Christmas, we had been through an experience that had almost everything.

By now the pattern of early-tour blues I experienced every time I went abroad with England was well established but manageable. For the first week I would be awful, sleep badly, feel agitated and miss home like mad and then, as soon as the cricket started, I would be able to put those feelings to one side and throw myself into playing or training. It was as though my sheer love of cricket, the simple thrill I never lost of hitting a ball with a bat and everything else that went with it, would conquer all ills. It also helped me no end that, in our opening warm-up match, against the Sind Governor's XI in Karachi, I made my first century for England, and we were straight into a three-match one-day series which, though short, was crammed full of incident.

We won the opener, in Karachi, with Freddie batting magnificently for 84 to help us reach a stiff target of 304. In the second, at Lahore on 27 October, we were first befuddled by Shahid Afridi's leg-spinners – he took five for 40 but was then reported by ICC referee for a suspect action – then he bashed 61 in no time, and our evening was made complete when we were attacked by a swarm of insects, attracted by the humidity and the floodlights if not by the standard of our bowling and fielding. Gough swallowed a mouthful when he ran up to bowl, and the bowlers appealed at their peril. All of them wore sunglasses and White bowled in a cap. One of the little sods climbed up the middle stump and paused for a close-up on the stump camera, and, to millions of horrified TV viewers, the magnifying effect made him look like the cockroach that ate Cincinnati. In the last match in Rawalpindi, again won by Pakistan, the main distraction was acute physical pain. So many spectators had arrived intent on getting into the ground without tickets, even though the ground was full of those who had them, that the local police decided to try and disperse them with tear gas. The trouble was the wind picked it up and blew it right across the field just as Thorpe and me were trying to dig us out of the mire. Nasser had already been given out to the worst lbw decision of the century when Wasim Akram's slower ball pitched about two foot outside his left-stump and had chosen to release his frustration by smashing in the glass door of the dressing-room fridge with his bat.

When the gas came it felt like all the saliva had been removed from your mouth and throat and then your eyes stung like someone had thrown salt into them. It was bloody horrible.

Afterwards, and prior to the start of the Test series, Duncan spoke to me and asked me if I would be prepared to join the tour management committee alongside himself, Nasser, Alec and Gough. I was pretty taken aback, but it seemed a reasonable idea. Duncan wanted the views of all the players to be heard, even the new boys, and this would give me a chance of being their voice. Nasser particularly wanted me to keep an eye on any possibility that a player might be suffering from too much mickey-taking. I loved getting involved in dressing-room banter, even though I took my fair share of stick. But I'd spoken to him about my feelings as regards bullying. If ever I felt it was going too far I hated it and would often try and intervene. Nasser wanted me to take responsibility for this in our dressing-room and I was happy to agree.

By the time the first Test started, a fortnight later on 15 November, I would realise what I had let myself in for.

Just prior to coming out to Pakistan and then again on arrival we had been briefed on two important subjects. First, the issue of match-fixing was very much alive. A report by a Pakistan judge, Justice Al Quayyum, had named a number of Pakistan players as possibly being implicated. Secondly, a report by the Delhi Criminal Investigation Bureau into allegations made by a man called MK Gupta, an Indian bookmaker who claimed he had paid various international cricketers for seemingly innocent information over the past few years, was about to be published. The other issue was our behaviour. This was the first time England had played in Pakistan for 13 years, since the infamous row on the field between the England captain Mike Gatting and the Pakistan umpire Shakoor Rana. So it was absolutely vital that the series was played without any kind of incident. The Pakistan people had been affronted by Gatting's comments about Shakoor and the slightest thing might spark big trouble.

If anyone in the party hadn't been paying attention, from the moment we arrived at the Pearl Continental Hotel in Rawalpindi at the end of October to prepare for our first first-class match against the Pakistan Cricket Board's Patron's XI, they were now. I noticed a strange mood around the place when I came down to breakfast on the first morning. It didn't take long to find out why.

Alec Stewart had been named in the Delhi police report as one of those international stars, and the only England player, who MK Gupta claimed he had paid money to for information; £5,000, to be precise. It was a bombshell none of us had been expecting. When the Quayyum report had been released, Sir Ian MacLaurin, the ECB chairman, said that any player named should be suspended from all cricket until his innocence was proven, or otherwise, and that applied to Pakistan's Wasim Akram, Waqar Younis and Inzamam ul Haq. Inevitably, the media were asking why this should not now apply to Alec. He stayed at the hotel for most of the match, rested in advance of the news breaking out, but you could see the whole thing had a terrible effect on him. He just looked pale and unwell for the entire time we were there. We all believed him to be totally innocent, but the strain must have been almost intolerable. He spent all week defending his integrity but it took him a long time to recover and by the end of the year the knock-on effect nearly brought his England career to a premature end.

And then, in the next match against the catchily named North-West Frontier Province Governor's XI, Caddy behaved as though he must have been staring idly out of the window during our pre-tour reminder about best behaviour.

I made 93 in our first innings, just failing to reach my first first-class hundred for England, but we were well on top and on the way to bowling them out cheaply in their second when Caddy had an appeal for a catch at the wicket turned down. He went too far, with the umpire Sajjad Asghar claiming afterwards he had made derogatory comments 'about my country'. Caddy said that was a misunderstanding, although he later apologised for his outburst.

Nasser appeared on TV afterwards to defend Caddick with what some thought was rather too much passion. Little did anyone outside the dressing-room know the reason why. Some time in that second innings Graham Thorpe shelled a pretty straightforward catch at slip. When Nasser had a go at him, Thorpe reacted by hurling the ball towards him, which made the skipper even more annoyed. Later in the dressing-room the two of them squared up and a five-minute, full-on, massive row ensued, with fingers jabbed in chests, insults exchanged and kit everywhere. Nasser wanted our level of intensity to be as high as possible all the time, Thorpe's attitude to practice matches was less about the match and more about the practice. I just sat there in the corner thinking: 'Oh my God. We haven't even started the Tests and this team is falling to bits.

But the incidents did seem to help us all let off steam, and from then on the team pulled together so strongly that, after drawing the first two Tests in Lahore and Faisalabad, our resolve to leave after the last in Karachi unbeaten was massive.

In order to do so, after conceding 405 in the first innings, despite my first and, amazingly, only wicket for England – Imran Nazir, in a spell of one for 34 off fourteen overs at first change – Atherton had to be at his obdurate best.

By this stage of the tour I had realised that if I was going to be playing my cricket at this level and in these conditions I was going to have to get much, much fitter. The penny finally dropped when I went for a run around the outfield with Phil Neale, our operations manager, and I was blowing out of my arse to keep up with him, even though he was old enough to be my dad. Phil had played many years for Worcestershire and as a footballer for Lincoln City and had always kept himself in shape, but this was ridiculous.

By now I was knackered, pure and simple, so watching Athers bat for nine hours and 38 minutes to score 125 from the dressing-room couch was just what I needed. When we bowled them out for 158 on the final afternoon – Ashley Giles spinning out Inzy the previous evening had been the breakthrough and he finished the series with 17 wickets – leaving us 176 in a minimum of 44 overs, Ath's marathon feat of skill and endurance became more than mere defiance.

I had just about enough energy to make 24 in our run chase, but then Thorpe and Hick brilliantly took over. The Pakistan skipper Moin Khan tried every trick in the book to slow up the game; he knew what time it got dark in Karachi at this time of year and the shadows were lengthening fast. Soon enough the sun dipped behind the stands. We were still scoring at a good enough rate, with Thorpe and Hick running them ragged, but it looked as though we were bound to run out of time, balls, and light.

Yet the umpires, Steve Bucknor and Mohammad Nazir, clearly miffed by the delaying tactics, seemed determined to carry on, come what may.

In the dressing-room we were all going crazy. As per usual cricket superstition dictated that no one was allowed to move from their position. Nasser was doing his nut about the time-wasting, worst of which was the bowlers changing from round the wicket to over again ball after ball. It was taking so much time for the groundstaff to wheel the sightscreen into position every time the bowlers changed over, that Matthew Hoggard ran out of the dressing-room and started pushing it himself. And when Hick was out and Nasser went in with only a few needed to win, the light was all but gone. Trying to spot the whereabouts of the ball was nigh on impossible. The only clue you got was when one of the fielders moved and in the end it was so dark nobody did.

I had no idea where Thorpe's winning runs had come from until we watched the finale on TV much later. But when they did we celebrated in somewhat surreal fashion, by spraying bottles, grand-prix style, all over the dressing-room. No one seemed to mind much that they contained 7Up and Coke – no alcohol allowed, of course – but there wasn't a drop of British Airways champagne left when we arrived home the day after.

Playing for England? Another bottle of that, please.

Chapter 6

ONE HUNDRED FOR EDDIE

*'I looked at the scoreboard, just to make sure
no one had miscounted and there it was
— M E Trescothick 100 ... I raised my eyes to the sky
and said quietly: "Cheers, Eddie."'*

My deep satisfaction at our victory in Karachi was tempered by the knowledge that I had a massive amount of work still to do to establish myself in the England side and stay there.

Clearly, my fitness was lacking, but, against Pakistan, so was my batting. I was fine against the quicks, but I had struggled against top-class spinners like Saqlain Mushtaq and Danish Kaneria, and, on the upcoming tour to Sri Lanka, starting in February 2001, I was about to face one of the most dangerous who ever lived, Muttiah Muralitharan. I knew full well that the way I batted against him in the next few months would decide whether I would be given the chance to play against Australia in the 2001 Ashes series in England. And Shane Warne.

Duncan knew how much needed to be done. And he believed he had developed just the method to help me, his 'forward press'. Duncan's theory was that, when batting against spinners, if you made a small but positive move onto the front foot before the ball was released, you would put yourself in a better position to go either fully forward or fully back depending on the length of the ball. It was unorthodox and some batsmen never really got on with it, preferring instead to stick to their own tried and trusted technique against the turning ball, but for those who mastered it Duncan's explanation made sense: 'If you are going to catch a bus, it is better to arrive at the bus stop early enough to read the number on the front, rather than at the last moment when you have no choice but to get on and find out later if it is going where you want to go.'

As I didn't really have a technique to speak of, except to sweep as much as possible, and, failing that, slog, I was the perfect blank canvas for Duncan to work on. I had tried putting the theory into action during practice in Lahore, but I hadn't managed to get to grips with it all. I 'pressed', then simply got stuck.

Now, when we got to Sri Lanka, I told Duncan I wanted to have another go. He agreed and I threw myself into it. I was glad of it for two reasons. First and obviously, I liked playing at this level so much I wanted to do it for years to come. Second and less so, I had my first real experience that the feeling of uneasiness at being away from home was more than the usual mix of run-of-the-mill homesickness, jet lag and sleepless nights. I didn't know quite what the problem was; all I did know was that the feeling wasn't right. It was just a shadow of what was to come later, but chilly enough and Nasser picked up on it, as a matter of fact, though in all probability he wouldn't have had a clue he did. After practice on one of the first few days of the tour in Colombo, he came up to me asked: 'How you feeling, Tres? You don't seem yourself.'

'I'm fine,' I told him. 'I just need to get into the tour, that's all.'

That I did, spending so much time in the nets with Duncan that the other lads started asking me if he was my dad. Duncan's lad they called me. Some have speculated that he invested so heavily in me in terms of hours and energy because it was perceived that I was his pick and therefore his reputation for being able to identify talent and nurture it rested on my becoming a success with England. Knowing Duncan I'm pretty sure all he wanted was the best for me and therefore the team. Seeing him shun the limelight on so many occasions in future years when his England teams won series after series, there is no way on earth you could describe Duncan as a glory-hunter. In fact, his painful shyness was often misinterpreted as plain rudeness, and sometimes vice versa, by the way.

But he could coach, don't worry about that. I pressed and pressed again, and suddenly it all clicked into place, like it had with Peter Carlstein in Perth.

The second aspect of my batting that required improvement was my concentration when nearing a century. In county cricket I had often had trouble in the nervous 90s and, meeting up with the England sports psychologist Steve Bull for the first time, he recommended I try and practise batting through them by creating the scenario in my mind. Starting a net as though I was on 90, I would try to play my way through the next ten runs, a single here, two there, maybe a boundary if the shot was on and risk-free, so that I would know how to approach the task next time, if ever, I got within sight of three figures.

I have no hesitation in saying that I owe the first of my 14 Test hundreds, in the shadow of the old Dutch fort on the headland jutting into the crystal blue waters of the Indian Ocean in Galle, and probably quite a few of the rest as well, to Duncan, with a bit of Bully thrown in as well.

The day I was able to keep my promise to Alan Gregg, Eddie's father, 24 February 2001, the third day of the first Test against Sri Lanka, was bloody boiling hot from the start. We had spent the best part of six sweltering sessions in the field watching Marvan

Atapattu score a double-ton and Aravinda de Silva 106 and only once during that time did our mood briefly lift, when Caddy tried to sledge de Silva with hilarious consequences. 'Harry', well known on the county circuit playing for Kent as one of the most pleasant and inoffensive blokes of all time, had just cut a shortish ball for four over the covers and Caddy let him have a barrage. 'F***in' 'ell, mate,' he began, as he always did, in his unmistakeable Kiwi twang, 'are you ever going to learn to play that shot properly?' To a man, we winced because we knew what was coming next and Caddy certainly didn't let us down. He bowled the exact same ball and de Silva leant back and hit it harder than I have ever seen a cricket ball hit before, straight along the deck, to the cover boundary.

'You're right, Caddy,' de Silva called back, 'but maybe, if you keep bowling those long-hops, I'll get the hang of it in the end.'

The heat and humidity were so energy-sapping I drunk gallons of energy drinks to keep me going, with the unfortunate result that by the time I got back to my room to sleep I found I was caffeined-up to the eyeballs.

I was still wide-awake when, after they finally declared on 470 for five, I had my first chance to put the forward press to the test, as Murali grabbed the new ball to open the bowling with Chaminda Vaas. It was the first time I had ever faced the snake-eyed assassin and before then I had considered the idea that he put so much spin on the ball that you could actually hear it coming as nothing but one of those old cricketer's tales. But I swear it really is true. I actually did hear the thing fizzing as it burned a hole in the air on its journey towards me. The eerie noise, like a whistling mosquito, only added to the hypnotic overall effect Murali had on the best batsmen in the world. And this was before he had even thought of inventing the doosra, the ball that looked like an off-break but which, on landing, turned the other way, like a leg-break.

Controversy over his action had dogged him throughout his career and we did some practice against our off-spinner Robert Croft just chucking the ball from 19 yards, not because we thought Murali did it as we were quite happy to accept the findings of the ICC in that regard, it was just that no other bowler alive could turn the ball as much as he did, simply by bowling it. Actually, as time passed, I grew to appreciate that views in the dropping room on whether he chucked the ball tended to depend on whether he had just got you out and for how many.

Soon enough I settled into my plan; a slight forward movement then pause, then spot the length. If the length was good I played straight on the basis that the top-spinner or arm-ball would hold its line, and the off-spinner would turn so much it was bound to go safely past the outside edge. I would be patient, forget the sweep completely, but if the ball was up I would drive straight or punch for singles and if it was short enough I would sway back and cut and pull. The fact was I couldn't pick Murali's different deliveries for love nor money, but, with Duncan's expert help, I had developed a plan to play according to the law of probability and it worked. When I got to the 90s I then tuned myself into the practice sessions suggested by Steve Bull and flicked on the memory switch.

Murali helped no end when he dropped one short and let me pull him through mid-wicket for four to get to 99. And then, of course, standing one run away from a Test century for England, the biggest moment in my career, and probably my life, the bloody plan disappeared into thin air. Murali bowled the next ball in about the same area, but slightly fuller, I started to go back for the pull, realized it wasn't short enough, panicked, then sort of shovelled my bat at it in a now quite desperate attempt to turn it into the leg-side for a single. In the end, hours of work in the nets came down to closing my eyes and hoping for the best and when I opened them again I saw the ball squirt sideways out off the leading edge at a comfortable catching height towards backward point on the offside. Only there was no backward point, so I ran and Robert Croft ran past me and I'd done it.

I looked at the scoreboard, just to make sure no one had miscounted and there it was – ME Trescothick 100.

I raised my bat towards Hayley, sitting in the main stand, and to the dressing-room, then raised my eyes to the sky and said quietly: 'Cheers, Eddie.' And soon, at the close of play, I was enjoying the moment with two more of our mates from school who had come all the way over to watch me play, Lee and Mark Cole. We sank a lot of beers that night in memory of a good friend.

Later, when I rang home to speak to mum and dad, I noticed dad didn't sound too well. He didn't say anything himself but, when I spoke to mum afterwards she told me why. With a substantial time difference between Galle and Bristol, they had both come down to the living room to watch the cricket on Sky in the middle of the night, well before the central heating fired up to battle the February chill. Dad had dressed for the cold, wrapped in pyjamas, socks and a thick dressing-gown and mum had also wrapped up warm. The difference was that, because dad was educated in the ways of cricket superstition, when the central heating system came on and mum went upstairs to change into normal clothes, as long as I was batting dad had to sit there in what he was wearing and not move. By the time play ended for the day in Galle he was sweating like a horse. He had obviously been on the point of heatstroke when we spoke.

The next day I was finally out for 122, but a combination of Murali's brilliance and some shocking umpiring decisions did for us, all out 253. We counted seven bad ones in the match, of which the worst was suffered by Alec Stewart, leg before to a ball from Sanath Jayasuriya, bowling left-arm over, which pitched a yard outside legstump. And though the 'press' worked for me again in the second innings, helping me make 57 as we followed on, we lost by an innings and some.

Nasser's pre-tour assessment, that we were 'a mediocre side but improving' may have been his way of dousing expectations after our win in Pakistan. But it suddenly sounded a bit too close for comfort and, after months of poor form with the bat, his own position in the team and as skipper were under scrutiny, especially as it was clear Michael Vaughan's promotion could not be delayed a moment longer than necessary. And now, in the second Test in Kandy, Nasser showed exactly what he was made of and exactly what he wanted from his team. He had some luck, or rather, a lot. The umpiring by the local man B C Cooray and the South African 'slow-death' Rudi Koertzen was even worse than in Galle, with something approaching 15 errors in total, but, unlike in Galle, almost all of them went in our favour, prompting a local newspaper headline claiming 'BC bats for England,' and rumours that he had received death threats and his house had been attacked, both of which, happily, turned out to be nonsense.

The unfortunate BC first gave Nasser not out to clear bat-pad catches twice on his way to a pretty ugly 109, and Hicky was also reprieved twice by him before he had got off the mark in the first innings. The second, bowled Jayasuriya for 16, turned out to be his last in Test cricket. Hick, my inspiration as a teenager, played 65 Tests and enjoyed many good days. But did his record in international cricket do justice to his immense talent?

There is no doubt we were up for a fight, and on day three, so were the Sri Lankans. Trying to peg back our first innings lead of 90, they found themselves two for 2 when Caddy, who along with Gough and White bowled really well and really fast throughout, drew Jayasuriya into a big booming drive. The ball flew like a rocket to third slip where Thorpe took off and clung onto an amazing catch. But when Sanath stopped about three quarters of the way back to the main stand, we knew something was up. Their players had seen on the TV replays that Sanath had actually smashed the ball hard into the ground, and gestured to him to stay put, but with no way within the rules of using the TV evidence to prove his case, he ended up registering his 'disappointment' in spectacular fashion, taking off his helmet and hurling it into the turf at his feet. That provoked uproar among the travelling Barmy Army on the upper tier of the stand. They then started booing him and, for a few moments, it looked as if Sanath might actually invite one or two of them down to sort it out man to man.

Later the already fractious mood boiled over again with Atherton and Sangakkara blowing up on the pitch and afterwards, along with a fine against Sanath of 60 per cent of his match fee, these two were issued a severe reprimand by referee Hanumant Singh. So the final acts of the drama, with us needing 161 to win in the fourth innings, were played out in an atmosphere that wouldn't have seemed out of place in a spaghetti western, which was perfect for Thorpey, as cool as Clint Eastwood, to go out and nudge and nurdle 46 precious runs and for White and Giles to take us home by three wickets.

How knackered were we when we got to Colombo to play in the third and now deciding Test just four days later? Gone at all levels, as were they. We traded first innings scores around 250 in the first innings, with me getting out in ridiculous fashion when I smashed a short ball towards the boundary, looked towards the rope to see whether it had gone for four or six, then heard Russell Arnold at short leg screeching like a banshee. Upon inspection, he had found the ball in the billowing sails of his loose-fitting shirt, grabbed it and claimed a perfectly legitimate, if utterly bizarre catch.

The exhaustion of all concerned manifested itself on the third and last day, 17 March, when 22 wickets fell at the Sinhalese Sports

Club in absolutely scorching heat, many of them, including mine, to very tired-looking shots indeed. Years earlier, nearly to the day in March 1993, Duncan's namesake Keith Fletcher had seen his side become the first England team to lose a Test in Sri Lanka and commented afterwards: 'It is very nearly too hot here, at this time of year, for Europeans to play cricket.' To me, it was very nearly too hot for *any* human life to survive.

Vaughan was a tad fresher than the rest of us, coming in for Hick, and he made our second top score next to the amazing Thorpe, who dragged up 113 from his very essence. Then the bowlers, again huge in the inferno, skittled them out for 81. Giles and Croft shared 11 between them in the match and Caddick and Gough were also superb. And Thorpe was just brilliant in calming things down when it looked like we might keel over before we reached the finish line, making an unbeaten 32 out of 74 to win, with six wickets down. He virtually had to be carried off the field at the end and spent the rest of the evening battling dehydration.

We celebrated our fourth series win on the trot, and our second successive victory in hostile conditions in rather more appropriate fashion than we had done in Karachi, and the Barmy Army caught our mood. *'Bring on the Aussies'* they sang all evening, and the theme from *The Great Escape*, and how good did all that sound?

* * *

We simply had nothing left with which to contest the one-day series that followed. But it only took a short break at home to perk me up for the start of the 2001 domestic season with Somerset, during which a combination of finally batting on pitches where the ball came onto the bat and my new technique allowed me to score millions. On 7 May in our Benson & Hedges Cup win over Gloucestershire at Taunton I hit my fourth century in six innings, and my third in that competition in seven days.

We won the first of two Tests against Pakistan, at Lord's, thanks mainly to Caddick and Gough, who put memories of the previous season's spat to bed as they both celebrated Darren's first five-for at Lord's and the Yorkshireman's 200th Test wicket.

To me, Goughy was the most instinctively clever bowler I ever played with. In later years he may have suffered with his dodgy knee and then carved a niche for himself as the first cricketing champion of *Strictly Come Dancing* before Mark Ramprakash; he might have come across as a bit of a showman from time to time; and he was prone to the occasional gaffe, as in 'Why do they call me rhino? Because I'm as strong as an ox'. But he was also quite simply one of the best and most consistent bowlers in the world, not express pace, but skiddy and quicker than he looked. Where Caddick, while brilliant if the pitch was right for his back-of-a-length bowling, only really had one way to bowl, Gough could switch and change to suit the conditions. He seemed to have a plan and a ball for every batsman he came up against. He knew just when to bowl a slower ball or a bumper. In the way he was always probing for a weakness and, if he found it knew exactly how to exploit it; in the way he was always at you, he made me think of how Shane Warne might have operated had he been a pace bowler rather than the best leg-spinner the world has ever seen. It was no coincidence that the pair of them got on so well.

By the time we played in the second Test against Pakistan, at Old Trafford, where Alec took over as captain in Nasser's absence through injury, Vaughan made his first Test hundred (120) in a first innings stand of 267 with Thorpe (138) and I was helped to my second Test ton in our second innings by Athers. Whether it was eyesight or merely my lack of ability, I found myself having a lot of trouble dealing with the reverse-swing of Wasim, Waqar and Abdul Razzaq. So Ath, who could see it a mile off, suggested the following system. When he was batting at the non-striker's end he would

look closely at which way round the bowler was holding the ball in
his hand, a sure sign of which way it would swing. If the ball was
going to swing in towards me, he would hold the bat handle in his
right hand as he faced me, indicating the ball would be moving
from my left to right, and vice versa. The result was my second Test
ton and my first at home, 117 in the second innings, earning me a
spot on the dressing-room honours board. It was a brilliant plan, so
brilliant that, rather carelessly, and to Atherton's wry amusement,
I couldn't stop myself from sharing it with the nation in my newspaper column for the *Mail On Sunday* the following week, with rele-
vant details and diagrams. I still had a lot to learn about dealing
with the media, but, amazingly, this eventually turned out to be
only my third most controversial offering of the season.

Somehow, on that final day, we contrived to slither from 213 for
four on my dismissal to 261 all out and lost a match we should have
drawn without thinking, or even possibly won.

The trouble was in our approach to being set a target of 370 in
112 overs. In later years, with other characters in the side, I believe
we would have gone for it from the start and given ourselves a
good chance of getting there. Now though, the mindset of 'what
we have, we hold' was still ingrained deep in the psyche of some
of this group of players and in the mindset of the captain, so used
were they to being burned for failure in their earlier years. Instead
of thinking 'Right, 370 to win the game', we were thinking 'Christ,
we've got to bat all day to save this.' We'd made up our minds
before the innings started that we would have to scrap for the draw
that would secure us a series victory. Who knows if that thinking
made a difference? Maybe they were just better than us on the
day, but it didn't take much for our balloon to be pricked. Afterwards I recall thinking that, despite everything we had achieved in
the previous year – wins over West Indies, Pakistan, and Sri Lanka
– this stupid collapse meant we were still not quite strong enough

or confident enough when the pressure was on us to express our-selves freely and positively; thinking that people were still too insular and fearful, that individuals were still more interested in themselves than the team and that we had to change that mentality or we would end up going nowhere.

And now we had to play Australia, experts in the theory and practice of doing your head in.

*   *   *

The world champions arrived in England in early June with Steve Waugh at the helm and war on their mind, or rather *The Art of War*, by the ancient Chinese warlord Sun Tzu, which their coach John Buchanan used as his coaching manual. No prisoners were to be taken and anyone or anything that stood in their way was to be brushed aside. And the talking started almost as soon as they got here. I can't recall who said or wrote it but one of them described me as being about to find out my honeymoon period was over and the words stayed with me for the rest of the summer.

The highlights of our triangular one-day series with Pakistan and Australia were the 69 I scored against the Aussies at Bristol on 10 June and the 137 I made against Pakistan at Lord's two days later, though both matches were lost. In the immediate aftermath of making that hundred at Lord's I was in a pretty weird mood. I'd enjoyed the innings hugely, because it was a bloody battle from start to finish and I made my first one-day ton for England, but as time passed the realization grew that, in the end, I had probably cost us a victory I had done so much to earn.

Chasing 243 to win, I started by running out Nick Knight for one. We then lost Alec for four and Vaughan for a duck and were 36 for three when Middlesex's Owais Shah came in and played brilliantly on his home ground for 62. He was out at 196 for four, then three more wickets fell in quick succession and, at 205 for seven, it was down to me, with only Caddy, Gough and Alan Mullally for company. When the final over began we were 234 for eight, with nine runs needed and two wickets left. I looked up at Caddy at the other end, with the absolutely terrible Mullally to come, and considered my options. I plumped for going for broke and tried to launch Saqlain into the Mound Stand for my third six of the innings. I knew I was cooked the moment the ball left the bat because I just hadn't got enough of it. I watched in despair as Shahid Afridi positioned himself for the catch at mid-wicket, then in hope when Shoaib Malik, who hadn't heard his call, ran straight into him and knocked him flying. Sadly for me, Afridi got up holding the ball in his hands, Caddy was out stumped soon after and we lost by two runs.

I resolved, there and then, that if I ever found myself in a similar situation I would make sure I finished the job. But any disappointment at not doing so here was soon replaced by embarrassment at finishing the tournament with scores of 15, 0 and 0, the last one, bowled McGrath, and at some comments I made in my *Mail on Sunday* column. Bad behaviour by certain sections of the crowd, sadly mainly the young Pakistan supporters, had led to nasty incidents of pitch invasions, including an assault on Nick Knight. When Australia's Michael Bevan, standing on the Lord's balcony at the end of their NatWest final win against Pakistan, was hit on the side of the head by a full lager can thrown from the crowd in front of the pavilion, the fall-out was hard to contain. And I didn't help by going into print to suggest, reasonably I thought, that anyone caught behaving like that at a public sports event should be heavily fined and 'banged up for a night in the cells.' Thank you, Nelson Mandela.

My columns were becoming unmissable, by now. But the best was yet to come.

The prospect of taking on Australia was exciting but incredibly daunting. We were up against it from the start, with injuries removing Thorpe for four Tests, Hussain for two and Vaughan for all five, and it took Waugh & Co. just 11 playing days to achieve the three wins they needed to retain the little urn, once again.

Initially, I allowed the 'honeymoon' comments to worm away in my head. As I prepared for my first Ashes experience, at Edgbaston, I wasn't thinking about facing Glenn McGrath, but GLENN F***ING McGRATH, which is probably why, after Atherton called me for a leg bye from the only ball he bowled me, I edged the first one I received from Jason Gillespie to Shane Warne for a two-ball duck and they said thanks for coming.

We made 294, thanks bizarrely to Caddy and Alec Stewart putting on 103 for the tenth wicket. The pressure was off in the second innings, but only because Steve Waugh, Damien Martyn and later, brutally, Adam Gilchrist all made hundreds in their 576, and their lead of 282 meant we were doomed. So I relaxed and hit an encouraging 76, and shared a second wicket stand of 95 with Mark Butcher who scored 41. Slightly less encouraging was the fact that the next highest score was nine, three blokes made ducks, Nasser broke his finger, and we were all out for 164, losing in four days by an innings and 118 runs.

Until the series was over as a contest, on the third day of the third Test at Nottingham, we never looked forward.

There was indecision over who should lead at Lord's in Nasser's absence. He did already consider me as a possible long-term successor but it was too early for me now. Alec said he didn't want to do it again, so Atherton agreed, somewhat reluctantly, that he would have a go if there was no one else. There was no one else.

They slaughtered us by eight wickets there and buried us by seven at Trent Bridge even though we twice were on top and Steve Waugh had to be carried off on a stretcher in their second innings with a torn calf which everyone presumed would force him out for the rest of the series.

It was at this point that I produced my most significant column to date, in which I freely admitted that the Australians were far superior to us in all departments and had been playing cricket from another planet. Not exactly rocket science, surely. But I got such a hammering the next day for my defeatist attitude I resolved to put my laptop away for the time being at least.

Our batting was down to the bare bones by now, but with Nasser due to be fit for the fourth Test at Leeds a major issue had developed over who should make way. It was decided that Butch had to go and not just for cricketing reasons. Butch had always been a sociable type and his method of winding down after a day's play was one used by generations of cricketers before him the world over – he had a few beers. This time, however, he had over-stepped the mark. One night in Nottingham, and probably not the last night of the game, he had taken things to excess and Duncan wanted to drop him to show he would not tolerate it. Nasser agreed, but as the management meeting broke up Duncan indicated he wanted to make a couple more phone calls before coming to a final decision. Good job he did. Butcher's brilliant 173 not out in the second innings at Headingley of the fourth Test was an innings of genius; anything short he cut and pulled and he even came down the track to drive McGrath through the covers. He was inspired and led us to victory by six wickets. Twenty years on from the last time an Englishman played a similar innings here to win a Test against Australia against all the odds, Beefy would have been proud of him.

From my point of view the match was memorable for reasons unconnected with Butcher's brilliance.

By now I was firmly established as the man in charge of looking after the ball when we were fielding. It was my job to keep the shine on the new ball for as long as possible with a bit of spit and lot of polish. And through trial and error I had finally settled on the best type of spit for the task at hand.

It had been common knowledge in county cricket for some time that certain sweets produced saliva which, when applied to the ball for cleaning purposes, enabled it to keep its shine for longer and therefore its swing. As with most of the great scientific discoveries, this one happened quite by accident. While at Warwickshire, Dermot Reeve noticed that his bowlers somehow had the ability to keep the ball swinging far longer than any team they faced. The problem was no one in their side knew why. By process of investigation and elimination he realized the reason was that the player in charge of polishing and keeping the ball clean was his bespectacled top-order batsman Asif Din, or rather, what he did to keep his concentration levels up, chewing extra strong mints.

It took a while for word to get around the circuit but once it did the sales of sweets near the county grounds of England went through the roof.

I tried Asif's confection of choice but couldn't get on with them. Too dry. Then I had a go at Murray Mints and found they worked a treat. Trouble was, even allowing for trying to keep one going as long as possible I still used to get through about 15 a day and the taste soon palled. Still, at least I never had to pay for them. Once Phil Neale came on board as our operations manager it was one of his jobs to make sure the dressing-room was fully stocked at all times. We even tried taking them on tour a couple of times until we realized that they didn't work as well on the Kookaburra balls used overseas as the Dukes we used back home.

On the first day of the match in Leeds, an unfortunate fielding incident almost gave the game away to the Aussies for the first time, as I dived to gather the ball at square leg, landed on my side and a shower of Murray Mints spewed out of my trouser pocket all over the grass right in front of the umpire. Fortunately, neither he nor the two batsmen seemed to take much notice as I scrambled around on all fours trying desperately to gather in the sweets before they started asking awkward questions.

But our celebratory mood soon dipped again in the final Test at The Oval where Steve Waugh made it his business to rub our noses in it and prove once and for all that the common or garden Pom is gutless and weak.

There was no way Waugh was fit to play. But, apparently he had been so riled by comments Thorpe had made about not being able to play because of a broken finger, he decided he was going to take the field in the fifth Test even if it killed him. His batting in their first innings was incredible whichever way you looked at it. Making 157 not out, without a runner, when he was limping and in great pain, said everything about his extraordinary resolve and will. At the same time we did question his judgement because his almost obsessive desire to prove his point could have resulted in the injury becoming far worse. And in the end it all seemed to be less about Aussie pride and more about his. Still no one could argue with his contribution to their 641 for four declared or, despite Mark Ramprakash's excellent 133, the result, another hammering. Four-one, Thanks for the series. See you next year.

As if Duncan and Nasser didn't have enough on their plate, now Alec Stewart and Darren Gough hit them with the news that they wanted to take a break from touring in the winter. Neither wanted to go to India, though Gough said he would be available for the one-dayers there, but they were happy to pitch up in New Zealand in the early part of 2002.

In Alec's case there was speculation that he didn't want to travel to the country where the allegations about his involvement with the bookmaker MK Gupta had originated the previous winter, though Alec insisted he wanted to take a break to spend more time at home with his family and undertake surgery on his elbows.

Duncan wasn't buying any of it, for any reason. As far as he was concerned he didn't want players picking and choosing tours to suit them and that was non-negotiable. And then, almost as soon as the squads were announced, with both names absent, an event took place that made such matters appear less than infinitessimally important.

The terrorist attack on the twin-towers of the World Trade Center in Manhattan on 11 September 2001 and the reverberations even impacted in a small way on cricket. When the great grey cloud had settled, security was suddenly elevated to the top of everyone's list of waking thoughts, and attention was inevitably drawn to our winter commitments.

A short five-match one-day series in Zimbabwe in October should present no problems and it didn't. We won all five, with Freddie and Ben Hollioake putting in very promising displays with bat and ball and, when Nasser decided to have a breather, my appointment as captain of the fourth match in Bulawayo seemed another clear indication of future thinking.

But travelling to India was another matter entirely. The Foreign Office advice to travellers had made it crystal clear that, while they were 'unaware of any specific threat', India was one of a number of travel destinations where Westerners should 'keep a low profile'. Those of the squad who were married with children felt particularly vulnerable and altogether five of the selected squad, myself, Andy Caddick, Ashley Giles, Craig White and Robert Croft, expressed doubts about going. It's all very well for people sitting in offices to be brave about these things or for people to start writing in the newspapers about not giving in to terror, but we are cricketers, not professional soldiers. In the end, for some of us it was a case of 'Well, I don't want to go, but if you're going, I'll go and let's get it done.' Only Croft and Caddy pulled out, for reasons we all sympathised with and understood. Cricket was our livelihood and our passion, of course, but it was only cricket after all.

It turned out to be a tour of mediums and lows. We lost the first Test in Mohali by ten wickets and Thorpe flew home in distress the day before the second in Ahmedabad to try and patch up his marriage, which gave Vaughan a way into the side but meant Butcher had no option but to play despite being sick as a dog. He and I put on 124 for the first wicket and I still don't know how he made 51 because he was actually throwing up moments before the start and again all the way through lunch, shouting at the toilet for about half an hour. I fell on 99, annoyingly one short of my third Test ton, and soon afterwards Craig White played brilliantly for his first and only Test century.

Then, when India batted, I got my first taste of what Sachin Tendulkar meant to his people. The crowd swelled from about a tenth full to completely full and outside the ground a near-empty wasteland was suddenly covered in dust, bicycles, tuk-tuks and mopeds.

Inside, when one of their openers got out, the crowd cheered and cheered until they noticed that the batsman coming in at No.3 was not Sachin but Rahul Dravid, at which point they booed and booed.

But from the moment he got off the mark to the moment he was out for 104 it was all cheers and the result, a tame draw, seemed utterly immaterial to his supporters. We even won praise for our resilience.

However we won nothing from the locals for what happened in the final Test in Bangalore when, after Vaughan was given out handled the ball for 64 in our first innings 336, we adopted tactics designed to stop Sachin scoring that for some went too close to the line separating fair and unfair play. In essence Fred bowled round the wicket at his head and Ashley bowled over the wicket into the rough about a foot outside his leg stump with seven fielders on the onside, plus the wicket-keeper James Foster.

We didn't care. It may not have been pretty and Sachin did manage to make 90, but it took so long and the match was so badly hit by the weather and some of us were so knackered that we were merely grateful not to be chasing leather again and very happy to be home, on Christmas Eve.

When I finished eating and sleeping my way through my Christmas day birthday, I reflected on my first full year as an England cricketer. From my own perspective, though I still wanted more and more, maybe the occasional break might not go amiss. As far as the team was concerned, I wondered whether our performance in the final Test in Bangalore might turn out to be a significant turning point. Did we, deep down, employ those tactics against Sachin because we thought it was okay to settle for a 1–0 defeat? And did that mean Steve Waugh was right about us being weak and gutless? And what were we going to do about it?

Chapter 7

A GUT-FULL OF CRICKET

'All I got for my trouble in pointing out these dangers was a hammering in the papers and a bollocking from Duncan. It wasn't that he was unsympathetic. It was just that he felt such thoughts should be kept within the dressing-room.'

There were occasions, probably four in my entire career, when batting became so easy for me it was almost frightening, when everything seemed to be happening in such super-slow-motion that I felt like the master of my own laws of time and space.

For a few moments during my first Test hundred in Galle in February 2001, and my second, against Pakistan that summer, that feeling settled on me briefly. But in my first England innings of 2002, in the opening one-day international against India at Eden Gardens, Kolkata, it was with me for every single ball I faced.

Chasing 282 for victory under lights, I batted like I was in a scene from *The Matrix*, picking up the sight and the flight of the white ball, then moving so fast and freely that it felt like I had about a week to play each delivery. No matter who was bowling or what they were offering up, I felt like I could have done the shopping in the time it took for the ball to arrive down my end and that I could take my pick of about a hundred different shots for each ball. Fair enough, I might have been a tad light-headed that day, what with 92,000 people in the ground and me suffering from the effects of a gastric virus, but I had a sense of utter dominance. And it was especially pleasing that it happened for me against the veteran Indian pace bowler Javagal Srinath. I've nothing at all against him personally and we always found him a determined but charming opponent. It was just that, as I recorded earlier, when county pace bowlers were getting me out for a pastime in the late 90s, Srinath had once made me look so bad it was embarrassing, making me play and miss at about five balls an over in a Benson & Hedges match.

Now I found myself able to play him, and all the other bowlers, not with slogging disrespect but with risk-free disregard. The ball was as big as a beachball and my bat was as wide as my car, and I reached the fastest ever one-day hundred by an England batsman, from 80 balls. I'd hit 121 from 109 and felt sure I was going to bat through to the end, as I had failed to do against Pakistan at Lord's the previous summer; in fact I was batting so effortlessly that it felt to me like I was going to score almost all of the required runs myself, when I was on the wrong end of a complete shocker from umpire S.K. Sharma, given out lbw to a ball from Srinath, bowling over the wicket, that pitched at least six inches outside my leg stump. It wasn't the only one but it was the main reason why the management later presented a letter of complaint to the match referee Denis Lindsay about the standard of umpiring. Needless to say, once it became public, that went down with the locals like a plate of cold biriyani.

The innings was not a revenge mission, just an indicator to me of how far I had come in a relatively short space of time. Ironically, but typical of my tendency to over-analyse my batting at times, as

I reviewed the innings later I was struck by the unsettling feeling that, if batting was that easy, something must be wrong.

Over-analyse? All the time. In my quest for batting perfection I would leave no shot unexplained and my contributions in the rest of the series reflected that ability I had to disappear up my own coaching manual. But I did manage to regain my focus in the last of the six games in Mumbai, on 3 February, in which I made 95 in our 255, and in which Fred made a very mature 40, adding 37 with Gough for the last wicket.

Fred had struggled with the bat in the Tests but, in the last one in Bangalore, he had started to show how good he could become with the ball, and he had been consistently fast and straight throughout this series, mainly as first change behind Gough, Hoggard or Caddick. We needed to win here to earn a 3–3 draw and to pick up some momentum halfway through an already gruelling winter, and they needed six from the final two balls when Fred bowled Srinath for his third wicket, promptly ripped off his shirt and started waving it around his head. It was a spontaneous gesture of celebration which captured his and our mood. Unbeknown to us it enraged the Indian skipper Sourav Ganguly, who made a mental note to give some back at the earliest available opportunity.

Our subsequent tour to New Zealand started strangely for me, perked up in the middle, then petered out in tragic circumstances, and during it I underwent my first, but by no means last experience of the phenomenon known as burnout which later contributed so much to the illness that finally ended my career.

There was no doubt I was physically tired when we arrived in the land of the long white cloud and things were about to get cloudier still. At the time we were conducting ongoing experiments with the balance of the one-day side and, when we arrived at the Westpac stadium in Wellington, the home of the local rugby league team, to play the second of five matches, we put into practice the latest idea, which was for me to replace James Foster as wicket-keeper. I did all right with the gloves, as it turned out, taking my first of a career total of four catches behind the stumps to dismiss Brendon McCullum off Fred. In the break between innings, the Kiwi film director Peter Jackson orchestrated the crowd as they made grunting, howling and roaring noises for him to record and use for the battle scenes in his upcoming movie *The Lord Of The Rings*. It clearly had an effect on our batting as we slid to 89 all out, our second-lowest total in 344 one-day matches, with me starting things off with a big fat zero. Maybe we were scared that, if it looked as though we might win, Jackson might set the Orcs on us.

But my batting in that one-day series was shocking; my scores were 1, 0, 41, 0 and 5 and we went down 3–2. End of experiment.

By the time we arrived in Queenstown for the pre-Test warm-up against Otago, I was absolutely knackered and made the grave error of saying so to the press. I was merely trying to add my voice to what we all considered should be an ongoing discussion about the physical, psychological and emotional effects of life on the road as an international cricketer; and, particularly, life on the road for an England cricketer for whom the unique demands of playing every northern hemisphere summer at home as well as every south-ern hemisphere summer on tour, meant we now spent almost 12 months a year living out of suitcases and in hotel rooms. Of course the lifestyle was considered luxurious, our every off-field need was catered for by a solid back-up staff including a doctor, nutritionist, sports psychologist etc., we were very well paid for our efforts and it beat real work any day. But whereas in the past players could enjoy the countries they were visiting in much more leisurely and relaxing fashion, with the tours now so truncated, all you did on them was play, practice or travel, and grab the occasional game of golf on a rare day-off. That, coupled with the four-wall fever that can strike you when you are stuck inside a hotel bedroom complete with en-suite bathroom for days on end prior to moving onto the next one, was simply not a natural way to live. It creates extraordinary strains for the players not to mention their wives and families.

All I got for my trouble in pointing out these dangers was a hammering in the papers and a bollocking from Duncan. It wasn't that he was unsympathetic. It was just that he felt such thoughts should be kept within the dressing-room. His attitude was that we all knew what the problems were but by airing them in public it gave people the opportunity to attack you, to claim such thoughts were a sign of weakness, of giving in. Just another whingeing Pom. So, from then on, I kept them to myself, for the time being, though I did manage to earn the next match off and I bloody needed it too.

The opening Test in Christchurch was just extraordinary. It was my first experience of playing on a 'drop-in', pre-prepared pitch and it started wet, not damp. Both Mark Butcher and I were out for nothing in Chris Cairns's first over and only Nasser Hussain's dog-fighting 106 got us to 228. New Zealand did even worse, Hoggard taking seven for 63 as they made just 147.

Then the pitch dried out and turned into a road. Whereas 375 runs were made in the first two innings, 919 were made in the last two in just over two days. Thorpe, back again and by now in better mood, hit 200 not out, the fastest double-hundred for England against the Kiwis, from 231 balls faced. He put on 281 for the sixth wicket with Fred, who made his first Test ton, 137, as we declared on 468 for six, setting them a ridiculous 550 to win. At 333 for nine, with 217 still needed for a New Zealand win, Nathan Astle's 134 seemed merely a bold effort in a losing cause. By the time he reached his double-ton, from 153 balls, taking 61 off four overs with the second new cherry, he had smashed Thorpe's 24-hour-old record. He went from 101 to 200 in a scarcely believable 39 deliveries and the harder we tried, the further he hit it. When he was last out for 222, they had cut the target to 99 and we were extremely relieved to win by 98, towards the end of a four-day Test that will never be forgotten by those who played in it or watched.

From such highs we were cut so low by the news that reached us, at 10.30 a.m. on 23 March, as we were preparing to field on the third day of the second Test at the Basin Reserve in Wellington. Ben Hollioake, our friend and a member of the one-day squad in New Zealand less than a month before, had been killed in a car crash in Western Australia in the early hours of the morning. He was 24.

I was sitting in the back of the dressing-room when Duncan told me Ben was dead. In fact, he had to tell me twice before I could actually take it in. Naturally the Surrey boys, Ramps, Thorpe and Butcher took it hardest. But everyone shared their pain. Ben was just one of those rare individuals no one ever had a bad word for, we all had our own personal memories of the guy and none of us really wanted to carry on playing that day.

As a cricketer I believe it would only have been a matter of time before Ben realized his huge potential. He could do things with the bat that no one else could. Ever since he played his first match for England as a 19-year-old in a one-dayer at Lord's against Australia in 1997, and scored an elegant 63, he had been marked for special things and, after hard work and encouragement from his brother Adam, he appeared to be on the verge of making the final breakthrough. All we wanted from him now was consistency and he would have been a certainty for the squad for the 2003 World Cup in South Africa a year ahead, and from then on the sky might have been the limit.

As a bloke, Ben was a beauty, laid-back, seemingly always serene and calm and always caring about other people as much if not more than himself. Once, in Zimbabwe the previous autumn when Thorpey was having terrible emotional problems dealing with the break-up of his marriage, Ben scoured Bulawayo for supplies and came back with a sack of the best local hand-rolling tobacco and a bottle of proper Scotch to help ease his mate's pain. I still find it hard to believe that such a wonderful young man should be taken so long before his time.

No one actually suggested calling the game off, but from time to time the action just stopped as, one after another, much of us succumbed to tears. By now the Barmy Army also knew that Ben had crashed his 924 Porsche after a family dinner, just prior to flying home for pre-season training with Surrey, and that his girlfriend was fighting for her life. When they started to sing *'One Ben Hollioake, there's only one Ben Hollioake'* I just thought to myself: 'Right. Let's call this game off.'

As we lined up for a minute's silence the following morning Butch could have filled the ground with his tears. In the circumstances, the fact that the match ended in a tame draw was probably for the best.

I don't think the cloud ever lifted for the rest of the tour; the final match, in Auckland, was pretty farcical, rain affected and lost. The weather ruled out all but 50-odd overs in the first two days and time was running out for any kind of result to be achieved when somebody, somewhere decided they could turn the floodlights on at 5.50 p.m. on the fourth evening and play until about midnight, which might have been fine with a white ball and coloured clothes, but with whites on and a red ball to try and pick up was just plain mad. Nasser complained a few times that we could barely see the ball and Usman Afzaal, fielding as sub, very nearly got cleaned up by a skier that missed his head at deep square leg by an inch. The umpires Venkat and Doug Cowie wouldn't listen and were only prepared to offer the light to the batting side, who stayed on, slapped a few and ended up setting us a target of 312 in 105 overs, which we never looked like getting on a dodgy pitch and didn't.

Mark Ramprakash, batting at No.6, made 9 and 2 and never played for England again.

Many observers are still wondering why. Why, when he was by streets the best batsman in county cricket, could Ramps not do what was necessary to make himself a successful Test player? I would not presume to offer a definitive answer, except to say that the reason I think I managed to settle in so comfortably was that I just absolutely loved everything about the experience. For me the England dressing-room, the field onto which we stepped and the atmosphere generated by the crowd meant international cricket was not just the place to be, it was the *only* place to be. Maybe Ramps and even Graeme Hick just didn't feel so much at home and a story told by Mike Atherton may furnish some clues. During the second Test of England's 1998–99 Ashes tour in Perth, Ramps was batting under pressure for his place, as he so often seemed to be. As Glenn McGrath ran up to bowl, he prepared by moving slightly forward onto the front foot. The ball slipped out of Glenn's hand and turned into a beamer which was heading straight for Ramps' head at around 82 mph. Sighting conditions were perfect, but, instead of ducking or taking evasive action or trying to fend the ball off, Ramps carried on moving towards the ball and finished off in perfect position for an immaculate forward-defensive shot, head down and over where a good length ball would have pitched. The only problem was that the ball was by now wedged hard in between the bars of the grille on his batting helmet, having flown straight from the bowler's hand at head height, without bouncing. It was lodged so far in that it had to be manhandled out by one of the Aussie fielders. Michael's theory was that when Ramps was under the pump he actually lost focus, albeit temporarily, to the extent that, when he first went in, he was virtually playing blind and only if he somehow survived the first few balls would he then have a chance to make a score. I've no reason to argue with that assessment and can only offer sympathy that someone could get himself so wound up that all the ability in the world could not help him.

* * *

When we crawled home to England at the end of the first week in April, some of us were ready for a long break. Since the end of the previous summer, those who were in the side for both forms of the game were spent. A few had been on three tours, to Zimbabwe, India and New Zealand, and if I was knackered in Queenstown, I was on the floor by now. Yet there seemed no real respite. Another month slipped by, with a few games for Somerset and then another Test series, against Sri Lanka, which we won 2–0 after drawing the first at Lord's despite following on. And I didn't find any real form until the final of the NatWest triangular event at Lord's against India on 13 July, in which, once again, I made a one-day century in a losing cause.

The match actually revolved around two of our veteran performers, Hussain and Thorpe. We had been inconsistent in one-day cricket for some time and there were calls for changes to be made, for some of the older players to be replaced by younger guys to liven up the fielding. Duncan was keen on introducing new blood but he was also aware of the value of experience. In fact, he used to go on and on about how little we had compared to other countries.

Nasser had taken a lot of stick from commentators like Ian Botham who suggested that his grafting style was not what England needed at No.3 and that he should drop down the order, to let Fred go further up to take advantage of the fielding restrictions in the first 15 overs. What is more, the critics pointed out, Nasser had not yet made a one-day hundred in 71 attempts. Nass wasn't happy with the added pressure but, as so often in the past, it gave him something to kick against, though he seemed to me so keen to prove his critics wrong, that it may have blurred his thinking as captain.

In that final he wasn't at his most fluent, but he supported me brilliantly in a second-wicket stand of 185 in 177 balls. I reached my third one-day hundred from 89 deliveries, but, when I was out, Nasser and Fred took us to a huge total of 325, England's fourth highest, and on the way completed his first ODI hundred in his 72nd match. At this point he took off his helmet and, after raising his bat to the dressing-room, raised a three-fingered salute to the media centre and to Botham in particular, then turned his back and pointed to the number 3 on his shirt, leaving no one in the ground in any doubt as to where he felt he should carry on batting. It would have been the perfect gesture by Nasser to his critics, except that when we needed cool heads to shut out the game with the ball and in the field, mayhem was allowed to take over; Yuvraj Singh and Mohammad Kaif saw them home with three balls to spare, at which point Ganguly removed his shirt on the Indian balcony and could not stop himself doing a Freddie in celebration. Nasser may have won the argument about his batting position, but at what cost?

As for Thorpe, we had all known for some time that, after trying but failing to keep his marriage together, he had been struggling to maintain his focus and enthusiasm, and he had lost his place in the starting line-up as the series went on, but that day he did something which made a deep impact on me. He retired from one-day international cricket with immediate effect.

I was still pumped from having taken part in such an amazing match, from scoring another hundred at Lord's and having won, albeit rather fortunately, the award for the man of the series. And, even though my initial wide-eyed enthusiasm about playing for England was being tested by the demands placed upon us all, I was still utterly and completely convinced that there could be no better feeling in professional life than to play cricket for England and to score a century for England, at the home of the game.

So, as we sat on the dressing-room balcony taking in the noise and commotion of the crowd, I asked Thorpey: 'Mate, why would you ever want to give all this up? You don't think you'll miss it?'

'Tron,' he replied, 'I'm ⬛⬛⬛⬛⬛ but I couldn't give a f⬛⬛⬛.'

Clearly his mood was as low as it had been for a while, and though he initially made himself available for the upcoming Ashes tour that winter, he subsequently pulled out, once again putting his future career in jeopardy.

Knowing then what I do now, of course, to Thorpe the question must have sounded simply absurd.

I did manage to take a break for the second half of the summer, as it happens, though not quite the way I would have planned it. Fielding for Somerset against Worcestershire in a Cheltenham & Gloucester quarter-final at Taunton in the week before the first Test against India at Lord's, I was standing at extra-cover when Hick belted a ball with a touch of slice on it and, as it skidded across the turf it pushed back my left thumb and shattered it. The first effect was that I had to cancel a few precious days of holiday with Hayley as I went to have my thumb re-set and put in plaster. And I missed about seven weeks in all, which took out the first three games of the series, which I watched at home on the box, ironically not enjoying my enforced rest at all, but thinking 'this is horrible'.

Just before I was fit enough to come back Hayley and I did manage to get a week in Marbella, which meant I had to miss Somerset's C&G semi-final against Kent. You can imagine how thrilled Hayley was that I spent virtually the whole of that day texting and receiving texts from the boys at the ground as we scored 344 for five and Kent got closer and closer until they were finally all out five runs short.

Quite a bit had gone on in my absence from the England side, with Kent's Rob Key being given a go at the top of the order and doing enough to get himself on the plane to Australia, and debuts awarded to Simon Jones and Steve Harmison, two up-and-coming young pacemen. With Gough and Caddick starting to creak, the time had come to cast the net around for the next generation of young quicks, especially as we would need something pretty special in terms of firepower to unsettle the Australians that winter. Fred and Hoggard took the new ball in the first Test against India at Lord's in which Jones, well known to Duncan from his days as Glamorgan coach, made his debut. He had proper wheels and could bowl good reverse-swing as well. He was raw but busting a gut to succeed and though as Welsh as Tom Jones, bowling for England was in his genes. His dad, Jeff was a lively left-arm quick who toured West Indies in the 1960s but had been forced to quit early through an elbow injury. Alex Tudor was also back in the running and Harmison was known to a few of us who had faced him at Durham as a bowler who could make the ball take the elevator from just short of a length and at express pace. He clearly needed a lot of work and his confidence boosting at all times, but if he could develop along the right lines he had everything, and he made a promising start with five wickets on his debut in the second Test at Trent Bridge.

It was just now, towards the end of August, that I also came across another young paceman who I thought was destined for great things. I'd never seen the lad before I travelled to Blackpool with the Somerset squad as twelfth man to get myself ready to return to the England squad for the final Test with India, but the 19-year-old rookie swing bowler they called the Burnley Express more than lived up to his nickname. He took six for 41 as we rolled over for 140 in our first innings, and another three for 16 in seven overs as they routed us in the second for 71. In the middle of all that I rang Duncan, making no attempt to hide the excitement in my voice.

'Fletch, I've just see this lad Jimmy Anderson and I'm telling you we've got to pick this bloke now because he was magnificent. You've got to take him to the ICC Champions Trophy and keep him in mind for the one-dayers in Australia and the World Cup after that. He's only 18, but I'm telling you he is that good.'

Duncan said he would bear it in mind and Jimmy ended up being drafted into the England Academy squad for work down under that winter, which meant he was in exactly the right place at exactly the right time when opportunity knocked a few months later.

For the time being the series ended in a 1–1 draw and a drawn match at The Oval. Vaughan completed an amazing series, in which he made 615 runs at an average of 102.5 with his third hundred in seven innings, 195 to set alongside his 197 at Trent Bridge. It was his fourth hundred of the summer in all as he had made one in the very first Test against Sri Lanka. He was performing with the kind of ice-cool, consistent, yet understated brilliance you would have expected from a man with the nickname 'Virgil', pilot of Thunderbird 2.

Sadly, when we arrived in Australia after a soggy and disappointing Champions Trophy in Sri Lanka, we very soon discovered we were beyond even the powers of International Rescue to save us.

As usual for visiting Poms we were beaten up from all angles almost from the moment we arrived. The smile of satisfaction that they were better than us at cricket and the scowl of contempt at our general uselessness was only later replaced from time to time by a raised eyebrow of respect for the fact that they weren't better than Vaughan, who had an utterly brilliant series that settled the issue of who should be England's next captain firmly in his favour.

Things started badly, at Lilac Hill in Perth when Steve Harmison began an over that at one stage, littered with no balls and wides, looked as though it may take him the rest of the tour to finish. Fred never made it because of complications following a hernia operation that had kept him out of the final Test against India and when Goughy's knee ruled him out, we were right up against it as we went into the first Test in Brisbane.

Nasser has always taken responsibility for the decision to stick Australia in to bat that first morning of the 2002–03 Ashes series. He wrote later (about two days later, in fact) that he took one look around the dressing-room and saw something approaching fear on the faces of one or two of the players and that persuaded him to give up first use of what turned out to be a very good batting track. It's about time I held up my hand and admitted my part in the start of our and maybe Nasser's eventual downfall.

It is true that Nasser was worried that some of the younger lads might not be up for it that day, and that it might be better to field first if only to avoid the possibility of us getting rolled. But that was only after he had asked me what I thought we should do. I had just been batting in the nets which had definitely been doing a bit and when I went out to the wicket to take a look and try and make an educated guess as to how it might play the surface looked identical. I said to Nass that I felt our best chance of making an early impact was to bowl first.

By the end of the first day, the green tinge had long gone, the sun had dried the track out to burn it into a belter and Australia were 364 for two. We didn't help ourselves by dropping four catches, but we might have made a better fist of things had disaster not struck Simon Jones only seven overs into his Ashes career.

Coming on at first change after Caddick and Hoggard shared the new ball, Simon had quickly shown he had something a bit extra. His pace was good and he was certainly not overawed by the occasion and when he had Justin Langer caught behind by Alec Stewart for 32, a little spark of hope briefly flared.

We had been warned in advance about the possible dangers of diving on the newly-laid and sandy outfield, but Simon was such a wholehearted lad that he must have just forgotten for a moment when, after chasing a ball to the long-on boundary he attempted to slide alongside it and pull it back before it hit the rope. Even from where I was standing, 90 yards away at slip the other end, you could tell there was a big problem, when he went down and stayed down. When we got there we found out that his studs had stuck in the ground as he dived and his whole body weight had gone through his right knee, causing massive damage to his knee ligaments. Simon was in agony and it was here that the uglier side of the Aussie mentality took over and he was barracked by sections of the crowd. Clearly, they were unaware of the seriousness of his injury but they didn't think to stop and find out before they let him have a barrage. 'Get up, ya pommie pr***!' was about as sympathetic as it got. One kind soul even offered him a drink, or rather threw a full can of coke at him. It took Simon more than a year to rebuild his knee and restart his career and I know those memories made him even more determined to come back and even more delighted when he made such an impact in the 2005 Ashes series.

The effect on us was immediate and clear, like letting all the air out of a balloon. When they reached nearly 500 in their first innings we all just felt the series was more or less over before it had really got going. I was happy enough with my 72 in our reply of 325, but us being bowled out for 79 in the second innings didn't help, nor did the newspaper headline the following day which marked our defeat by 384 runs by asking: 'Is there anybody left in England who can actually play cricket?'

Fortunately there was. Vaughan. From here to the end of the series he batted like the best player who had ever lived. Every time they pitched the ball up he smashed it through the covers. Every time they bowled short he pulled it for four or six. I remember thinking they could not bowl at him, and the 'they' were bloody Glenn McGrath and Shane Warne.

Following on from his century-filled summer in England, he hit 177 in the second Test in Adelaide, which we lost by an innings and 51 runs. They blew us away in the third in Perth, by an innings and 48 runs, which I suppose amounts to an improvement of sorts, but meant once again the Poms were beaten within eleven actual days' playing time, on 1 December. Brett Lee bowled a spell during which I came as close to being physically frightened on a cricket pitch as I have ever been in my life.

Vaughan then hit 145 in the Boxing Day Test in Melbourne, after which we were 4–0 down after four, but saved the best until last, a wonderful 183 in the final Test in Sydney to put us in position to grab a consolation win, despite Steve Waugh, in his 156th and probably last Test match, completing a century that provoked one of the loudest roars I had ever heard on a cricket field. Caddick had a brilliant match as well, taking ten wickets and finishing the second innings with seven for 94 as we bowled them out to win by 225 runs.

I did my best to join in with the celebrations. Unbeknown to everyone but Steve Bull I was struggling badly with burnout that stayed with me all the way through to the end of the 2003 World Cup in early March.

I can't actually recall much of what happened in the VB series with Australia and Sri Lanka, except that we carried on playing, travelling and losing to Australia. I was delighted that Jimmy Anderson made such a big impact that he won himself a place in the World Cup squad, but my last two innings in the contest were 0 and 0 in the finals and I was that good.

*   *   *

From the moment we pitched up in South Africa for the World Cup, our initial experiences at the premier one-day competition in world cricket were sheer torture.

The question was should we play against Zimbabwe in Harare, or not. Many wanted us to pull out on moral grounds alone and the issue was aired within the squad over and over again. One newspaper back in England equated the publicity indeed a visit would represent for the President Robert Mugabe as akin to England footballers being photographed giving the Nazi salute to Adolf Hitler when playing a friendly match in Germany in the 1930s. But the ECB made it clear they wanted us to go ahead and play. Even when the concerns over security grew, to those who might see our match there as an opportunity for peaceful protest, as well as ourselves, and the death-threats started to arrive, no one seemed to be listening to our concerns at all, until Richard Bevan, the chief executive of the Professional Cricketers' Association was asked to get involved.

Nasser was particularly upset that neither the ECB nor the International Cricket Council seemed to have any other response than a very heavy-handed 'go and play and get on with it'.

Meeting followed meeting. No one really knew what the hell to do. Some of the players were keen on carrying on because they might never get another chance to play in a World Cup. Some were dead against it full stop. Others were just bewildered. And the uncertainty dragged on and on until matters came to a head in quite farcical fashion.

It had come to light that Tim Lamb, the chief executive of our Board had received a letter as early as January from a group called the Sons and Daughters of Zimbabwe, denouncing the ECB for letting the team be used by Mugabe for his own publicity purposes and telling him: 'Our message to you is simple: COME TO ZIMBABWE AND YOU WILL GO BACK IN WOODEN COFFINS!

'Mugabe's thugs and a huge opposing group are like two chemicals waiting for a catalyst to spark a violent reaction. Your visit to Zimbabwe will provide precisely that catalyst and there's going to be one mighty bang. The England players and a load of Zimbabweans will die in the carnage.'

It went on 'Come to Harare and you will die. And how safe are your families back there in the UK? Even if you survive, there are foreign groups who are prepared to hurt you and hunt your families down for as long as it takes.

'Our advice is this: DON'T COME TO ZIMBABWE OR YOUR PLAYERS WILL BE LIVING IN FEAR FOR THE REST OF THEIR LIVES.'

Initially the South African security forces merely ridiculed the letter and its contents, even questioning the existence of the Sons and Daughters. When information later reached them that not only did they exist but they did in fact present a credible security threat, one show of hands in the room was all it took to confirm that, as far as we were concerned, we weren't going anywhere near the place.

For the point of view of our chances of progressing in the tournament it was a big shame. Jimmy had bowled brilliantly against Pakistan in Cape Town, taking four for 29. Had we beaten Australia on 2 March in Port Elizabeth, we would still have gone through to the next round. When they plunged to 48 for four with Caddy taking two for 4, then 135 for eight chasing 205, we were sure we were going to as well, then Andy Bichel kept Michael Bevan company and they ended up squeezing home with two balls to spare.

Nasser was on his knees at the end of the match, inconsolable. Soon afterwards, and to no one's great surprise, he quit as one-day captain.

Almost immediately after getting home I was extensively quoted in an article in the *Mail on Sunday* explaining exactly how

I felt. By now, even if the words wouldn't go down well with Duncan or the management, I couldn't hold back any longer.

I'd had enough of playing cricket for England non-stop. I'd had enough of travelling and packing and unpacking and travelling and unpacking and living inside four-star prisons. The article highlighted: 'A winter schedule that began on Tuesday 12 September 2002 – 72 hours after the fifth day of the final Test against India at The Oval – left the regulars in both forms of international cricket staggering through the arrivals hall at Heathrow on Thursday 6 March 2003, looking like extras from *The Night of the Living Dead*.'

I spoke as honestly as I could, without fear of the consequences, because while I so wanted to carry on loving the experience of playing for England, I now knew exactly what Thorpe had meant the previous summer. Some days I just didn't give a f*** either. There comes a time when you just want to stop; stop playing cricket, stop training, stop travelling, stop putting yourself out there, a time when you just want to not be doing what you've been doing over and over again for so long, a time when you make nought and feel nothing or make fifty and still feel nothing, when you just don't want to be with the same sixteen blokes on tour, on the bus, at breakfast, out to dinner, in the bar; when all you want to do is remove yourself from where you are. And I hated the feeling.

'I've had such a gut-full of playing cricket over the last five months that I just want to get it out of my system,' I said. 'I get so much enjoyment from the game and I love it so much but, at the moment, I've reached the stage where a bit of enthusiasm has gone. I am experiencing something I never have before and I thought I never would. I've stopped enjoying it.'

Little did I know I was about to embark on the most rewarding period of my whole career.

Chapter 8

NEW ENGLAND

*'Vaughan made good use of an upbeat press
conference to give Fred something to think about
… When asked by one of the cricket writers why it
had taken so long for Fred to start to fulfil
his potential, Michael uttered one
single word: "Beer."'*

Michael Vaughan's fantastic Ashes tour of 2002–03 meant he
was the media's hot favourite to take over as England's one-
day captain following Nasser Hussain's resignation at the end of
the World Cup. Everyone within the camp knew that whoever got
it would all but be nailed on for the job of Test skipper as well, as
and when the vacancy arose.

Until Michael began his incredible run of form at the start of the
home summer of 2002, most observers had considered me to be
the more likely choice; I had captained the one-day side in Zimbabwe, Nasser had appointed me his vice-captain in Australia and
we had grown very close over the past year or so. Strictly speaking,
my record in one-day cricket might have swung the vote in my
favour as captain for the shorter form of the game, especially as
Michael's one-day form was patchy. But, after a calendar year in

which he had scored 1,533 runs, including seven hundreds, and 633 runs with three sparkling centuries in a losing Ashes campaign, no one was betting against him.

Yet I must admit I did feel a certain sense of disappointment that his form with the bat might have been the reason he was chosen ahead of me.

I realized I wasn't going to get the job the day before the official announcement was made. The media had been informed that the new one-day skipper would be unveiled on 6 May, when Somerset were due to fly to Edinburgh to play Scotland in a C&G third round match the following day. As no one had rung me beforehand to ask me to cancel my travel arrangements, I reckoned, rightly as it turned out, that was that, though, after the match was over I did notice I had missed a call from David Graveney. As it was timed shortly after Michael's appointment was announced I didn't have to guess what he would have told me had he managed to get through.

My nose would instantly grow a foot in length if I said I wasn't disappointed to have been passed over. Who wouldn't have wanted the chance to be England captain? For someone like me, whose childhood dreams were only about things like that, absorbing the probability that my chance had gone for good was hard.

I had no problems whatsoever with Michael's appointment. I knew what sort of bloke he was and how well he would succeed. And I made sure I made contact with Michael straight away because the last thing I wanted was the merest suggestion of any problem between us. I might have been disappointed and my pride hurt, but that was irrelevant. The most important thing was for the team to move on and for us to move on.

If Duncan or David Graveney had said to me: 'Look, we think, all in all, he's the better man for the job' or 'We think he will be better tactically', or even raised the issue of that memorable moment in the World Cup when my inability to keep track of the Duckworth–Lewis

122 | Marcus Trescothick: Coming Back To Me

target meant we might have lost to Namibia, that would have been 100 per cent acceptable.

But it took another month for anyone within the management, or selection committee, to discuss the issue with me face to face, and the first conversation I did have, with Duncan Fletcher, as it turned out, confirmed my feeling that the decision had been for one reason and one reason alone; that Michael had had a great tour of Australia and I hadn't.

The first Test of the summer – against Zimbabwe, of all teams – had come and gone with us winning by an innings and 92 and Jimmy Anderson taking five for 73 to put his name on the honours board on his Test debut. A week later, on 3 June, two days before the start of the second Test, I was standing outside the dressing-room at Chester-le-Street when Duncan called me to one side for a chat.

Not a word about Michael's strengths as a leader or tactician, but all about the fact that he had had a good trip down under and I hadn't done as well.

I was disappointed and a little annoyed. But all that changed soon enough.

Nasser was still in charge of the Test side, for the time being, and still, apparently, keen to hold onto the job. In an article in the *Sunday Telegraph* he spelled out his remaining goals. They were 'to earn 100 caps, captain the side more times than Mike Atherton and lead England to more wins than Peter May.' Mike Gatting, the last man to lead England to an Ashes victory, on the 1986–87 tour, was quick to climb in, saying Nasser's words showed he cared more about himself than the team. I know Nasser had occasionally been accused of selfishness as a player and captain. In my judgement and in my experience, I believe every single thing he did and every waking thought he had when captain of England was intended for the benefit of the team. I know he had sleepless night agonizing over all kinds of team affairs. It hurt him badly that England had become the laughing stock of world cricket when he took over in 1999 and he made it his mission to make sure the laughing stopped. No wonder he occasionally came across as moody or was prone to the odd explosion, even with a long-time friend like Thorpe on that last tour to Sri Lanka; he carried a lot on his shoulders and his partnership with Duncan was vital in restoring pride in the England team.

But, from the moment Michael took over the reins for the and the transition that followed, the whole mood changed. Just as Nasser's often inspirational but always wholehearted and passionate leadership style was a reflection of his 'Mr Angry' nature, so was Michael's – calm, intelligent and with a smile that reflected the sense of enjoyment he wanted his players to play with Michael still expected passion from his players, but he wanted us to be inspired more by the thought of what we might achieve if we expressed ourselves freely on the pitch and off it, not driven by the need to avoid failure, to prove we weren't as bad as people thought we were. He wanted togetherness and unity and a sense of common purpose and he also wanted dynamism and athleticism and, if that came at the expense of experience, so be it, most obviously in the replacement of Alec Stewart by Nottinghamshire's Chris Read.

So when we won eight of the nine completed one-dayers in between the end of the Test series against Zimbabwe and the start of the next, beat Pakistan 3–0 in the NatWest challenge and defeated South Africa in the final of the triangular NatWest series with them and Zimbabwe that followed, the line of succession to the Test captaincy was virtually confirmed. Any hangover from the fiasco of the World Cup was instantly cured and any lingering feelings of burnout I had experienced were gone, for now.

Two innings against Pakistan were particularly satisfying for me. First, at The Oval, on 20 June, Pakistan were bowled out for 185 with Jimmy Anderson taking England's first-ever one-day hat-trick, Abdul Razzaq, Shoaib Akhtar and Mohammad Sami. Shoaib was really fired up when they came back at us. During the World Cup he had been clocked officially as bowling a 100mph ball, though later some doubt was cast on the accuracy of the speed gun. Now he sent down bowling as fast as I've ever faced, maybe even faster than Lee in Perth.

But the faster Shoaib bowled now, mostly around 95 mph, the more I enjoyed it. Tests conducted by scientists with nothing better to do established that when a fast bowler sends the ball towards you from 22 yards away at that pace, the time it takes to arrive is fractionally less time than the human brain actually needs to be able to register what to do and to tell the rest of the body to do it. The time lapse is made up by instinct, experience and some kind of sixth sense and today I had all three. This wasn't a *Matrix* moment, more a Superman day. I used the pace on the ball first to batter, then to deflect, and one of my sixes I carved up and over the slips and watched as the ball just kept going and going. If gravity had not kicked in, it would be passing Uranus about now. I felt so Krypton-strong throughout the innings that he could have bowled 200 mph and it would have made no difference. Shoaib got more and more cross, the crowd got noisier and noisier and by the time I was out, we were 109 for one in the twelfth over and I had made 86 in 55 balls. Vikram Solanki, no blocker he, had made eight.

The next match, at Lord's, was even better for me. Not seeing the job to its conclusion in that final against Pakistan on the same ground in 2001 had bugged me ever since. This time, in very similar circumstances, I managed it, batting all the way through our innings for 108 not out. Just like in 2001 we were struggling in a tight run-chase with wickets falling regularly, 154 for six needing 230 to win, but now Chris Read joined me in a partnership of 77 that took us home with nine balls to spare. Chris, who also had a point to prove about his ability with the bat, jumped into my arms at the end and we celebrated as though we'd won the World Cup. We did exactly the same three weeks later at the culmination of our successful NatWest series campaign, the highlight of which for me was our victory over South Africa at The Oval. Carrying my bat again for my sixth one-day hundred was good enough, and I had a brilliant time batting with Vikram who also made a wonderful stroke-filled hundred in our England record opening stand of 200, but as I had taken over from Michael on the morning of the match due to a back injury, the fact that it was a captain's innings as well as a winning one was extra special.

As we gathered in Birmingham to prepare for the five-Test series with South Africa there was a discernible feeling that change was in the air. Alec Stewart was back, but had announced he would be retiring from all cricket at the end of the season. Caddick was still injured, but though Darren Gough returned after a two-year absence and a serious knee operation, his colleagues in the pace department, Anderson, Harmison and Flintoff, made him look even older than they joked he was.

Nasser Hussain later claimed he noticed almost as soon as he entered the dressing-room that we all seemed to be taking our lead not from him but from Vaughan. When discussing where our guys should bowl to their batsmen, even Duncan, joined at the hip to his captain ever since they came together in 1999, kept asking Vaughan what we had done in the one-dayers.

Unsurprisingly Nasser was in a strange, tentative mood throughout the match. In the build-up he had been asked for his thoughts about Graeme Smith, the young new South African skipper and had suffered a temporary brain freeze over what his first name was. The best Nass could come up with was 'what'sisname', which apparently riled Smith so much that he later made reference to it helping him focus during his nine-hour 277 in their first innings, at which point several papers joked that Nasser might remember his name for some time to come. It was a cheapish shot but fairly harmless, yet it got right up Nasser's nose – though that, of course, was never a difficult thing to do – and when Vaughan then made a majestic 156 to help save the game and Nasser a first innings 1, his mind was made up.

The atmosphere in the Edgbaston dressing-room that Monday evening was fairly sombre, even though Vaughan's innings made sure of a draw. From a personal point of view I was pretty cheesed off because I had broken my right index finger while fielding in the slips and was concerned that I might have to miss a Test or two at least. But that became somewhat less of a priority when we heard Nasser had decided to give up the captaincy, though Duncan had managed to talk him out of his initial intention to retire from Test cricket. And Vaughan, typically, barely paused in between mouthfuls of the bacon sandwich he was munching at the time to accept Duncan's offer of the job. Goodbye, Mr Angry. Hello, Mr Hungry.

This time neither of us needed to say a thing. His appointment was so obviously the right decision, and he knew I was ready to support him in any way I could. In fact, when people later analysed the dynamic of the team, it was a more-or-less unanimously held view that the combination of Vaughan as captain and me as his No. 2 worked perfectly and much better than it might have done the other way around.

Mind you, that all looked some way off when Vaughan's tenure as captain began disastrously in the second Test, which started three days later at Lord's. They had given me a ring-block injection in the base of the damaged finger to enable me to carry on, and six straight sessions in the field did at least give it a chance of further rest as well. During that time Smith proved his first double-hundred had not been a matter of personal revenge against Nasser's supposed slight by scoring another one here, 259 out of their 682 for six declared, and they won by an innings and 92 runs. The biggest cheers of the match were reserved for Fred, who responded to Vaughan's encouragement to express himself by making a sensational 142 from 146 balls, hitting 18 fours and five sixes. We'd known for some time what Fred was capable of and we'd seen it in his first Test ton in Christchurch, but we all hoped this would be the start of something big and, thanks to some inspired man-management by Vaughan as time progressed, it turned out to be just that. But our biggest fears now concerned Nasser, who just wasn't with us on the field at all for so much of the match, had dropped Smith on 8 and spent most of the rest wandering around in a foul temper. At one stage he ran up to Jimmy as he was about to get to the end of his run-up from the Nursery End, gave him a clear 'gee-up' and the rest of us looked on in faint embarrassment. Maybe that was not how Michael wanted things done from now on. Goughy decided he had made one comeback too many and retired from Tests straight after the match.

Michael knew he had to do something about Nasser to make sure he would be able to come back aboard a ship of which he was no longer master and commander, not least because we needed him and his cussedness with the bat. After clear the air talks Nasser was back to his battling best in the next Test at Trent Bridge, and he and Butcher made hundreds to help us to a first innings lead, then the whole team only made 118 in the second before we bowled them out in the fourth dig, thanks to six for 34 from James Kirtley, and we won by 70 runs. Kirtley had been under scrutiny over his action for some while but, after modification, was cleared at all levels and he bowled beautifully that day, swinging the ball at a decent pace. Ed Smith, who couldn't stop scoring hundreds for Kent was also given his Test debut and made a useful half-century. And the presence of a man who had achieved a double-first in history at Cambridge certainly lifted the average IQ in the dressing-room. It was a shame Goughy retired when he did as I can imagine the two of them discussing matters of great import. Ed was so clever they called him 'two brains'. Later he wrote a book on baseball and another called *What Sport Teaches Us About Life* that was described as a magisterial thesis. Yeah, but he didn't have a GCSE in drama did he?

We took another beating in the fourth Test at Headingley, where Martin Bicknell was called up for his third Test, ten years after his second, and Kabir Ali was given his debut, and I got a pasting in the press for taking the umpires' offer of bad light when we seemed to be well on course to overhaul their first innings 342. Butch and I were in the middle of a stand of 140-odd for the second wicket and had just collected 54 from the previous ten overs when a dirty great big black cloud came over the ground and Billy Bowden and Simon Taufel offered us the light. I said to Butch, 'Mate, I think we should go off here,' he didn't say no and I got absolutely nailed for it in the papers the next day. In hindsight, I have to admit it looked a shocking decision but at the time I was convinced I was right and given the same circumstances I would do the same again. My decision was based on the conviction that the light was so bad we would be off for the rest of the day. Therefore we should stick now so that we could twist in the morning. If we had stayed out and a wicket had fallen, the new batsman would have had pretty dodgy light to deal with – it had to have been poor for the umpires to have offered it in the first place – one wicket could easily have led to a clutch and we would have been in the cart. Trouble was we came back out again after half an hour during which Graeme Smith got in the ear of his bowlers and, when we faced up, both Butch and I went in quick succession anyway, we lost momentum and eventually the match by 191 runs to trail 2–1. By the time the post-mortems had been conducted, it turned out that it was all my fault.

So much for my tactical nous, wrote the papers, and for the new spirit of adventure. I was still getting letters about taking the light a year later and whenever the issue of why I was overlooked for the captaincy cropped up, people would say: 'What about when he took the light at Headingley against South Africa, then?' and everyone would nod sagely and say. 'Exactly.'

We knew how much was at stake when we arrived at the Oval for the fifth and final Test, beginning on 4 September. Anything but victory and the merchants of gloom who were busy gathering themselves for another debate on *'What's wrong with English cricket?'* might have moved to dismantle everything we were trying to build. Already a group of cricket worthies known as the Cricket Reform Group, which included Mike Atherton and Bob Willis, were circulating a manifesto advocating massive changes to the structure of the English game and who knew where their work might end?

With Nasser again absent due to his brittle fingers, Vaughan decided the time had come to see if Thorpe could do a job for us again. The selectors had mixed views; Thorpe's last contact with them had been 11 months before, when he told them he was not available to go on the previous winter's Ashes tour only a week or so after assuring them he was and, if he succeeded here and so put himself in line for the winter tours to Bangladesh, Sri Lanka and West Indies, how could they make sure he wouldn't land them in it again?

Admittedly his selection was not exactly a sign of the brave new world, but those of us who had played alongside him in the England dressing-room in places like Sri Lanka and Pakistan knew his potential worth. We wanted him there even if one or two of the selectors took some persuading.

At the start of day two, however, with South Africa on 362 for four and one of them the run out of Smith for 18, we looked a massive price to win. Bookmakers were offering odds of 40–1 and no one was banging the door down to get a bet on. And then a total fluke occurred that changed the match, the series and everything. Shaun Pollock drove hard and straight back towards Ashley Giles and Jacques Kallis was left stranded when the ball deflected off his fingers into the stumps. From 419 for six, they slumped to 484 all out, and the stage was set for my best innings for England to date, my first and only Test double-hundred, which here and now I would like to dedicate to Eminem.

Prior to that match I had not been in the best of nick. Even though the injections had numbed the pain in my finger, I still felt restricted and that was affecting my confidence. In the build-up I had a few sessions with Steve Bull to try and sort out my head, during which we discussed what I might do to help myself maintain focus. I told him about the fact that, often when I had batted well in the past I had found myself listening to music or singing inside my head. Plenty of players listen to music to relax themselves before going into bat. I remembered reading an article in which Glenn McGrath had talked about singing songs to himself to help relieve pressure in tight situations, like the death overs of a one-day international. Steve suggested being more proactive about it; if I felt I needed to focus or calm down or I was clutching for form during an innings, instead of waiting for the music to start up, perhaps I should pick a tune and start singing.

And how I needed it now. I'd practised really hard in the build-up, but when I went out to bat that day I was all over the place.

I scratched around for the first ten or twelve runs and I recall standing there at the crease, looking down at my boots, muttering out loud, 'What the f*** am I doing?' I was thinking so much about my hands, about my head, about my feet that I had forgotten to do the most important thing – watch the ball – and the more

I thought the worse I batted. Finally I said to myself, 'Forget all that. Just sing something.'

Ever since leaving school I had been into 'gangster rap' music and artists like Snoop Dog, Warren G and Eminem. Now, I picked my favourite 'Lose Yourself' from the album *Eight Mile*, and so I did, repeating various lines from the song, in no particular order, over and over again.

'Look,' I said to myself in my own mind as Shaun Pollock ran up to bowl, with the bass thumping in my brain, 'if you had one shot, one opportunity to seize everything you ever wanted – one moment – would you capture it or let it slip?' And the longer the innings went on, the more I lost myself in the music, and the more I did that, the more the super-slow-motion effect kicked in again. I stopped thinking through the processes of batting and just batted. I knew, almost in advance, what ball was about to be bowled and where. No one could bowl at me. How do you bowl at someone who is batting in a different time zone to you anyway? After 374 balls and 219 runs, I made my first and only mistake, holing out to Jacques Rudolph off Makhaya Ntini. 'Lose Yourself' may have been wearing thin by then, but I had made my highest Test score and featured in a stand of 268 with Thorpe, who made a brilliant 124 on his triumphant return, to take us past their total. A year later I persuaded Michael Vaughan to try 'Lose Yourself' as our one-day batting theme tune.

Though absolutely delighted for me, my dad was quietly delighted for himself when I was out because it meant he could finally get rid of the single piece of gum he had been chewing for the entire nine and a half hours of my innings. After we had managed to crowbar his jaws apart, he told me later he had started chewing it when I went into bat the previous day, chewed it until the close, took it out of his mouth and put it in a safe place overnight, then popped it back in his gob when we resumed the following morning and was still chewing it when I was out at 489 for six. In total he had chewed it for 570 minutes. That's devotion. Daft sod.

And then up stepped Fred with licence to thrill.

On the fourth morning, with the forecast predicting bad weather we were eight down and only 18 ahead, a position which, under previous regimes might have led to much agonizing over how to proceed.

'Go and have a hit and enjoy yourself,' Vaughan told Flintoff, which was like handing a kid the key to the sweetshop and unwrapping all the chocolate bars for him. Fred bashed and battered 95 in double-quick time with reverse-sweeps for six and the kitchen sink as well, 85 of his runs coming off 72 balls. At the other end Steve Harmison, with whom Fred was developing a very close friendship, made an invaluable contribution to their ninth wicket stand of 99 – precisely three – which enabled a by-now hysterical Vaughan to declare on 604 for nine, a lead of 120.

This was Freddie not only at his best but his most influential, because it changed the emphasis and transformed the expectations within the two camps. South Africa would have been irritated by my innings, knowing they probably could not win once we had matched their score. But Freddie hurt them because he opened up the chance that they might lose and at the same time gave us belief that we might actually win. And now we piled in, Harmison, the Durham rookie and Martin Bicknell, the Surrey veteran, taking four wickets apiece as we bowled them out for 229, then knocked off the 110 required to win the game and square the series in quick time. Finishing on 69 not out with Butcher 20 not out, I made a grand total of 288 runs in the match, but more importantly I had made a real contribution to a result that gave the new captain and the new team some much needed space in which to breathe, think and plan for the next stage of its development.

Afterwards, after Alec, who ended his Test career in victory just as he had started it, had been lifted shoulder-high by Fred and all of us doused in bubbly, Vaughan made good use of an upbeat press conference to give Fred something to think about as he pondered which way his career was going to go from here.

When asked by one of the cricket writers why it had taken so long for Fred to start to fulfil his potential, Michael uttered a single word: 'Beer.'

In the circumstances, no one thought twice about such an apparently throwaway and jokey remark but Vaughan rarely did things like that for no reason and if Fred was in a fit state to read the papers next day he would have reckoned so as well. Mind you he probably wasn't and nor were the rest of us. The next morning I woke up giggling thinking of the game of football we had played on the outfield, after the crowd had long since departed, with one of those huge rubber stretching balls, all p***ed out of our minds in the pitch-black of the South London night. And for the first time in ages, I slurred to myself, 'Ishn't thish great?'

Chapter 9

THE JIGSAW

*'Looking back I should have taken some more time
and trouble to discuss the problems he [Harmy]
was going through, but at the time I just thought
he was being soft. If you don't want to play, I
thought to myself, why don't you just p*** off and
we'll bring in someone who does.'*

No disrespect to Bangladesh, who had lost 23 of their 24 Tests thus far, but from the moment we arrived at the start of October 2004 to begin a potentially testing winter there, in Sri Lanka, then after Christmas in the Caribbean, the cricket was something of a sideshow.

Michael and Duncan had firm ideas about the kind of players we needed to find if we were to make real progress from this point on. We wanted real high pace from our quick bowlers, and we were hopeful that, with time and work, the 6ft 5in Steve Harmison might develop into a real, out-and-out strike bowler and the leader of a very strong attack, featuring Fred, and maybe even Simon Jones, now well on the road to recovery after his horrific knee injury and due to be available for the tour to West Indies.

When Steve bowled well he was one of those guys you would find any excuse you could think of not to face in the nets. Horrible bounce off a good length, straight into the ribs or your chin, at a top speed of 93mph. Lovely to watch, especially from the slips. Terrible to bat against.

Fred was capable of bowling even a notch or two quicker, his huge effort ball zeroing in at the right-hander from over the wicket or at guys like me from around with no possibility of evasive action. Fred was accurate as well and was beginning to get to grips with the mysteries of reverse swing.

Jones had skiddy pace with excellent reverse and normal swing.

To me, there was one other place up for grabs for a conventional swing bowler and it was between a clutch like Hoggard, Anderson, Kirtley, Richard Johnson and Martin Saggers.

Duncan had always needed some persuading about Matthew Hoggard, but Vaughan thought he might be the most likely if he could just crank up his pace. Jimmy, unfortunately, was having a few problems adjusting to a slightly remodelled action, recommended after experts agreed that his natural bowling style would lead to injury problems if left uncorrected. Ashley was wilier than he was given credit for as our spinner, and valuable as a batsman and in the field as well. Read would be first up to take over from Alec on a full-time basis and, given enough chances, a pecking order would eventually be established among the batsmen inside and on the fringe of selection. Not that we were thinking as far ahead as the 2005 Ashes at this stage, but Michael and I were agreed on one thing; there was no way we wanted to go through what we had experienced last time.

What Michael emphasized in Bangladesh was the need to get super-fit and we threw ourselves into it there like maniacs. His message was: 'We've got to move on from where we are and if we are going to get better we need to get fitter.' Michael spoke at length with Duncan and they set up a new and punishing regime with the physiologist Nigel Stockhill, which formed the basis for everything we did from then on.

It was too much for Fred, who had to go home and missed the two Tests, and it soon became obvious that his best mate Harmy was missing him. He took nine wickets in the first Test in Dhaka, but was utterly miserable throughout, complaining about the place, the heat, the humidity, everything. With my experience of burnout I should probably have been more sympathetic, but I wasn't. My attitude then was pure and simple: 'This bloke is swinging the lead' and I was even more frustrated because I knew how good he could be for us and how vital.

I knew all about burnout and homesickness but I also felt that if *I* could get through a tour like this, so could he. The team unity Michael was searching for depended on everyone sticking together and if someone couldn't hack it, or seemingly didn't care enough about what we were doing to get fully involved then, no matter how important he might be to the side, he deserved no sympathy. Looking back I should have taken some more time and trouble to discuss the problems he was going through, but at the time I just thought he was being soft. If you don't want to play, I thought to myself, why don't you just p*** off and we'll bring in someone who does. One or two of the press picked up on the feelings within the camp and they were spot on. As with my earlier thoughts about Thorpe retiring from one-day cricket, it was an attitude I had cause to reflect upon in later years. Harmy went back to England suffering a back strain and didn't help matters when, on being told he could leave, started behaving like a kid on the last day of school, enjoying the fact that he was getting out of there rather too much.

At that stage quite a few of us within the camp needed some persuading Harmy was worth persevering with, but, fair play to him, although he stayed at home for the Sri Lankan leg of the trip, while there he threw himself into training with Newcastle United and got himself fantastically fit for bowling in the Caribbean, with spectacular results, as it turned out.

But he was only picked after we made absolutely sure he was up for it, and a crucial change of approach from Michael worked wonders in that regard, as it did for Fred as well.

Our immediate problem, however, was all about Murali, or rather the mystery ball he had developed since we last met, the 'doosra', literally 'the other one', the ball that looked like an off break but turned like a leg break. I had had enough trouble picking his regular varieties but I wouldn't have been able to pick this one if you'd tied a ribbon round it.

We battled hard enough and, knowing we were outgunned, determined to go back to the Nasser way of 'staying in the game', drawing in Galle and in Kandy, where our former skipper Nasser got into strife for sledging Murali after the Sri Lankans went running to the match referee Clive Lloyd to complain.

But we ended up losing the final match in Colombo by an innings and 215 runs, and the most memorable aspect of our crunching defeat was comedy fielding of the highest order. I think I dropped Samaraweera three times, though I lost count in the end. We couldn't catch a bus and after I was out cheaply, an England supporter gave me a gobful for not trying. I'd like to have seen him have a crack at Murali.

Fortunately that bloke didn't have much to moan about from that point on, as it turned out to be the last time we ended up losing a Test series for two years. In fact, we were about to start a run of six wins on the trot that culminated in the greatest prize of them all, the 2005 Ashes.

Hayley and I took the chance of some time off between tours to get married in January 2004. We'd been living together for some time and I finally succumbed to her giving me earache on a beautiful crisp winter's day at Trull Parish Church, near Taunton on Saturday 24 January. I couldn't decide which of Jason Kerr or Steffan Jones to ask to be my best man so I asked them both. The only hitch came afterwards when the heating broke down in the marquee in the middle of a field for about half an hour as all the guests sat huddled together in the deep winter evening fighting the effects of hypothermia.

After a rather warmer honeymoon in Florida, I arrived in the Caribbean in mid-February for the first of the six-in-a row, the four-Test series against Brian Lara's side during which several more pieces of the jigsaw were hammered firmly into place.

First, a combination of brilliant man-management from Vaughan and Duncan and the arrival on the scene of our new bowling coach Troy Cooley made sure the potentially problematic brotherhood of Fred and Harmy was brought onside.

I'm not saying they were disruptive but Fred, in particular, liked doing things his own way. He had always been a big social animal and his stamina and capacity for enjoying himself were legendary but when Vaughan had mentioned 'beer' back at The Oval the previous summer, everyone understood what he meant. Now we needed him to change, slightly, and Harmy quite a lot, or this side's progress could easily stall.

Troy, a former state player with Tasmania, was initially hired by Rod Marsh to work at the ECB National Academy in 2003. He soon graduated to a more specific role as the England first-team bowling coach, instantly gaining the trust and respect of the bowlers for his ideas and approach. He got them thinking as a team within a team, which let Duncan concentrate on other areas. If the quicks really felt they needed to work on something, or even occasionally take a day off, they could be treated in isolation and Troy could be the conduit. Rather than Fred or Harmy asking Duncan for a

break, or being nervous about doing so in case they were perceived to be skiving, Troy could step in and recommend to Duncan
they be rested. They felt better and so did Duncan.

Furthermore Michael and Duncan made the decision to stop
trying to persuade, cajole or even bully the pair of them to fall in
with our ideas about the importance of the team ethic and unity,
but to give them a bit of licence. A number of conversations took
place in which, instead of saying, 'We need you to do this or you
must do that,' Duncan and Michael said, 'Show us that you really
want to be part of what we are trying to do. Show us you really care
about playing for this England team.'

And, match-by-match, our four-man pace attack grew into itself
with fantastic results.

In the first Test in Jamaica, we made 339 first up, thanks to extras
top-scoring on 60, as a result of the number of no-balls and wides
sent down by the fiery but wayward pacemen Tino Best and Fidel
Edwards. We led by 38 on first innings and, remarkably, it was
nearly enough for us to win without batting a second time because
Hurricane Harmison turned up on the third morning and just blew
them away. This was the day everything clicked into place for him.
On a fast and bouncy Sabina Park surface, with his pace, bounce
and growing aggression, he was unstoppable, taking seven wickets for twelve runs from 12.3 overs as we flattened them for 47.

One photograph of me taking a catch at first slip to dismiss
Adam Sanford said it all. Standing next to me was a second slip,
then a third, a fourth, a fifth and a sixth, and next to him, two gul-
leys. We had nine men and the keeper behind the bat, which, with
a short leg plus Harmison bowling, meant we had no one in the
outfield at all.

Every ball came down like a bouncing bomb, the batsmen
appeared utterly terrified and hearts were pumping fit to explode
in case the next edge came to you, not only because you wanted to

make sure you caught the ball, but because if you didn't take it cleanly there was every chance it might take a finger with it to the boundary. It was one of the most gruesomely exciting passages of play I have ever experienced.

I can't recall Harmy bowling a single delivery anywhere other than exactly where he wanted it to go, and when he bowled like that he just got you out, even if your name was Brian Lara, as Harmy then did twice in the next Test in Trinidad, among another seven scalps in the match.

In Port-of-Spain, Jones earned his reward after 16 months of agony and bloody hard work since Brisbane by taking five for 57 to set up another easy victory, celebrating his achievement with tears of pure Welsh emotion, with Jeff, his old man, beaming with pride from the sidelines.

Simon's dad knew, as we all did, that if we could make it 3–0 in Barbados we would be the first England team since 1967–68 to win a series in the Caribbean, when he was a key member of their attack. And now Fred, in the first innings with five for 58, then, after Thorpe's wonderful hundred, Hoggard in the second – with a hat-trick to remove Ramnaresh Sarwan, Shiv Chanderpaul, and Ryan Hinds – made it happen, completing a four-timer of match-winning performances by a four-wheeled pace wagon that had run down everything in its path.

Afterwards the celebrations we shared with the Barmy Army left all the bars on the island frantically searching for more supplies of the venerable Mount Gay. And now might be a good time to apologize to the residents of St Laurence's Gap for the noise we made falling out of the bus many, many hours later when we were driven back from The Kensington Oval to our hotel. Blame Freddie, if you like. But Thorpe knows he was the one singing loudest.

Whether the drink was responsible I cannot tell, but it was about this time, at the press conference on the eve of the final Test in

Antigua, that a Sunday newspaper reporter who shall remain nameless asked Lara if, in view of his run of low scores, he was concerned that his glorious talent might be on the wane.

Three days later Lara declared the West Indies first innings closed at 751 for five. He was not out 400, setting a new record for the highest individual score in Test history, as he had done on the same ground against England in 1994, that time scoring a mere 375. He had batted for 778 minutes, faced 582 balls, hit 43 fours and four sixes. The special thing about Brian was that if he made up his mind to score a hundred there was generally very little you could do to stop him. In this instance he just happened to have made up his mind to score four hundred. Thanks, Reg.

Despite this, we left the West Indies happy that the bowling pieces of the puzzle were now in place. We had also taken the unusual step of changing a winning side after Barbados, bringing in Geraint Jones to keep wicket instead of Chris Read. Read hadn't done an awful lot wrong and anyone taking over from Alec was bound to suffer by comparison not only to him but also to Adam Gilchrist, but Duncan had noticed that he was occasionally reluctant to go for catches to his right beyond a certain distance. He also felt Jones might be a better bet with the bat.

So, five bowlers – Harmison, Hoggard, Flintoff, Giles and Jones – were now in place, though Simon's unhappy knack of picking up injuries at regular intervals meant there would still be opportunities for Anderson and Saggers to displace him in the coming months, and Geraint Jones soon established himself as No.1 choice with the gloves. Just the batsmen to finalise now and the jigsaw would be complete.

And we found the next one almost immediately, during the first home Test of 2004, against New Zealand at Lord's, starting on 20 May.

The first thing that happened when we arrived at HQ was to get together for a session of goal-setting. Duncan was keen on the players sitting down together and talking about team and individual targets and, at this meeting, in the MCC Committee room in the old pavilion we all decided, virtually as one, that the goal we should set ourselves for the summer was to win every single Test match, three against New Zealand and four against West Indies. Seven Tests, seven wins. That was our target. We weren't being arrogant. This wasn't bravado talking, or booze. We truly believed we could do it.

The second thing that happened was that Vaughan twisted his knee in the nets trying to sweep a ball from a 19-year-old left-arm spinner called Zac Taylor and collapsed in a heap. It looked awful at the time, even so we all assumed the problem was only a temporary one. Little did we know this was in fact the start of a long-running battle that almost forced him into premature retirement.

For now, Michael's misfortune was my good luck as it gave me the chance to captain England in a Test match, and at Lord's. I made sure I breathed in every moment, but what I actually ended up noticing most was how my new opening partner was taking to the demands of Test cricket like he'd been doing it for donkey's years.

A couple of seasons earlier Andrew Strauss had considered giving up playing cricket for Middlesex and going into the city to earn proper money. Now he batted like a million dollars as we put on 190 for the first wicket in response to New Zealand's first innings 386, making a faultless 112 on his debut out of our 441. Everything about him just looked right from the first moment I saw him; he netted right, practised right, prepared right, even walked out to the middle with me right, enthusiastic but utterly focused. And how right did he bat that day? There are some people whose potential to play at the highest level you can spot a mile off. Strauss was one of them and no one needed to say a word. Whoever had to make way for Vaughan's return for the next Test, Strauss wasn't it.

Our efforts to bowl them out within reasonable bounds hit a snag when Chris Cairns teed off against the quicks and hit Jones, Harmison and Flintoff (twice) out of the ground.

We set off in hard pursuit of 282 to win, but when I and Butch were out at 35 for two it looked all over.

Instead, from the moment Hussain joined Strauss at the crease it was clear he was a man on a mission. Their partnership had grown to 108, with Strauss only 17 away from a century in each innings of his debut, when Nasser managed to run him out by miles.

Nass was distraught, but, instead of crumbling, took it upon himself to bring us home, and, with Thorpe, one of his best mates in the game at the other end, did it with a glorious cover drive with which he also reached his 14th Test century.

It was clear that Nasser had been thinking what everyone else had been thinking. Vaughan would be fit for the next Test at Leeds. Strauss could not be dropped. Something would have to give.

As Hussain got closer to the finish line so the feeling grew inside him that batting us to victory would be a pretty special way to go and afterwards he spent the next hour or so canvassing opinions from Duncan and Thorpe. Was he seeking support for his idea to call it a day or opposition that might persuade him to change his mind?

For the next two days the silence was deafening, except from Shane Warne, who came up with his idea of the perfect solution in his column in *The Times*.

'Selection can be simple at times, but on other occasions it needs a bit of thought and a lot of guts. Unless England drop a batsman at Headingley, they will be fudging the issue,' he wrote.

'Andrew Strauss must stay and so should Nasser Hussain. The best way to keep both and still maintain the balance of the team is to leave out Marcus Trescothick.

'Trescothick is a very good one-day player, but I think he has been found out at Test level over the past two years. You do not need to be Einstein to work out the way to bowl at him and his technique does not seem to be adaptable.'

And he advocated that if Hussain were to wait until the end of the summer to finish 'it will enable Trescothick to go back to Somerset and learn how to play again.'

All I can say is this was typical Warne bull****. It annoyed me then and it still annoys me now that players feel they are entitled to go into print to try and destroy a fellow professional. Warne may think what he did was all part of the game, that he was being clever by trying to f*** with my head. I think it is just disrespectful. We all love playing cricket for a living and on the field we will go at each other as hard as we can. Of course, Warne is one of the greatest bowlers who ever drew breath and a master at winding people up on and off the field, but this was a personal and scornful attempt at belittling me. It might have been more understandable if he had done it during an Ashes series. And I know that if you are being paid to write a newspaper column you have to earn your money by saying something that is going to attract attention. But advising me to go back to Somerset to learn how to play again was crap. Saying I had been found out at Test level was crap – he must have missed my 219 against South Africa at The Oval and ignored the fact that I had made 1,000 Test runs in 2003 (even though I was batting with a broken finger for four of the five Tests against them that summer), as I was to do in 2004 and 2005. And saying you didn't have to be Einstein to work out the way to bowl at me was obviously literally true, but more crap nonetheless.

He would keep, though. For a year, anyway.

In the meantime, Nasser confirmed what I think we all knew by now and quit, and, in the next Test at Headingley, I pulled out a brand new bat when we went out to respond to their 409 and made 132, the first of my three Test hundreds that summer. Fred made 94, Geraint Jones 100 and we scored 526, bowled them out for 161 and won by nine wickets.

We completed the first part of our pre-season target at Nottingham, winning by four wickets, thanks to another top ton from Thorpe, now relishing his second chance, who finished 104 not out. Three-nil against New Zealand.

We pretty much blew up in the triangular series and failed to qualify for the final which was somewhat embarrassing.

But a double-hundred by Rob Key, in for Butcher, who had suffered whiplash in a car accident, put his name among the live contenders for a regular spot and Vaughan returned to his brilliant best with a hundred in both innings in the first Test against West Indies at Lord's which we won by 210 runs. Four out of four.

We made it five in a row at Edgbaston, where I repeated Vaughan's trick and made centuries in both innings. I was gutted to have run myself out in the first innings, for 105. Don't tell Warne, but I did struggle a bit against their quicks that summer, though not for any reason Einstein would have identified. I just found Fidel Edwards quicker and skiddier than he looked. And with Tino Best, search me. I just didn't have a clue where the ball was going to land, at my feet, at my head or possibly at my head, without bouncing.

Neither of them were playing here, so I really wanted to cash in when I reached three figures and enjoy myself, get to the 'matrix' moment, kick on and score a massive one. Still, the view of Fred bashing the ball everywhere for 167 to help us to 566 for nine declared was a reasonable consolation, for now he wasn't only one of our brilliant pace attack, his improved batting meant he was now a fantastic all-rounder as well. Another piece in place...

We duly completed wins No. 6, at Old Trafford, and No. 7 at The Oval, where, after a quietish summer, Harmy took nine wickets in the match as we bowled them out twice and left ourselves one to win in the second innings, which I managed from the third ball with a pretty four.

Our confidence had grown as the summer and the run of seven progressed. By now we just felt we could win almost any game from almost any position. All we thought about was winning. Even if we found ourselves up against it, it wasn't how are we going to get out of this one, but what do we need to do to win from here? Score 500 in 100 overs and bowl them out for twelve? Okay then, crack on.

And when we came up against Australia in the semi-final of the ICC Champions Trophy at Edgbaston on 21 September, that was exactly the mentality we took with us onto the field.

For most of the recent past an Australian score of 259 would almost certainly have been enough to do our nut in. This time, definitely spurred on by Warne's words, even though he himself was absent, I was completely determined not to allow that to happen. Michael and I batted positively, I hit 81 in 88 balls, we shared a second wicket stand of 140 and Strauss came in at No. 4 to finish off the win with a calm 52 not out. A year later, as we prepared for the 2005 Ashes, Duncan told us to use this result and this performance as proof not only that Australia could actually be beaten, but they could actually be beaten by us, and comfortably, too.

What could possibly go wrong now?

Two things; the spectre of another tour to Zimbabwe was looming. As usual, the ECB contrived to drop the burning hot potato in our hands, insisting that, without government orders to stop us going to Zimbabwe, we could not pull out of the short one-day series there prior to a trip to Namibia. Sensing we were all going to be left high and dry again, Harmy decided to announce in his *News of the World* column that he wasn't going on moral grounds, not knowing Duncan had intended to tell him he was going to be rested that very same day. When we arrived at The Oval to play West Indies in the Champions Trophy final, rumours of who was going to Zimbabwe and who wasn't were buzzing around and served only to unsettle everyone.

I had already received a phone call from John Carr, the England team's director, telling me I was going to be rested, for which I was extremely grateful as I was getting very close to burnout again and needed a proper break before going to South Africa that winter.

First I had also been told he wasn't going and so had Ashley Giles. But the Board then decided that, as captain, Vaughan had to go, come what may, no ifs or buts, personal choice, concerns about the state of his knee or wishes of the selectors or coach, in order to keep up appearances and keep ECB sweet with the rest of the ICC. When Giles heard that Vaughan was being made to go, he offered to go as well and I was placed in an awful position. On the one hand I wanted to support Vaughan and the rest of the players. On the other I was dog tired. I felt really guilty about not offering to go. I felt I was letting Michael down. But I knew that, in the long run, the best thing for me and therefore the side was for me to just stop. And, of course, what really pissed us all off was that we were once again put in a position where we were the ones having to make these kind of decisions. Despite all the talk and all the assurances, the bottom line was that nothing had changed since the World Cup fiasco the previous year.

And the other thing that could go wrong? We lost the Champions Trophy Final to West Indies at The Oval in near darkness, on 25 September, the latest date international cricket had ever been played in this country. I made 104, bloody run out again, of our 217, then, after reducing them to 147 for eight with the light fading fast, we lost the plot and the match as Courtney Browne and Ian Bradshaw put on an unbeaten stand of 71 to win with seven balls to spare.

A summer of such brightness had ended, once again, in murky gloom. Less than twelve months in the future, however, we would experience the sunniest days of our lives.

Chapter 10

JERUSALEM

*'Cue the madness. Seas of champagne, cameras,
songs, "Jersualem". More champagne, KP
managing to pour almost half a bottle of it into his
eye. The Ashes. Vaughan holding the Urn. Us
waving at the girls, Tears, loads of tears.
Even more champagne. "Jerusalem" again.
Sleep? What for?'*

When I retrace the story of my fight against the illness that finally ended my International career, I cannot escape the feeling that it first revealed itself to me during the period immediately before and immediately after I joined England's tour to South Africa in the winter of 2004–05.

Though it had an instant and disturbing effect on me, it was only a fleeting visit, then it flapped its black wings and flew away until it knew I was ready for the taking. I had no idea what it was or what it might lead to. And when it went I thought no more about it. But I can recall the time it arrived to the very moment.

Hayley was around five months pregnant with Ellie at the time, a few days before I was due to join up with the rest of the squad. We were at the big multiscreen cinema complex near where the road out of Taunton meets the M5 motorway, watching a movie with friends. Neither of us was particularly enjoying the film, in fact I can't actually recall what it was we were watching, but I do remember at one point we both turned to each other simultaneously and I said: 'This is awful. Shall we leg it?'

We decided to stay because our mates seemed to be enjoying the experience more than we were and then, a few moments later, Hayley turned to me again, this time with a little more urgency in her voice and said: 'Marcus, I feel really funny …,' and then she passed out.

Already super-sensitive because of her condition, I vaulted over the vacant seats in front of us and ran to call 999 for an ambulance. When we got to the hospital, the doctor performed various tests and what he told us sent a shiver down my spine. 'Mrs Trescothick,' the doctor began, 'your baby is fine. But we have detected what may be a murmur in your heart. This is not uncommon for pregnant women and is almost certainly nothing to worry about, but we would like you to come back for an electrocardiagram, an ECG, from which we will be able to get a much clearer picture of what is going on …'

Even though the words were spoken with calm compassion, inevitably it all sounded utterly terrifying.

I tried not to show my fears in case I made Hayley feel worse than she already did. The first thing I had to do was contact the Board because the ECG was set for the following Thursday, the day after I was due to fly out. They were very understanding and told me to take as much time as I needed to sort things out.

The day of the ECG turned out to be about the happiest of my life. There was no problem, we were told. All clear. Hayley's heart was having to work double-time to look after her and the baby, and what had happened to her was pretty normal. I was cleared to travel the next day.

When I got to South Africa, however, I very soon realized that something was wrong. As I have said, feelings of homesickness mixed with the disruption to normal sleep caused by jet lag were a regular early tour condition for me, and always in the past, once the cricket had given me something to focus on, the problem became manageable.

Not this time, not at first anyway. When the feelings persisted for a couple of bad days and shocking nights, I spoke with Kirk Russell, our physio and Steve Bull, our sports psychologist and told them: 'I don't feel right, here. I don't feel myself.'

I told them I felt worried, more so than usual. I told them I was struggling to get a grip on what was happening, that I was sleeping poorly and not really eating much. I told them I was feeling very uncomfortable about being away from home and away from Hayley, that I was concerned about what had happened to her just before I left, that I couldn't concentrate or get into the cricket, that I was struggling.

I was pretty miserable for the first six days of the tour, and it didn't help that we were once again stuck in a four-star prison in a shopping 'city' in Sandton, a concrete and glass suburb of Johannesburg, which was decorated in every shade of brown you could think of.

I never said to anyone I can't hack this or I've got to go home, and I never told Hayley how I was, but I remember just battling through it all feeling like crap and thinking I wish I didn't have to do this. And worrying about how things were at home, how Hayley was, how our baby was. After a couple of sleepless nights left me exhausted, I asked for and was given some sleeping pills, which at least helped in that regard. In the next year or so I found Zopiclone; it's better than Horlicks.

What probably worried me more than anything else was that the cricket didn't seem to help like it had in the past. In fact, though I briefly felt better after making 85 not out in the match against Nicky Oppenheimer's XI, a couple of low scores in the opening first-class match against South Africa A at Pochefstroom sent me spinning back down again, now also nagged by the thought that I might actually have started a slow but possibly terminal decline in form.

Steve Bull advised me to start writing down these thoughts in a diary but to end my daily entries with a few self affirming thoughts, and gradually it seemed to do the trick. As I wrote down all my stats, the number of runs I'd scored and the number of hundreds I'd made, the feeling dawned on me that maybe I wasn't such a no-hoper after all.

My batting still wasn't 100 per cent, but I did manage to get my mind back on the cricket enough to make a decent contribution in the first Test in Port Elizabeth, sharing an opening stand of 152 with Strauss, whose 112 made him the first batsman to score a century in his first appearance against three consecutive opponents, and his 94 in the second dig ensured we won by seven wickets. Eight out of eight.

Hayley had arrived by the time we reached Durban for the second Test starting on Boxing Day 2004. It was still early enough in her pregnancy for her to travel and a couple of days after we were reunited I woke up one morning and realized I was okay. Whatever the problem had been, it was over.

My batting, on the other hand, was still well short of okay and it took a crucial intervention by Duncan to help me regain my form and confidence. In fact, it enabled me to take a huge step forward.

I went to him and told him I felt unbalanced at the crease, that the bat wasn't coming down straight even though I was trying my hardest to make it do so, and that I couldn't figure out what was wrong. After I was out for 18 in the first innings and we fell for just 139, he took me to the nets and just watched me for about five minutes. The he brought the practice to an end, walked over to me and said: 'Just relax your right arm, and slightly open your shoulder so you are a fraction more front-on to the bowler.'

I did as he advised, the bat started to come down and through the ball much straighter and I found I was absolutely smoking it. And, of course, it was not just my batting that felt better. My confidence soared. It is a dreadful thing to feel that your batting has got stuck; self-analysis, a surfeit of which I was always prone to, and self-doubt can take you over. What if I can't solve this? What if I can't bat anymore? And then a just a look or a word from a team-mate or a passer-by can set you off. And when you are in that frame of mind even an innocent question like: 'Everything all right?' sounds like 'What the hell is wrong with you?' Mere hard work is not always the answer, so a vicious circle can easily suck you in. Then comes the advice, some better informed than the rest and, in your desperation to cure the problem you listen to everyone and everything and your brain aches with the weight of it all. Sometimes simple rest can be a cure. More often than not, all you need is for a second pair of eyes connected to a good cricket brain. Five minutes with Duncan's eyes and Duncan's brain was all I needed. Shane Warne may joke that the coach is what you get on to drive to the ground. I wasn't laughing much before our coach sorted me out here.

At the time I carried this slight technical adjustment with me onto the pitch in the second innings at Durban; we were in trouble, trailing by nearly 200, but, from the start, I was timing the ball better than ever before. You probably wouldn't have noticed any change between how I looked at the crease now and how I had looked all summer, so small was the change I made, but the difference in how I felt was huge. Early on I recall playing an off drive against Shaun Pollock and it was almost like I had played the most perfect shot of all time. Instantly I wasn't thinking about my troubles on or off the field, I was once again back online with the Vaughan principle of searching for victory in the wreckage of almost certain defeat. Now, where was I? And how are we going to win this match?

Strauss and I put on 273 for the first wicket of which I made 132 and he 136, Thorpe got our third century of the innings, Geraint Jones and Fred smashed a hundred partnership and suddenly South Africa were the team under pressure. We made 570 for seven declared, but from 370 as well and I picked them off at regular intervals until, at 268 for eight, they looked doomed when bad light came to save them.

Relieved to have escaped and roused by a brilliant 149 from Jacques Kallis, they then hammered us in third Test in Cape Town by 196 runs.

We traded scores of 400 plus in the first innings of the fourth Test in Jo'burg, even though the track was always helpful to the seamers and Pollock in particular. Our bowling was pretty scratchy first up. Matthew Hoggard bowled nice and tidy, but Fred seemed to be limping, the first sign of the ankle injury that forced him home at the end of the Test series, for surgery. Harmy was also struggling with a calf injury and poor Jimmy Anderson was having a nightmare, spraying the ball all over the shop, in his first match after five months out with back problems and more remodeling of his action, and getting caned by Herschelle Gibbs. Indeed when Jimmy finally had Gibbs caught by Hoggard he shed tears of embarrassment. A measure of how desperate we were was that Vaughan threw a still fairly new ball to me on the Sunday morning and then kept me on for five whole overs.

But when it came to our turn to bat again, it happened; my next taste of batting in *The Matrix*, an innings of 180 that was the most memorable of my career thus far.

I experienced that super slow-motion effect almost from the first ball I faced and now, with my new improved technique, I just felt the ball had not yet been invented that could actually get me out.

Because the match situation and the regular fall of wickets demanded it, I proceeded at first with something like caution. Even so, at the end of the fourth evening I was 101 not out, but we were only 189 ahead with half the side out and, while the draw was favourite an England collapse might let South Africa in through the back door.

Once again, though, the Vaughan principles came into play; of expression and positivity, of backing your ability and of looking to win at all times, no matter how lousy the view. I attacked and attacked and, with each falling wicket, attacked again. Ashley Giles, batting down the order at No.8 after dislocating his thumb two days earlier in the field, stuck around with me towards the end, helping me put on 50 for the seventh wicket and Harmy made another mammoth contribution to a tenth wicket stand of 58, once again unwrapping the score he saved for all such occasions, namely three.

And I had a blast, running down the track to hit Pollock over extra-cover for four and launching the left –arm spinner Nicky Boje out of the stadium with a massive slog-sweep. More, more, more.

When I was last out at 332, the draw was probably still favourite, especially as the South African skipper Graeme Smith had suffered concussion in fielding practice and was under doctor's orders not to bat.

The fact that he later ignored them and did, making 67 not out in a last-ditch counter-attack coming in at 118 for six, was entirely down to Hoggard who was just magnificent, outbowling the hugely experienced Pollock and Kallis by finding exactly the right length to bowl and peppering it. He ended up with seven for 61 from the finest 111 balls he has ever bowled to secure a dramatic win and a 2–1 lead with one to play. Even Duncan, who never quite seemed to be on Hoggy's wavelength, had nothing but praise for him that day.

When we held onto the advantage in the fifth and final Test at Centurion and secured our fourth series win on the bounce, people inevitably turned the Ashes hype up to full blast.

*   *   *

Reviewing the lessons thrown up by the tour so far, we could see nine virtual certainties for the series with Australia, including our batting: Andrew Strauss, Marcus Trescothick, Michael Vaughan, Andrew Flintoff, Geraint Jones, Matthew Hoggard, Ashley Giles, Steve Harmison and Simon Jones.

Graham Thorpe was considered by everyone outside the camp to be a shoo-in for one of the two remaining batting spots, and on ability and experience he had no rival. But a few of us had noticed that his back problem seemed to be affecting him more and more. Some also thought his eyes and his reactions might be slowing down, though I don't recall ever thinking that myself. Rob Key and Mark Butcher were also still in the frame for the two remaining batting places. Rob was highly rated by many Australians who he had impressed on the 2002–03 tour down under and had proved he could concentrate as hard as he could whack the ball in his double-hundred against West Indies at Lord's. Butch had been suffering from a wrist injury since being hit in the first Test at Port Elizabeth and almost certainly would have carried on had it not taken most of 2005 to even start to heal properly. Ian Bell, who made his Test debut in the final match against West Indies at The Oval the previous summer and made an assured 70, was also considered ready for elevation soon, but some feared putting him in against Australia might be a baptism of fire that could leave him badly burned.

But even though we were mullered in the one-day series that followed, losing five out of seven with two washouts, another young batsman we had been waiting to see for some time played with such breathtaking panache that he instantly propelled himself near to the top of the list of contenders.

Kevin Pietersen was born in South Africa and played most of his young cricket there, but had abandoned his native country due to what he perceived to be the lack of opportunities resulting from the South African Board's quota system.

Now the home crowds and some of their players, including Graeme Smith, showered all over him every name under the hot African sun associated with treachery and defection that they could think of.

And his reaction was just amazing. He scored 108 in the second match in Bloemfontein. He scored 75 in the fourth in Cape Town. He scored exactly 100 in the fifth in east London in 69 balls, beating my 80 balls against India and Srinath at Eden Gardens as the fastest century in a one-day international for England. And finally, he scored 116 in the seventh match at Centurion, by which time the booing and carping from the crowds had long been drowned out by the cheers and even the on-field sledging stopped.

All of which meant that when we got around to the serious planning for the task ahead, the one thing we knew we had to do was somehow get him in. Two things struck me most about KP. First, that while some players take time to get used to the environment he made it his own, running down the wicket to the spinners in particular and smacking the ball out of the park, and secondly how he fed off the stick he was getting. A positive attitude against spin and the ability to take stick. Now, against whom might those qualities come in handy?

Ellie was born on 23 April 2005, St George's Day, bouncy and beautiful and, despite the early scare, Hayley was fine. But the first few days after they came home were a real bolt out of the blue for me. No sleep for Ellie meant no sleep for Hayley and no sleep for me. All three of us were exhausted, for very different reasons, but there just seemed no end to the tiredness. Hayley was very emotional and prone to crying and the whole business of being first-time parents was a massive shock to the system.

When I went back to play for Somerset at the start of the season, and I was asked to captain the side against Essex on 27 April, just four days and four sleepless nights after the birth, I just couldn't get going at all. I had been suffering terrible migraine caused by a combination of lack of sleep and worry about Ellie and Hayley. And after a net session just before the start of play on day two, I walked into one of the vacant rooms in the clubhouse after about my worst net session ever, put my head in a towel and cried my eyes out. I was feeling the usual strains all new parents go through, but I found the emotion of it all really wearing. We were due out on the field soon afterwards and I told the coach, Mark Garraway, 'Sorry, mate. I need to take five here. I'll be all right but I've got a migraine and I just can't go on the field right now.'

Then I saw Mike Burns drop a catch standing at first slip, the position I should have been standing in, and I felt considerably worse.

The next match, against Durham at Stockton-on-Tees, was even worse. By now my GP had put me on betablockers for the migraines which had the effect of making me incredibly sleepy. I couldn't seem to get up in the morning. I couldn't seem to get myself out of bed. I couldn't run and, when batting I could barely see the ball.

The day of my first innings against Steve Harmison I was absolutely cacking myself because he was bowling very fast and I was basically blind.

I was obviously concerned because the first Test series of the summer, against Bangladesh, was about to begin, not to mention who was coming next. But I came off the medication straight away,

Ellie started sleeping better, as did Hayley, and things started to settle down well enough for me to see the wood from the trees again. I was still struggling for rhythm, though, and it took a couple of long sessions in the nets with Tim Boon, our new assistant coach, just hitting ball after ball to help me into some kind of form. Finally something clicked and, at the end of May and start of June, I scored 194 in our victory at Lord's by an innings and 261 runs by noon on the third day, and 151 at Chester-le-Street as we won there by an innings and 27.

The Ashes selection issue was by now a topic of huge debate. Thorpe had been retained and won his 100th cap at the Riverside, making 66 not out in our only innings. Bell made his mark against the inexperienced Bangladesh attack, making 65 not out at Lord's and 162 not out up north, but the most unfortunate aspect of these mismatches from our point of view was that they were two of only five batsmen to actually have a bat, along with myself, Strauss and Vaughan. And that meant that the only international cricket players like Fred, back and fit again after his ankle op, Geraint Jones and the tail would have before contesting the Ashes would be the one-day stuff that came next.

Even so, when we pitched up at Southampton to play Australia in the first ever 'Ashes' Twenty20 match on 13 June it was clear we were not the only team with problems.

The talking and planning had been going on for some time. Strategies for how to bowl at their batsmen had been developed, all kinds of people had been studying tapes of their batting and no suggestion was ignored. More detailed planning would take place a month hence when we met up before the first Test at Lord's. For now the priority was to make a positive statement of intent.

Duncan and Michael had both spoken about getting in the space of the Aussie players, not overtly offering them outside, of course, but challenging them at all times, trying to make the Ashes experience as uncomfortable for them as it had been for so long for us.

We tore into them at the Rose Bowl, after making 179 for eight, having them 31 for seven with Gough, still playing one-dayers for us even though he had packed up Test cricket twelve months earlier, absolutely on fire, taking three for 16, including the two openers, Adam Gilchrist and Matthew Hayden. Jon Lewis took four for 24. When the crowds taunted: 'Are you Bangladesh in disguise?' they didn't see the funny side.

I enjoyed myself in the first match of the NatWest triangular series, against Bangladesh at The Oval on 16 June, making 100 not out in my 100th ODI and my ninth one-day ton which took me past Graham Gooch's England record of eight. When Australia then lost to Test cricket's newest member in Cardiff on 18 June, after having dropped and fined Andrew Symonds for turning up the worse for wear after a big night out in the Welsh capital, we just p***ed ourselves.

Next day we beat Australia again by three wickets in Bristol, thanks to an innings from KP that was to have huge repercussions.

We had known, of course, that KP would have to be fitted into our Ashes Test side; but this innings of 91 not out from 119 for four, chasing 253 to win, showed us and them what he might do when he got there. It was confident, aggressive and brutal and it came off 65 balls. The final piece of the jigsaw was ready to be rammed into place. The only problem was, with Thorpe and Bell apparently also certain to play, we now had one too many. The one-day matches continued in breathless fashion, with Australia stunned by their early reversals, now showing why they were the world champions at all forms of the game. They beat us twice in succession to qualify for the final, but not before an incident at Edgbaston in a washed out day–night match on 28 June.

If 'get in their space' had been one of the orders of the day, the other was 'none of us stands alone', and now a clash between Simon Jones and Matthew Hayden gave us the perfect opportunity to carry out both. Simon had already dismissed Gilchrist and when Hayden played a ball defensively back down the pitch towards him, he picked it up and hurled it in the general direction of the stumps as a warning that if he was going to bat in front of his crease he had better make sure he got back in time. Unfortunately, or rather, fortunately, as things turned out, Simon's aim was dreadful and he accidentally threw the ball at around 100 mph straight into Hayden's shoulder. Simon, a little shocked by what he had done, spluttered an apology straight away, but Hayden, clearly ruffled, reacted aggressively, letting fly with a barrage of f-words.

What happened next was a big statement on our behalf. In other times, that might have been that and we would probably all have shuffled back to our places. This time, four or five of us rushed to the scene to back Simon up. I was on my way as well, but Paul Collingwood's flame-red hair right in front of the colossal Aussie batsman, seemingly big enough to swallow Colly whole, was a sight for sore eyes. The message: bully any one of us and we will come right back at you, and bring our mates.

At Lord's in the final of the NatWest series, an amazing match gave us all an indication of what kind of excitement was to come. Gough, Jones, Fred and Harmy shared the wickets as we bowled them out for an eminently gettable 196, but when we slumped to 33 for five, the crowd's sense of resignation and disappointment that they might just be too good for us after all, quickly spread. As for me I was unsettled by an unintentional 90mph beamer from Brett Lee – sorry I killed you, mate – then got out by Glenn McGrath for the third time in our three meetings. Good job Warne wasn't playing, I thought to myself. But Colly and Geraint Jones put on 116 for the sixth wicket, Gough clattered 12 before being run out and with three needed off McGrath's last ball, Giles and Harmy scrambled through for two leg byes to level the scores.

Sadly a very different kind of drama hung over our next clash, the first of three one-dayers at Headingley on 7 July.

News of the terrorist atrocities during the London rush hour was filtering through to us all morning up in Leeds. No one could tell for sure how many casualties had been caused by devastating bombs on the London transport system, but loss of life was expected to be heavy.

There was no solid discussion about not playing the game, though it was very hard to get into it as whenever a new snippet of information came through all thoughts drifted back to the capital. But I switched myself off mentally, concentrated on what I had to do and made my first hundred against Australia at any level, and my tenth in all one-day cricket as we won easily.

The Aussies were clearly just as stunned as we were by events in London and the final two matches, on 10 July and 12 July, were scheduled for Lord's and The Oval.

I personally would not have blamed them if they had upped sticks and gone home there and then. I tried to put myself in their shoes. Heaven forbid this ever happens, but what if we had been touring Pakistan, or Sri Lanka, or anywhere for that matter, and 56 people had died in the city in which we were due to play not one but two matches in the next week? We would probably have been out of there in a flash.

We lost them both, but in the circumstances, we were just glad to get this one-day series over and done with.

*   *   *

The final act in the construction of our Ashes team ended in cruel disappointment for Thorpe. He had been a fantastic batsman for England all over the world and he would have loved to have bowed out from Test cricket with one more Ashes series under his belt, especially as I think he quietly fancied our chances with the bowling attack we had at our disposal. But three batsmen into two places just wouldn't go and in the end it came down to a straight choice between him and KP.

Several factors swung it in KP's favour. First was the Vaughan principle of attack whenever possible, defend when only absolutely necessary. In Thorpe we had a batsman we knew we could rely on to bail us out of bad situations. In KP we saw a batsman who would be up front trying to win us the game before we got into a bad situation.

Second was the idea that the fewer players we had who carried the psychological scars of being beaten by Australia before, the better. We all respected Thorpe's Ashes experience but most of that was experience of losing to Australia.

And thirdly, Thorpe's back was clearly an issue and even if we discovered we really couldn't match them for skill the least we could do was field as well as they did.

Thorpe was cut up when he was told he was not in the squad for the first Test at Lord's and we all sympathized as we owed him a huge debt, especially for innings like his hundred in Barbados the previous spring which turned a tight match in our favour, his brilliant batting in my early career in Sri Lanka and Pakistan and his quiet friendly advice. True to form, he made sure he didn't outstay his welcome and retired from all cricket almost immediately.

But we were all tremendously excited by the buzz around Lord's and the buzz around KP, bizarre dead skunk hairstyle and all.

And by the time we prepared to walk out on the first morning of the 2005 Ashes series, even the usual 5–0 victory prediction from McGrath sounded less threatening than usual.

The first thing that struck us all was the noise inside the pavilion. Walking out of the dressing-room down the stairs holding the polished wooden handrail, we noticed a build up of noise like the thunder of an underground train approaching the next stop. At the moment we entered the Long Room the roar exploded in our ears. It felt like we were going out to fight Mike Tyson. 'Come on lads!' the members shouted. 'Come on!' And when we emerged into daylight the noise of the capacity crowd was just overwhelming.

And it never really relented from then until the end of the series.

Ricky Ponting said later the moment he knew they were in for a fight was when a ball from Harmy, who had already hit Justin Langer a fearful crack on the right elbow, pushed the grille of his helmet into his cheek, drawing blood and no one, but no one from our side went to check on how he was. It was quite deliberate, if near to the wrong side of the line we wanted to draw between us and them. But it had the desired effect. The fab four, Harmy, Hoggard, Fred and Simon, were quite brilliant that day, with Harmy taking five for 43 and blowing away the tail as we bowled them out to increasing mayhem in the stands, for 190. Maybe the best wicket of them all was Hayden, bowled Hoggard according to plans, tucked up for space from around the wicket. The most emotional had to be Simon's from his first ball of the match and the first he had bowled in a Test against Australia since the knee injury that nearly ended his career back in 2002, to have Damien Martyn caught behind. Payback time in grand style for those who barracked him when he was lying in agony on the Gabba outfield.

And now, Glenn McGrath didn't so much let all the air out of the balloon as stamp all over it. I'd prepared myself of course. In fact during the week before I had worked a lot with Steve Bull on staying calm in the cauldron. But I just wasn't ready for the quality of the stuff he sent down ball after ball, always at you, nothing to hit, moving the ball off the seam either way, at will. He made Straussy and me look like camels in clogs. I was his 500th Test victim and I felt like I'd been the other 499 as well. Glenn finished with nine wickets in the match.

KP, as we hoped he might, took to the place as though he owned it, and one day he probably will, by the way, but as the game progressed it was clear they were just too strong. Something was missing: in a word, belief.

By the time we arrived at Edgbaston for round two, we were all still trying to stay positive. It wasn't easy. Giles had taken a hammering in the press – 'playing against Ashley Giles was like playing ten men against eleven' according to one analyst – and was clearly concerned. And this is where Vaughan came into his own. He could sense how down we all were and how worried that we might turn out to be just another bunch of Ashes losers. But, instead of castigating us, pointing out the flaws in our performance at Lord's, telling us we had to do more of this or less of that, he employed reassurance and positivity to inspire us. That was Vaughan's trick. Steve Harmison once told me that one of Vaughan's strengths was that he was a great liar. If he believed it was the right thing to do, he would tell you what he thought you needed to hear to inflate your confidence, even though he may not have believed it himself. Now, at a team-talk in the Warwickshire committee room, he started by reiterating our goals, told us we had all the tools we needed to achieve them and urged us to go out and enjoy the experience. It worked so well that, by the end, we were thinking: 'Well, what the hell have we got to lose?'

Our spirits were raised even further when, an hour before play was due to start Glenn McGrath failed to spot a stray ball on the Edgbaston outfield and put himself out of the game.

The correct reaction would have been to say 'hard, luck, mate.' But inside Strauss and I and the rest of the lads couldn't stop ourselves from thinking unkind thoughts like 'You beauty!' And when Ricky Ponting made the barely believable decision to offer us first use of what looked a good pitch without his first choice paceman at his disposal, we all thought to ourselves: 'Now or never.'

And it was now. We went out and attacked. Just before lunch Brett Lee bowled me a couple of hittable balls and I hit them, taking 18 off the over, and when Warne came on to bowl his first over, I prepared to do something I had wanted to do ever since he told the world I had been found out as a Test player. I didn't say a word; I just hit him back over his head for six . It was a completely sublime moment, for which I owed some thanks to the ministrations of Merlin, the bowling machine we used to replicate the experience of facing Warne, which, unlike the real thing, had the great added virtue of not trying to get in your ear all day and all night. The wizardish machine had been on the blink at Lord's, but its recovery here came just in time.

I finished on 90 and KP and Fred carried on in the same vein as we reached 407 all out before the end of the first day.

I could sense a difference in Fred. At Lord's he seemed for the first time overawed. Now he was smiling and relaxed and about to turn the series on its head. He said later, sessions with sports psychologist Jamie Edwards had restored his ego.

Indeed, after taking a first innings lead, we got the jitters in our second innings and without Fred might have ballsed it up completely. But he just kept hitting and we ended up setting them a target of 282 to win, though a nasty looking shoulder twinge had us crossing everything that he would be able to bowl again in the match.

Our spirits wavered while Hayden and Langer started in some comfort and then Fred came on to bowl the 13th over of the innings, the best of his entire career and maybe the whole history of the Ashes.

First ball, to Langer, blocked. Second ball, fast and straight and climbing rapidly off a length, cannoned off his arm guard down onto his thigh and into the stumps. Third ball, swinging into new batsman Ponting's pads from outside off stump and a huge lbw appeal, eventually turned down by Billy Bowden. Fourth ball, another steeply bouncing ball arrowed into Ponting which he did well to steer into the gully. Fifth ball, another big inswinger, another appeal, another no from Bowden. Ponting left the sixth ball with some relief, but only because he didn't hear the cry of no-ball. And then the incident that changed everything. Fred turned the ball around in his hands at the start of the run-up and sent down the perfect outswinger that took the Aussie captain's outside edge and carried comfortably to Geraint Jones. It was sensational stuff. For six balls Fred had made Ponting look like he wasn't good enough to play him, and we're talking about one of the best batsmen who ever lived. The most sensational over of all our careers had come to an end with Langer and Ponting out, Australia rattled, and Fred, fuelled by Red Bull, adrenaline and desire, massive. As I passed him I told him, 'Fred, if you play until you're ninety, you'll never bowl better than that.'

There soon followed a brilliant slower one from Harmy to bamboozle Michael Clarke and, at 175 for eight, we were all but home and hosed. Except for Warne, Lee and Kasprowicz taking them to within three runs of winning.

Had they done it I'm pretty sure we would have been cooked for the series. We had high hopes and we had had our moments, some of them great. But Australia's enduring strength was winning the battles they really needed to win. Three more runs now and they would have done so again and the effect would almost certainly have been catastrophic for us. When Lee smoked a ball from Harmy through the covers towards the rope I was sure it was all over, but Simon Jones, stationed on the boundary cut it off and threw it in and moments later Harmy made one lift straight at Kasprowicz, he could only fend it off to Geraint behind the stumps and we all went completely berserk.

We should have won at Old Trafford where I made 63 and Vaughan rediscovered wonderful form. Simon Jones, the bowler whose pace, menace and reverse swing they just hadn't bargained for, took six for 53 to give us a lead of 142 and Strauss' second innings 106 and Bell's first half-century enabled us to set them too many to win in enough time for us to bowl them out. They were queuing for half a mile on the final morning to stand on home, and we got to within one wicket. Ponting was magnificent for them, making 156 when the next highest score was 39, and without it we would have won easily. Jones limped off with cramp at a crucial moment, however, and though Fred thundered in to take four for 71 we just couldn't finish the task.

But we did at Trent Bridge, in heart-stopping style. I made another 65 in our first innings and Fred a sensational hundred, his best-ever innings for England in my opinion, due to its importance in the context of the match and the series and his patience and intelligence throughout. Fred could slog and did, occasionally, and he loved doing it, but this time he put his cudgel away and used a sabre instead and he and Geraint, with whom he loved batting because he never let the game go quiet, put on 177 for the sixth wicket.

Simon again bowled beautifully to take five for 44, though the fantasy highlight was a full-length catch by Strauss to take Gilchrist off Fred, horizontal and several feet off the ground. After bowling them out for 218, Vaughan enforced the follow-on. This was a huge moment. This wasn't asking Bangladesh or Zimbabwe to follow-on but Australia, the team otherwise known as 'The Invincibles'. So enthusiastic were we to get amongst them again that we failed to notice that Simon was by now starting to limp and though he managed four overs in the second innings, his series was over.

Ponting made a prat of himself after being run out by our sub fielder Gary Pratt, carrying on like a pork pie and accusing us of cheating by overdoing the comfort breaks for bowlers, forgetting that Pratt was legitimately on for Jones who had already left for hospital x-rays. In any case, did he expect us to use bad fielders as subs?

The tension as it built up on the fourth day was almost unbearable. We only needed 129 but it soon felt like a thousand as Warne took over and nearly bowled us to death. Nerves, pure and simple, overwhelmed us. The prize was so big and so close but we seemed uncertain as to whether we were entitled to grab it.

With four needed, Giles played and missed a ball from Warne he was convinced had bowled him, which would have left us 125 for eight with Harmison the only fit man left, but Jones got padded up and was ready to bat on one leg if necessary. But the ball somehow slipped past his stumps and then, to total delirium, Warne bowled a ball of slightly fuller length and Ash drove it through mid wicket to the boundary.

At that moment I actually felt physically sick. The emotional outpouring in the dressing-room was quite overwhelming. Fred didn't know whose arm to punch first so he punched everyone's before launching Elton John's sodding 'Rocket Man' for the thousandth time that summer. Vaughan's veneer of ice-cold calm melted everywhere. Even Duncan smiled, or maybe it was just wind.

One more match, one more result and the Ashes would be ours.

For five days in September 2005 The Oval was the centre of the known universe. We knew that because it said so on the front page of the *Daily Mirror*. All week long, then all morning long on Thursday 8 September, no other news mattered except what was going on at the Kennington Oval.

The plan was simple. Win the toss, bat them out of the game, take the draw, get on that open-topped bus and kiss Nelson's Column.

And despite some incredibly harrowing moments, we carried it out, thanks largely to Strauss getting his most important 100 for England, 129, Fred making another big contribution with the bat,

72 and a massive one with the ball, five for 78 in 34 impeccable overs to bowl them out for 367, but eventually thanks to KP, we did it.

Pietersen was simply inspired. Tragically for Warne, he managed to shell a chance from his Hampshire team-mate at slip off Lee when KP had made just 15. By the time he was eighth out for 158, I wonder how many times KP had said I thinks, mates

And, after Giles made 59 to settle the issue, we were all of the same mind.

To be honest, I was so nervous I could only bring myself to watch KP's innings on the dressing-room TV.

Cue the madness. Seas of champagne, cameras, songs, 'Jerusalem'. More champagne, KP managing to pour almost half a bottle of it into his eye. The Ashes. Vaughan holding the Urn. Us waving at the girls. Tears, loads of tears. Even more champagne. 'Jerusalem' again. Sleep? What for?

I spent all of the night and half of the next morning attempting to counter acute dehydration by drinking more and more beer, and when I got back to our hotel around 4 a.m. I realized I was absolutely starving.

Sitting in the lobby I ordered a ham and cheese toastie and while waiting realized I had absolutely no chance of getting any sleep even if I had wanted to, which I didn't. So I decided to stay up and wait to see what Her Majesty's Press had in store for us.

The next bloke I saw was one of the journalists, who had been up drinking with Fred and Harmy in the hotel bar.

'What's up, Marcus?' he asked me.

'Mate, I'm so happy. I'm so excited. I cannot wait for the open-top bus ride.'

'But that's not for ages. What are you doing here now?'

'I've ordered all the papers and I'm waiting for them to arrive,' I explained.

'At four-thirty?'

'As long as it takes,' I said.

*　*　*

We'd done it. We'd bloody done it.

Up on the open-top bus, Fred looking terrible, unable to open his eyes. Even more 'Jerusalem'. Sunglasses as standard issue for sore heads and to keep the glare of KP's hair out of our eyes. Hoggy, chortling and getting ready to take the piss out of Tony Blair at the No.10 reception, at which I was so soaked I could barely string two words together. 'What do all these photographers want, I wonder?' asked the PM. 'A photo, you knob,' replied Matthew, who is from the North.

Harmy flying. Vaughan still fairly cool, Duncan suffering from Smileyman's disease. Ash still shaking with emotion. Geraint Jones faintly embarrassed, so too Bell and Collingwood, in for Simon Jones who was there, on crutches, legless. Strauss eyes-glazed but still somehow focused.

Me? Gone, mate. Absolutely gone. Hayley, get me to bed before I wake up. All this, a seat at Ashton Gate, an MBE and the freedom of Keynsham – surely nothing could stop us now.

Chapter 11

DOING THE 'RIGHT' THING

*'Looking back, I almost cannot believe that
I managed to persuade myself that my captain's
needs were greater than my wife's, that
the England cricket team was more
important than my family.'*

When reviewing England's disappointing tour to Pakistan in the autumn of 2005, the 2–0 defeat in the three-Test series and our 3–2 loss in the one-day internationals that followed, people claimed we had suffered some kind of hangover following our Ashes victory and the almost surreal outpouring of joy at Trafalgar Square; that we paid for our complacency against a young and largely inexperienced team and that, after beating Australia, we allowed ourselves to get carried away with our own publicity. To a large extent, all of the above was probably spot on and I number myself among those who had been seduced into believing we were the business.

However, for large parts of the tour such concerns pretty much passed me by. I should have come home early. I almost did, on two separate occasions. Had it not been for Michael Vaughan begging me to stay, I would have done, and, if I had, it is just possible that both the post-natal depression to which Hayley succumbed and the illness that subsequently overwhelmed me and ultimately ended my career as an England cricketer might have been kept at bay a while longer, or maybe even for good. What is certain is that the decision I made, twice, to stay on tour is something I deeply regret.

Ironically, even though this was my first trip away from our daughter Ellie, the start of the scheduled two-month tour had been a much more comfortable experience for me than usual. Initially I had had no problems at all with my sleeping because I could count on my by now tried and trusted Zopiclone tablets to put me away. One tablet and the next thing I knew it was morning. In any case, the buzz and the high from the Ashes celebrations made me want to get out on the pitch as soon as possible and prove what giants we were.

Leaving Hayley and Ellie was not pleasant, though my thoughts were eased by the knowledge that the new house in the country outside Taunton into which we had moved at the end of the summer was protected by the CCTV security cameras we had had installed. Even better for our peace of mind was that, using my laptop, I could log onto the system via the internet from anywhere we travelled should the need arise.

All in all, whereas the first few days on almost every other trip abroad with England I can recall were bumpy and painful, this time, from the moment we landed in Islamabad, my overriding emotion was excitement. We were amazing. I was amazing. Everyone told us so. And we believed every word we had read and heard.

Three days into the tour Vaughan, Ashley Giles, Matthew Hoggard and myself were brought down to earth with a crash when, in a visit designed to help raise awareness back home, we spent an afternoon in the Pakistan Institute of Medical Science, in the twin-city of Rawalpindi, witnessing at first hand the true scale of the human tragedy that the recent earthquake, whose epicentre was a mere 60 miles away, had left in its wake. As we arrived, so did a seemingly endless stream of military helicopters, still bringing in the survivors, and the dead. We were met by a couple of doctors and scores of photographers and were told incredible stories about the extent of the damage, how whole villages had been lifted off the ground, then fallen back to earth and disappeared from view. We were told that they had barely enough supplies to last for a further week. The situation seemed utterly desperate.

For me, the experience of meeting some of the children who had been left maimed and orphaned was particularly upsetting. One young boy, apparently in uncontrollable pain, was screaming and screaming and it seemed nothing could be done to calm him. I walked to the next ward, looked through the window and saw this tiny baby, both broken legs in plaster and stirrups. The shock hit me like a hard slap across the face. I remember cupping my mouth in my hands, then walking away from the scene as quickly as I could. Once I was away and out of sight of the others I broke down in tears. It took me five minutes to stop, but, once I did, I just couldn't bring myself to carry on with the visit. When we did the pre-arranged interview with Sky TV afterwards, I started to go again, at which point Hoggy quickly put his arm round my shoulder. When the camera stopped filming, I broke down a second time. The baby I had seen, I later learned, was less than a month old. His name was Ahmed. He had arrived at the hospital just five days into his life and, for three weeks, had been cradled by his young sister. Their mother had been one of the more than 50,000 victims.

Ash was also clearly moved by the event and what he had seen, and in particular meeting a young girl called Ashia, at two-and-a-half-years old, almost exactly the same age as one of his daughters.

Was my reaction an early sign of what was to come? Did that experience plant something in my subconscious, a link with the separation anxiety I was later to feel so strongly about being away from my own family, which later resurfaced to such devastating effect? Maybe.

In the meantime, however, I was quickly able to refocus. In truth, as a team, we were all just too pumped up to let anything get in the way of what we were there for.

Having beaten the best team in the world, we were determined to become the best team in the world. Last time we had toured here, five years previously, we had scrapped and battled and played patient, attritional cricket and nicked the series in near-darkness on the final evening in Karachi. Here things were going to be different. Here we would put our marker down. Under Michael Vaughan we had developed our own style of vibrant, powerful, aggressive cricket. We had employed attack as the best form of defence and won six successive Test series. And now we wanted to show the world we could beat all-comers on our own terms. Like Australia had been doing for so long, I wanted us to become so good that our reputation would intimidate opposing teams even before we played them.

We all know what comes after pride.

Prior to the trip, Simon Jones, our surprise package against the Aussies, had withdrawn through injury. But with Harmison, Hoggard, Flintoff and Giles all initially fit, we believed we had more than enough firepower to rattle an inexperienced Pakistan batting line-up. On the field the tour started as well as it could have done for me. On 31 October, the opening day of the trip, I batted from first ball to last in our practice match against the Pakistan Cricket Board Patron's XI in Rawalpindi, scoring 124 not out and putting on 118 for the ninth wicket with our reserve keeper Matt Prior, telling the press boys afterwards: 'After this, I am hungry to do well.'

In Lahore, we had a poor game against Pakistan A, losing by six wickets, made immeasurably worse by the injury Vaughan suffered on day two, 7 November, when his dodgy knee locked as he ran a second run with Andrew Strauss. It looked pretty bad straightaway, and by the time we reached Multan two days later for the first Test starting on Saturday 12 November, it had already been announced our Ashes winning leader was out of the match and I had been appointed to skipper the side in his place.

I was ready. For some time, I'd been Vaughan's unofficial No 2 and so drilled were we by now according to his and Duncan Fletcher's way of doing things that we were confident any effect would be minimal. Unbeknown to me at this stage, my appointment had been far from the formality it had seemed at the time. Not long after Vaughan had suffered his injury Duncan called Freddie Flintoff into his hotel room in Lahore and told him: 'If Michael is only going to be out for one Test, then Tres will take over the captaincy. If he is going to be out for the whole series, I want you to do it.' According to Fred, Duncan didn't really give a big reason for his thinking other than a vague reference to me not being 'in the right place', but Fred did describe the incident as being 'a bit cloak and dagger'. I didn't think that much of it at the time, but that does explain the tone of my subsequent meeting with Fletcher. 'Are you certain you want to do this job?' he had asked me. 'Are you clear about everything it entails?' At the time I just thought this was Fletch's usual trick of raising an issue in order to confirm the conclusion he had already come to himself. In hindsight it appears he was not totally certain I was the right man to lead the side in Vaughan's absence. Maybe he had seen something I was yet to recognize.

In the end, with the news about Vaughan more promising than at first feared, I was confirmed as captain and we played an absolute blinder for the first four days of the match and, from a purely cricketing perspective, it remains something of a mystery how we managed to end up losing by 22 runs.

What no one outside the team knew until the match was over, however, was that I had received a phone call from Hayley at the end of the second day of the match, Sunday 13 November 2005, which turned out to be the first in the sequence of events spanning from then until 14 March 2008 that culminated in my retirement from international cricket.

I got back to the hotel, the rather incongruously named Holiday Inn, in high spirits that evening. My first two days as stand-in for Michael had gone excellently. After losing the toss, we had managed to restrict Pakistan to 274 in their first innings, with Freddie taking up where he had left off in the summer, bowling fantastically well to take four for 68. By the close of play on day two we were well placed on 253 for three. I had already reached a century, my 13th in Tests for England and, as it turned out, my last but one. I was not out 135 and I was feeling in fantastic nick. As I said at the time, bearing in mind the pressure of expectation the side was under, the fact that Shoaib Akhtar was in the opposing attack and the loss of our best batsman and skipper, so far I already felt this was one of my very best innings and my mind was full of the possibility of helping establish a match-winning total the next day.

Hayley's first phone call was no more than mildly concerning. She was ringing from the house owned by her mum and dad, Sue and John Rowse, about five minutes' drive from our place, and she told me she was a bit worried because she couldn't get hold of her dad. He was always offering to do odd jobs round the house and this time had taken his ladder with him to clear out some of our guttering. Hayley had been trying for hours to reach him by phone but her dad's phone was just ringing out. It was way past the time when he said he would be back and getting dark. So she told me she was going to go to our house to find out what was going on and would ring me back when she did.

The next time I spoke to Hayley, she had just discovered her father, lying on our patio steps with his ladder nearby, cold, unconscious and in a pool of blood. She couldn't really tell me much more than that, except he seemed to have suffered some kind of accident and had a bad head injury. She was distraught, barely able to speak. She had managed to ring the ambulance and was waiting for it to arrive. I did my best to try and calm her, but it was hopeless. I felt helpless. Hayley needed me and I wasn't there.

Hayley next rang me from the hospital. By now John was in intensive care. When they had got to him, the paramedics said that, in view of how much blood he had lost and the seriousness of the blow to his head, they believed the only thing that had kept him alive was the cold. She sounded more calm now, though she was still half-sick with worry. There was nothing more either of us could do, except wait and pray. We spoke a couple more times, and I snatched an hour or two of sleep here and there. The next morning I told Duncan what had happened and, though the seriousness of the situation was still unclear, I began making enquiries about going home, if need be. At breakfast I spoke to Phil Neale, our tour manager, and I asked about the possibility of returning home in between the first two Test matches. This one was due to end in three days, on 16 November, and my first thought was whether I could fly home and back again to Pakistan in time for the start of the second Test, in Faisalabad, on 20 November. Clearly it wouldn't be possible. So I then asked Phil if he could look into me returning home indefinitely.

For now, I had to try and refocus on the match in hand which was just weird. At first, it was still all a blur. For obvious reasons the journey to the ground, a hair-raising 20-minute high-speed dash flanked by gun-toting security guards through streets cordoned off to the usual manic morning rush-hour, seemed a lot less like a funfair ride than normal and by now, because a couple of the players had been informed that there was a problem back home, the mood in the dressing-room was quite subdued.

I tried to find the switch to turn off my personal feelings but couldn't locate it. Yet I told myself I just had to try and concentrate on my batting. That was what I had to do because there was nothing else I could do. It was hard work. As I was warming up before resuming my innings I remember feeling very distant and detached.

Once play started, though, bit by bit, I found I was able to get on top of my feelings. By the time I was out for 193, my third-highest Test score, caught behind by Kamran Akmal off Shabbir Ahmed, I was actually enjoying batting again, especially putting on nearly a hundred for the sixth wicket with Fred including a straight six off the leg-spinner Danish Kaneria. And, though my wicket, in the third over after lunch, precipitated a collapse from 388 for seven to 418 all out, at the close of day three we were still winning a tight game.

By now all the players knew something serious had happened. Hayley was extremely upset when I got through on the phone that evening as her dad was in and out of consciousness and things were looking bleak. She never gave me the impression she thought her dad would not survive, but I'm certain she was just trying to protect me. What did emerge was that the doctors were unsure as to how John had received his injuries and they needed to know as much as possible as the circumstances could have had a bearing on how to treat him. Had he actually fallen from his ladder and struck his head on the rockery? Had an intruder hit him with something? Or had he actually fallen into a coma, or suffered a stroke or seizure, then suffered further injury when he fell?

It suddenly occurred to me that we could find out at least some of the answers by reviewing the CCTV security tapes. Clearly Hayley was not up to it, so that evening, in my hotel room in Multan, I turned on my laptop, logged on to the internet and re-lived my father-in-law's accident in harrowing detail.

I fast-forwarded the tape to the precise moment when it happened. Then, to try and work out the exact sequence of events, I watched the incident in slow motion. First I saw John erect his ladder, then climb up and lean towards the guttering. I saw the ladder collapse, folding in on itself. I watched John fall backwards and I saw him hit his head on the side of the rockery and lose consciousness. It was just dreadful. I rewound the tape to make sure of what I had seen. Then I watched on. Every so often I would see John appear to come round, sit up, then pass out again. This agonizing process continued over and over for about 40 to 45 minutes. It was almost unbearable to watch. Then eventually I saw him sit up and crawl round the rockery to the patio windows. I watched him as he tried to attract someone's attention. He was in such a state of shock that he was unaware the house was empty. At that point I saw Hayley arrive and as soon as I did, I turned off the tape. I didn't want to see any more. I didn't want to see her reaction. I didn't want to see her upset.

When it was over I sat in my room feeling sick to my stomach. It was like I had just driven past a car crash. I couldn't get the feeling or the images out of my mind.

I didn't speak to Hayley that night, but, in the morning, I told her what I had seen. She was incredibly upset and this was the first time she actually said what must have been in her heart all along. 'Please, Marcus. Can you come home?' she asked.

My instant, thoughtless reaction was: 'No, I can't.' Whether it was an inability to face up to the situation, or my feeling that, as England captain, that came first and everything else second, I can't tell. Was my response motivated by selfishness, by a sense of duty that now seems almost comically warped or just by not wanting to confront what I might find when I got home? All I am certain of now is that I was totally, completely and utterly wrong. I shouldn't have had to think twice. I should have gone home there and then. Forget the cricket, forget the match, forget the England tour, forget everything else. I should have got on the next plane and gone home to look after my wife. I am ashamed I did not.

As the conversation continued, with Hayley becoming more upset, I did change tack. I told Hayley I would try and see what I could do. I would look into the possibility of flying home and I did. I spoke to Phil Neale to keep the lines open about the possibility of leaving the tour, but I decided, come what may, I simply had to get through the rest of the match first.

I found I was better able to switch into the cricket now we were fielding. The target of bowling Pakistan out in their second innings cheaply enough to convert our lead into victory helped me channel my thoughts. In any case, after having more or less decided I was definitely going home after the match, I was able to put aside the reason for the moment. The tactical battles on the field were taking up all my attention. How to get out Inzamam, for instance, a batsman I regarded with great respect. As it happened, Hoggard did, lbw for 72, managing to get one to hold its line with the second new ball, then Fred nipped a couple more out in quick succession, and from 266 for three, they were quickly struggling at 295 for seven, a lead of under 150. Finally they were all out for 341, more than they should have got, but with 198 runs to win on a pitch that was still good for batting we ended day four confident of victory, even though I had gone for just five at the start of our chase.

By the same time the following day, we had lost, bowled out for 175 runs, 23 short of the target. At 64 for one it looked pretty much in the bag for us, but we contrived to lose three wickets in eight balls, Ian Bell, Strauss and Collingwood, then Fred hit a six or bust shot against Kaneria and was caught at deep mid-wicket and KP chased a very wide delivery from Mohammad Sami and was caught

Building sandcastles somewhere on the Devon coast.

Mum holding me, with sis Anna.

I want an ice-cream and I want it now.

What happens when I push his button?

Dad and me. Dig the shorts. On second thoughts, bury them.

Relaxing with Lex and Mini.

Anna liked it when I cut my own hair…

That's better; pudding bowl no. 1.

A pair of donkeys.

Wasn't me, mum!

Eddie Gregg, Mark Francis, Neil Roslee, me and Steve Durning at St Anne's sports day.

Young cricket stars

Steve Hill

Avon cricketers Ian March and Marcus Trescothick have both won places in the first-ever England under-14 squad, who will be coached by former international David Lloyd.

The batsmen will face their under-15 counterparts in a two-day match at Aundle, Leicestershire, next month after impressing for the West in a national schools' festival at Warwickshire.

"This is a quite staggering achievement," said regional selector Phil Webster.

"It count in the books

his Western League debut for Keynsham as a wicketkeeper-batsman, although England want the Sir Bernard Lovell pupil to concentrate solely on scoring runs.

March attends St Mary Redcliffe School and plays his club cricket for Frenchay. He captained the West at Warwickshire and will bat for England at number four or five.

Another Avon player — Neil Priscott, of Beechen Cliff — has been selected to tour The Netherlands with a West of England under-13 party of 15 in August.

The younger brother of Somerset professional, Stuart, is such an exceptional

along with March, has also
ted to a West under-14 trip to
the end of the year.
will climax with a two-day
inst Trinidad under-15s at the

MARCUS TO LEAD ENGLAND

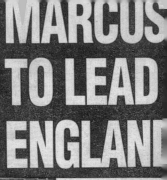

Trescothick U-19s skip

By CHRIS HEWETT

BRILLIANT Somerset batti
scothick w
name
England's
19 capt
this w
three-Te
the West

The 18-yea
whose family
Longwell
always a ho
honour when
Michael Va
promotion to
their tour of

Diffe

"I was qui
being named
Michael ma
but it's neve
to count yo
aid the
Bernard L
pupil.

"It's been
immer wh
d hopefull
carry th
Caribbea

EVENING POST, MONDAY, JUNE 28, 1992

POST CRICKET
escothick in form for Keynsham

MASTER BLASTER MARCUS

US
ay i
anna
er A
pow
3,73

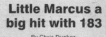

Marcus picked for England squad

YOUNG talented Keynsham left-handed
batsman and wicketkeeper, Marcus
has been picked for the England und
squad.

Marcus's father, Martin, played fo
and was on Somerset's books and w
Keynsham's 126-strong junior section

Trescothick signs for Somerset

BIG-HITTING Keynsham batsman Marcus Trescothick is to follow his father Martyn into full-time cricket with Somerset.

The powerfully-built 16-year-old, who lives in Oldland, joins the county on August 17 on a contract which will take him through the 1993 and 1994 seasons.

The county offer comes after Trescothick's performances for Somerset under-19s — including an unbeaten 158 against Warwickshire — and an appearance in the second XI against

earlier this
r the co
t the
week.

"He has
pener for
Grouse W
h he ha
ll he is sti

of him. P
he has al
old enoug
he has al
merset.
who is 6 ft
ynsham and
Avon Sc
ayed for Eng
vel, but a re
19 Sch
ruised thum
been playing
colts side un
r Robinson
named Yo
by the Cricke
nger, and dur
he amassed 4
ions, the final r
rthrow of the l

cthick, Somers
teps to strengthe
the capture
Folland, 28, on
best season.
hand-

TRESCOTHICK: Fine
season for Somerset

Neighbours call time on record breaking stand

D KEYNSHAM 15-
olds have made
cricketing head-
into the town
record books
a few neighbours'
books.
ing for Keynsham's
17 team against
end under 17s in Bris-
cketkeeper-batsman
Trescothick and
pace bowler Steve
y shared a magnifi
stand in their side's
victory.
ner England form

One ball crashed through a
window.

So great was their hitting
power, a shortage of cricket
balls was a growing possibility.

Said Tony Gurnsey,
father of Steve, and a member of the KCC Youth Com-
mittee: "As Marcus and
Steve sent the balls screaming into gardens, household-
ers refused to hand them
back.

"Then one of the house
owners, a woman, ran on to
the wicket and refused to
move out of the bowling line
until some kind of

Keynsham cricketers Marcus Trescothick and Steve
Gurnsey

Little Marcus a big hit with 183

By Chris Ducker

FORGET the Evening Post Top Man cricket award this week — we've nominated a Top Kid instead!

Marcus Trescothick, a pint-sized left-hander from St Anne's School, Oldland Common, is very special.

Until three weeks his best perfor ditable

Marcus's father is Martyn Trescothick, the Keynsham batsman and former club captain.

Said Dad: "The lad thinks of nothing but sport and has been good at all ball games since he was very young. He plays in goal for the Northavon soccer team and has been down to the enzenga Ground at

opens
12

EVENING POST, THURSDAY, SEPTEMBER 22, 1994

POST SPORT
Young gun earns rave revie

MARCUS AIMS FOR THE TOP

By RICHARD LATHAM

SOMERSET KEEN ON TRESCOTHICK

SOMERSET are poised to sign promising Keynsham batsman Marcus Trescothick on a two-year contra

The 16-year-old left-
hander, from Oldland, is
already a prolific scorer in
club cricket. Somerset
director of cricket Bob
Cottam describes him as
an immense talent."

Last summer
Trescothick was named
England young cricketer
of the year after hitting 13
centuries in a total of more
than 3,600 run

Trescothick takes top award

By Brendan Gallagher

MARCUS TRESCOTHICK, 15, crowned a season of phenomenal run-scoring at Lord's yesterday when Micky Stewart, the England team manager, presented the young Bristolian with The Cricketer and Slazenger Young Cricketer Award for 1991.

The powerful, left-handed opener has 750 runs to date, including 12 centu

His top score was an unbeaten double hu
dred for Keynsham Under-17s against Do
nend. He also scored 171 not out for Somers
Under-16s against their Worcestersh
counterparts.

He represented England Under-14s l
season but missed selection this year af
two uncharacteristic failures during t
trials.

Major scores this season: 200° Keynsham U-17 v Downend

Keynsham Under-15s featuring Eddie, first row ...elt, and me with the gloves on.

'When I grow up I want to be a handbag.' England Under-19s in Sri Lanka.

...e, as the third flowerpot man.

Receiving a *Bristol Evening Post* award from Jack Russell.

...ith the Somerset Under-15s; me extreme right, top row. Fantastic hair.

Posing with Angus Fraser of England and
Carl Hooper of the West Indies after winning the
Cricketer Magazine Young Player of the Year, 1991,
with England coach Micky Stewart in the second row.

My new
best
mate, err,
prize.

Ready for the
new season,
1992.

Posing for a
newspaper photo
in the local sports
shop.

Just possibly
sausages were on
the menu, here in
my first digs in
Taunton.

Being awarded my first Test cap by England skipper Nasser Hussain, against West Indies at Old Trafford, August 2000.

I spent so much time in the nets with our brilliant coach that my team-mates called me 'Duncan's lad'. Here I am trying and failing to master his 'forward press' for batting against spin in general and Murali in particular.

My maiden Test ton, 122 against Sri Lanka in Galle, 2001, dedicated to Eddie Gregg. Here, I sweep Sanath Jayasuriya.

My only Test wicket, Imran Nazir of Pakistan. The gun was waiting for him in their dressing room.

Fred's bowling in India 2002 was the making of him as an all-rounder.

Trademark celebrations for another Test hu

My highest Test score, 219, against South Africa at The Oval 2003.

Andrew Strauss and I leave The Oval after I hit the four we needed to complete seven straight Test wins in 2004.

Matthew Hoggard may have found his stubborn blocking funny, but opposing bowlers rarely did.

Hitting Omari Banks for runs at Edgbaston, where, in 2004, I scored hundreds in both innings against the Windies.

My 2004–05 tour of South Africa started terribly but this slog-sweep off Nicky Boje ended up the other side of the stand in the fourth Test in Johannesburg, as I scored 180 in our series-deciding victory. Mark Boucher looks on.

My long reach meant I could smother most conventional spin.

Celebrating the 2005 Ashes, open-topped bus style.

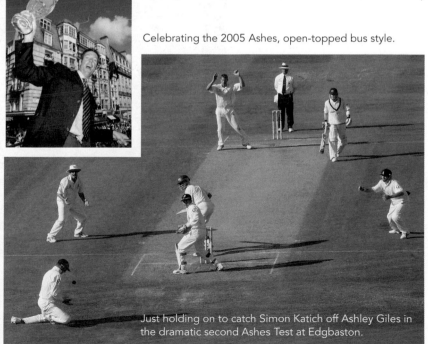

Just holding on to catch Simon Katich off Ashley Giles in the dramatic second Ashes Test at Edgbaston.

A quick look first before stepping off the bus in Karachi for a one-day international in 2005.

Below: When Michael Vaughan was ruled out of the first Test in Multan, I took over, made 193 and lost. Posing with Inzamam and the trophy before the series started.

Above: Once rivals for the England captaincy, but Vaughany never had anything less than my full support.

The strain starts to mount.

Ducking under a Shoaib Akhtar bouncer in Multan.

Making 100 not out against Bangladesh at The Oval in 2005, in my 100th one-day international.

I tried to sign them all during our one-day win over Australia at Bristol in 2005.

Move over, Sergio…

On safari in South Africa, 2005.

The fitness regime we adopted in Bangladesh in 2004 helped our Ashes effort enormously when the time came.

I missed playing for England, but Somerset were my first love and my great support.

Top: Getting in the dive in the Twenty20 match against Sri Lanka at the Rose Bowl, 2006.

Middle: Telling the press that my problems were behind me and I was fit and ready for the 2005–06 Ashes series down under.

Bottom Left: Nearing my highest first-class score, 284, for Somerset against Northants in May 2007.

Bottom Right: The award for the William Hill Sports Book of 2008 means as much to me as any cricketing gong ever has.

Where I'm happiest, surrounded by my family. Hayley holds Millie, with Ellie on my lap.

behind. When Ash was bowled by Shoaib Akhtar we were suddenly 117 for seven. Geraint Jones dragged us to 166, 32 runs short before Shoaib cleaned him up. Shaun Udal, at 36 our veteran second spinner, was bowled by Kaneria two balls later and though Harmy had a dart Shoaib had him caught by Younis Khan and we were sunk.

I was devastated, and though I tried to put a brave face on things in the captain's press conference afterwards, trotting out all the required lines about 'character', 'sticking together', 'team spirit', etc., the beer in Vaughan's room before we departed tasted especially flat and the plane trip to Faisalabad was particularly quiet. Trying to make sense of all that had happened was almost impossible. My father-in-law was lying in the intensive care unit at Frenchay Hospital in Bristol. Hayley was pleading with me to come home. I had captained the side, scored one of my best ever hundreds and we had lost. And there was more. To put a comical cap on all that, we were told after the match that Hoggy had been reprimanded and fined by the match referee Roshan Mahanama for failing to appeal properly, or at least according to the ludicrous ICC directive that insisted bowlers had to turn to the umpire after appealing for confirmation of the outcome before celebrating a wicket. The intention was to underline the authority of the umpire at all times, but a bowler instinctively knows when a batsman has edged the ball and has a pretty good idea of when an lbw shout is out and they have always reacted accordingly. The umpires also made themselves unpopular with the Pakistan team, reporting the bowling actions of Shabbir Ahmed and off-spinner Shoaib Malik. Shoaib Akhtar, who had already undergone remedial work to correct his action, was not reported.

Amid all the confusion and disappointment I had reached a decision. I was definitely going home as soon as possible. That night I spoke to Phil again and asked him to firm up some travel plans. I then spoke to Duncan and told him I felt I had to get back and help Hayley through the crisis. I said, 'Things are not good at home. I'm thinking about going home tomorrow.'

Duncan was very sympathetic. His only advice was to 'do the right thing'.

'Obviously we want you to stay,' he told me. 'You're a vital member of the side. You've just got 190. But you do the right thing by your family. No one can tell you what to do. Only you know.' I spoke to Nigel Stockhill, the team physiologist. He suggested I sleep on it.

I never actually told Hayley at that stage that I was coming home. In my own mind I rationalized that I should make sure all the arrangements were in place and the tickets booked before I told her. But maybe I was actually hanging on for a good enough reason to stay, or even an excuse.

When I woke up on 17 November, however, I was sure in my own mind. I was going home.

Because of the time difference between Pakistan and home it was too early to ring Hayley and let her know. I intended to speak to Michael Vaughan at breakfast, then confirm the arrangements with Duncan and Phil. But my plans were initially delayed when Andrew Walpole, our media relations manager, took me to one side to tell me that the information about me making plans to come home from the tour, and that flights had already been booked for the trip, and even a reference to the cause of my possible departure had somehow made their way into that day's edition of the *Sun* back home. To this day I have absolutely no idea how the paper had got hold of the story, and by now other media, radio and websites were discussing it.

I was irritated, to say the least, but not unduly perturbed as the only thing of any importance was to get home. I had intended to let Vaughan know at breakfast but I didn't see him there. Then, when

I got back to my room, he rang and asked if he could come round for a chat. He would have been involved in discussions with Duncan and was probably aware that I was about to make the decision.

I can't remember who spoke first, but when Michael did speak, he made his position crystal clear. 'We really need you to stay, mate,' he told me. 'I know things are really tough at home, but you're such a big member of the side at the moment. You've just got a hundred and nearly won us the game. I really need you to stay, just for these couple of weeks for the last two Tests. Try and dig it out and see what happens.'

I didn't say no straightaway and I didn't say yes. But the outcome of the meeting was that I changed my mind and I changed my decision. At the moment Michael came into the room, I was going home. When he left, 15 to 20 minutes later, I was staying. I don't blame him at all. It wasn't Michael's fault. It was my choice. From a purely selfish perspective staying was obviously the easier option. I would still have to deal with the phone calls from home, but I wouldn't actually have to confront what was going on there in person.

Now, by more or less begging me to stay, Michael had given me a way out and I took it.

I set about giving myself some support by reasoning that these were exceptional circumstances. We already knew we were going to be without Andrew Strauss for the final Test in Lahore in ten days' time as he had asked for and been granted compassionate leave to be at home with wife Ruth for the birth of their first child. If I went home and Vaughan failed to recover, I told myself, England would have gone into the third and possibly decisive Test, taking on Shoaib Akhtar and Kaneria without their three senior batsmen. That was good enough for me.

I told Phil, Duncan and finally Michael that I was staying and then I rang Hayley to tell her the news she definitely did not want to hear. It was a hard phone call to make, but once it was done, I felt almost relieved to be able to refocus on being on tour, so much so that by the time she rang again later that day, around 6.30 p.m. I was just preparing myself to belt out 'Jerusalem' at the top of my voice.

The day before we reached Faisalabad, the singer Keely had arrived at the hotel with a film crew to record a video of her and us singing the Ashes 'anthem', for release as a Christmas single. The idea was that the proceeds would be shared between the players and the PCA Benevolent Fund. But on the day we pitched up quite a few of the lads were anything but enthusiastic about giving up a precious day off. There was a definite feeling among some players that the commercial exploitation of what we had done in the summer might be getting out of hand, but persuaded that a good cause would benefit, a group of us agreed to go ahead. Then, with the music blaring out of the hotel lobby and deafening anyone who happened to be within a five-mile radius, my phone rang.

I saw Hayley's name flash up on the screen, left the recording session immediately and made my way through the hotel to the swimming pool. I remember the sun was going down and the mosquitoes were out in force. I remember being bitten to shreds by the little bastards. And I remember Hayley's voice, quivering with sadness, as she asked me once again to come home.

She never put me under any pressure. Obviously I knew what she wanted me to do and say and she was really upset that I didn't. I could hear her crying on the other end of the line. Even then, she never said, 'I can't believe you're not coming back,' but that message was clear in her voice. And I, stubborn, selfish and stupid, kept saying no, I can't.

Afterwards I again tried to persuade myself that I was doing the right thing for the right reasons. In fact, looking back I realize only too well that I knew all along what I should have done. I let Hayley down almost as badly as it was possible to do.

Hoggy had also left the recording to come out to see me because he could tell I was upset. He was sympathetic. He told me that things would improve and that time would heal everything. I think he was just trying to make me feel better. And then a thought struck me. It just came into my mind from nowhere. I thought to myself, if I had got nought and nought in Multan, I would definitely have gone home.

Andrew Walpole set about releasing a statement in response to the story in the *Sun*. It acknowledged that I had discussed the option of going home with the management, and revealed the reason as being John's accident. The statement described John's condition as stable and I was quoted as saying: 'The past few days have been very traumatic for my family and I am naturally extremely concerned for my father-in-law. Having talked with my family and the England captain and coach, I've decided to remain with the squad.'

Looking back, I almost cannot believe that I managed to persuade myself that my captain's needs were greater than my wife's, that the England cricket team was more important than my family. Now, if the same situation arose, I would be on the first plane home. No ifs or buts or maybes. Nothing else would matter. But at the time I didn't see it that way. Staying on tour was, without doubt, completely and utterly the wrong thing to do. I have carried the guilt with me ever since. It almost certainly contributed to the illness that was just around the corner. And I wasn't finished yet, by the way.

* * *

Michael was able to return to the side for the second Test, which relieved some of the pressure for me. And, as the days passed so John's condition began to improve. On the field, even though we were dominated by Inzamam's brilliant batting, which brought him centuries in both innings, we managed to draw a match full of controversy from start to finish. On day one Ian Bell took a catch off his own bowling to dismiss Mohammad Yousuf, when TV replays suggested the ball might have kissed the ground. Then, while Inzy carried on with his patient craft, the returning Shahid Afridi smashed us everywhere, hitting 92 in 85 balls. Inzy completed his 23rd Test ton, equalling the record of Javed Miandad for Pakistan, and soon after he drove the ball back to Harmison who collected it in his follow-through and, instinctively, threw down the stumps at the batsman's end. Harmy appealed and after deliberation the TV umpire, Nadeem Ghauri, gave Inzy out, to the obvious and noisy dismay of the 17,000 crowd. In fact, as Inzy was leaping out of the way of the ball to avoid getting hit, strictly speaking the decision was wrong.

People were still debating the issue when Pakistan were all out just after lunch on day two. But all the talking stopped an hour or so later, when the match was stopped in its tracks by the single most terrifying incident I have ever experienced on a cricket field.

It was a bomb, a dirty great massive, big, bloody bomb. From where I was standing, the middle of the pitch, with Shoaib Akhtar running up to bowl to me, and from the noise we all heard – *BOOOOOM* – there was simply nothing else it could possibly be.

We'd become used to the security issue by now. Post 9/11 all our overseas tours had been conducted under the tightest scrutiny and, as events in London earlier that year had proved, no one was immune from being in the wrong place at the wrong time. And in the moment this enormous noise blew a hole in the Faisalabad afternoon we all just instinctively thought this was the time and place and that the terrorists had succeeded in bringing their campaign of hate into our own lives.

In the dressing-room, behind glass windows that had rattled within their frames with the force of the blast, a number of players started to pack their bags, thinking the match and indeed the tour must be over. In the area surrounding the scene of the explosion, hundreds of spectators turned and ran towards the exits at the top of the roofless concrete stands, though there was minimal panic. Ian Bell, my partner at the time, and I waited for the plume of black smoke to clear skywards; now in an eerie almost unearthly silence, myself and all the players on the pitch asked ourselves the same thing: 'How many are dead?'. The next question that entered my head was that if this was a terrorist attack, what the hell might happen now? To put it bluntly, I was bricking it.

The umpires had taken us all to one side of the square, farthest from the site of the incident, and there, after what seemed like hours but was in fact a few minutes, word reached us of the real cause of the explosion. A gas canister, used to put the fizz in Pepsi, had blown up, destroying the stall it was contained in.

Mercifully, and almost unbelievably, there had been just one casualty, and as far as we knew, that was not thought to be serious. But it could have been, judging by the twisted heavy metal advertising board and the wreckage of the soft drinks stall it had left behind.

Eventually we meandered back to the wicket to resume the match, at 113 for three in reply to their 462 all out. But before we did I noticed something very odd. Just on a good length at the end where I was batting a saucer-shaped undulation about eight inches across had appeared on the surface of the pitch. I immediately worked out what had happened. In the confusion following the explosion, someone had decided to boot a few holes out of the pitch with their size nines, presumably to try and speed up the wearing process so it might offer their spinners rather more help than they might have expected at this stage of the match. The umpires, Darrell Hair and Simon Taufel took one look, called over Inzy, the Pakistan captain, and made it plain they were onto what had happened, even though the identity of the culprit was as yet unknown.

That only became clear when Sky TV's commentary team, their suspicions alerted by the behaviour of the umpires, asked for the technicians to run the tape from the static camera they have in position for general views of the ground to see if something untoward had happened during the enforced break. There, plain as day, was Shahid Afridi, walking onto the pitch, glancing around him to make sure the coast was clear, then pirouetting on the spot. His actions earned him a ban for one Test and two one-day internationals. Some suggested that, after trying to take advantage of a potentially tragic incident, he got off lightly.

When the dust settled, Bell and Pietersen both completed first innings hundreds, though it was ironic that Afridi was their most successful bowler, finishing with four for 95 as we were all out for 446, a deficit of 16. We were briefly in with a chance when we had them 187 for seven in their second innings, but try as we might, we couldn't shift Inzy, who declared their second innings at 268 for nine, as soon as he reached three figures, unbeaten for exactly 100. At 20 for four, with me, Strauss and Bell all out for ducks, we might even have lost, but Fred, KP and Geraint made sure we survived.

Then we fell to bits in the final Test in Lahore, starting five days later. Collingwood came in for Strauss, away on paternity leave, and made 96. But our 288 first up was swallowed up by their massive 636 for eight declared, Inzy making 97 and Mohammad Yousuf scoring a fantastic 223 and Kamran Akmal 154 from No.8; and we collapsed in our second innings from a comfortable matchsaving 202 for two (Trescothick an impressive two-ball 0 to Shoaib Akhtar) to 248 all out, to lose by an innings and 100 runs and the series by a comfortable 2–0.

And then I managed to let Hayley down again.

Michael Vaughan had been sent home to get his knee sorted, a painfully long process that was to take the best part of a year. And after assuring Duncan things were much better at home, I was duly appointed to lead the side in the five-match one-day series that followed. Two days before it began, in Lahore, Hayley rang me to tell me her granddad had died.

For the second time on the trip she asked me if I could come home. For the second time, I said no. I felt a little less guilty about doing so this time because Hayley's grandfather had been gradually passing away for some time, so his death seemed less of a shock than her dad's accident had been. And in any case, John was on the mend by this time. But again I misjudged the effect my staying in Pakistan would have on her, that is, if I thought about it at all.

'No, I'm sorry,' I told her. 'I'm the England captain now and I have to stay and get this job done.'

It seemed an easier decision to make to say no because I would be coming home anyway in ten or twelve days' time. Of course, as I understand now only too well, it made things much harder for Hayley.

By the time I finally did leave, at the end of the tour, a couple of days before Christmas, I was absolutely exhausted. And what I encountered when we landed at Birmingham airport hardly lifted my mood.

Hayley had brought Ellie to meet me and when I picked up our eight-month-old girl, I realized she didn't recognize me. I remember thinking: 'That's not right'. I'd been away for two and a half months. I remember holding her in my arms and she was looking at me as if to say, who are you? And I hated it. It was a horrible feeling.

Chapter 12

'SOMETHING'S WRONG ...'

'We arrived in Baroda on the evening of Tuesday 21 February. Within five days I would be flying home, broken and in bits.'

To say I had a bad feeling about England's 2006 tour to India is something of an understatement. The fact is, as early as a month in advance of our departure, during a training camp at the National Cricket Academy in Loughborough, I told Steve Bull, the team's sports psychologist: 'Something's wrong. I don't want to train. I don't want to play cricket. I don't want to do anything. And I do not want to go away on this tour.' Two and two does not always make four, of course. But I have often wondered how differently things might have turned out if I had taken more notice of those feelings.

There was nothing particularly unusual in me having concerns about going away from home. I had been travelling abroad with England on and off for ten years or so. And the time immediately before and after leaving home was always hard work.

But whereas my feelings of general unease would normally give way to the pre-flight build-up of excitement of actually playing cricket for England again, this time was different. The nearer we came to leaving the less I wanted to go. I couldn't shrug off the listlessness, the lack of interest, the feeling of just not caring.

I couldn't put my finger on why, in particular. At first I thought my state of mind was probably due to a simple mixture of physical and mental exhaustion caused by the gruelling schedule of playing and travelling we had undergone over the past year or so – burnout for short – and sadness at the prospect of leaving family and friends again.

Those feelings had obviously intensified because of Ellie's presence and, in the time leading up to the trip, I did revisit more than once the incident on my return from Pakistan to Birmingham airport when my beautiful little girl reacted to my embrace as though I was a stranger. I do also recall being a little worried about Hayley. I remember thinking, on a couple of occasions, she had a vague, distant look about her, that her face looked gaunt and her eyes black. I also remember noticing her crying a couple of times, and trying not to show it. And I was carrying around an amount of residual guilt over my intransigent attitude to Hayley's pleas for me to return home from Pakistan.

Yet I also remember trying desperately to switch back into tour mode, thinking to myself, 'Well, Hayley's probably got the baby blues, which is pretty normal. She'll be fine. And she and Ellie will be coming out to join me in Mumbai during the tour, so we won't be apart for too long.' Needless to say, I was fairly ignorant of the effects and symptoms of post-natal depression at the time. In any case, whenever Hayley had been to the hospital for one of her regular checks, she told me the midwife pronounced her well. What I didn't know at the time was that the midwife had actually put her down as 'borderline' and what I also didn't know at the time, however, was that if someone suffering from depression doesn't want you to know they can put on a bloody good act – something I was later to experience personally.

Looking back now, it is pretty clear to me that these signs and feelings I had experienced were warnings of a deeper malaise. Maybe I hadn't been able to recognize them for what they were. Maybe I just hadn't been willing to do so.

In retrospect I could say that going through with the India trip was the biggest mistake of my life. But that would be wrong. I never got as far as accepting there was a decision to make.

When it came to it, my sense of so-called 'duty', of having to do the right thing, and even my self-centredness prevailed. I had an England tour to go on. I was an England cricketer. That is what I did. In the end, instead of saying 'this is all too much, I'm not going anywhere', I shut out all the doubts, flicked the switch marked emotional attachment into the 'off' position, and persuaded myself that once I was in the swing of the tour, I would find all my fears had been unfounded; Hayley would cope without me, as she always had done before.

To try and counter the worst of being away, I had taken loads of video film of Ellie playing at home over Christmas and New Year to watch on my laptop in India whenever I started to miss her. And if I did have trouble sleeping when I got there, I always had my trusty pills to get me through the night, and my sounding-board diary to help me get through the down days.

For the first few days of the trip I did my best to carry out those intentions and get right into the tour, and up to a point I succeeded.

After arriving in Mumbai on the night of Monday 13 February, we quickly settled into our familiar pattern. With only two practice matches before the opening Test against Sachin Tendulkar, Rahul Dravid, Anil Kumble, Harbajhan Singh et al. in Nagpur on 1 March, we had little time to acclimatize to local conditions, and, as always when touring this part of the world, we knew our preparations were bound to be disrupted by the effects of the heat, the food and the occasional flu-like virus that, no matter what precautions we took, someone always fell victim to.

I looked on in sympathy, relief and a degree of schoolboy chortling, when the first to go down was Matthew Hoggard who had apparently passed out on the floor of his hotel bathroom. I wasn't laughing much a couple of days later, when it was my turn.

Mumbai was hot and humid and the normal five-hour sessions of full-on, intensive practice and training we needed to get up speed were taking their toll. The night before our first match, against the Cricket Club of India Board President's XI at the Brabourne stadium, I recall getting back to my room at the Taj Mahal hotel and suddenly feeling cold and shivery. As the night wore on I felt worse and worse. One moment I'd be boiling hot and sweating heavily, then the next minute I'd be freezing cold. I thought I might be suffering from heatstroke. Then I woke up in the middle of the night to go to the loo and the next thing I knew I was thinking 'what am I doing lying face down on the bathroom floor?'

This repeating pattern of shivers and sweats then set in properly. The doctor, Peter Gregory, attended me, prescribed paracetamol and placed me in quarantine in my room until the fever passed. The last thing we needed at the start of the tour was for this virus to spread any further. The problem for me was that being left on my own, more-or-less completely isolated from the rest of the squad while they went about their business at the Brabourne, was absolutely the last thing I needed at the time. Even when totally well, I always needed people around me in the early days of a tour, to counter my homesickness and jet lag. Whenever I had felt low about being away from home in the first phase of previous tours, my normal routine would be to fill my time with things and people, tire myself out in the gym or in practice then crash out through sheer tiredness, or if not, take another pill.

I actually dreaded the thought of being alone in my hotel room.

Apart from Peter Gregory I don't think I saw another soul for the best part of two days. With so much time on my hands I started to think. And I started to brood. I wasn't eating because of the symptoms of the virus. Once again I felt like a five-star prisoner, not really enjoying breathing the air-conditioned atmosphere, feeling physically dreadful and quietly going stir crazy.

To try and cope with the boredom and keep the dark thoughts away, I ran through my collection of DVDs. Initially I was reluctant to play the tapes of Ellie, mainly because in my current state of mind I felt the experience might be too painful. So I watched an entire series of *Spooks*.

Then I did load a DVD of Ellie playing at home and, almost immediately after it started, an overwhelming wave of sadness and anxiety swept over me. It was like someone had sucked my spirit out of my body. I stopped the tape within seconds. I couldn't watch another moment. The black wings fluttered. Exhausted, emotionally vulnerable, isolated and far from home, I was finally ready for the taking.

That night, I rang Hayley. I tried not to let on just how bad I was feeling, because if I had done so I knew she would start worrying about me and she was in a fragile enough state as it was. But I did tell her I was very homesick and missing her and Ellie like mad.

I managed to sleep on and off through a second pretty uncomfortable night, and, on waking, I realized the physical symptoms brought on by the virus had died down sufficiently for me to think about getting out of my room, which, by now, I was desperate to do. I cheered up even more when the doc agreed that I could get down to the ground and take part in the final two days of the three-day match.

As it had been agreed it advance that, with time and practice possibilities before the first Test so short, we could field all of our 16-man squad at some stage, there was no problem with me playing. No one inside the camp had the slightest idea that anything was wrong with me other than the effects of the virus and that was the way I wanted it to stay. Even though I was still pretty weak from the effects of the past 48 hours, I managed to top score in our second innings with 88, but my inability to run between the wickets caused me to stuff Kevin Pietersen by the length of the pitch. I ran two but by the time I gave up on the third he was about to lap me, so when I sent him back he was running his fourth in total to my two and never had a chance.

Just getting back into playing was good for me. As it had done on occasions in the past, my cricket was going to get me through, I tried hard to convince myself. But, truth be told, I was struggling again.

Michael Vaughan had clearly seen something. On one occasion, sitting by the hotel pool, Vaughan turned to me out of the blue and asked: 'Are you all right? You're very quiet. You're not saying much. What's going on?'

'I'm fine,' I told him. 'I'm not feeling great but it's nothing to worry about. I'm just getting into the tour.' I lied. Even the fact that he had spoken to me in this way deepened my sense of unease.

After the match, which we won easily by 238 runs, a load of us went out for dinner to an Italian restaurant and I just couldn't get into it at all. I was jittery, unsettled, shaky and very dull company. I felt like absolute shit and later spent a third successive restless night worrying, tossing and turning.

The next day, before we flew to Baroda, Strauss and I busied ourselves with confirming arrangements with the hotel for when the girls were coming out later in the tour. And, for the time being, I had other issues to keep me occupied as well. As part of the management group I was heavily involved in the discussion over how the team should line up for the first Test. In the absence of Ashley Giles, who had broken down prior to the one-day series in Pakistan, and, bearing in mind the necessity of playing two spinners when pitch and climate conditions dictated it, we had a selection issue over which of the two left-armers present we should pick to accompany Shaun Udal. The choice was between my county colleague Ian Blackwell and the young Northampton-shire bowler, Monty Panesar and I felt we should go with Black-well. I hadn't seen enough of Monty to be able to make an informed judgment over his ability with the ball. But my reasoning was that if we were looking for a like-for-like replacement for Giles, someone who could do a job with the ball when conditions were not in his favour, an even better one when they were and give you something with the bat and in the field, as he had done in the Ashes series, then Blackwell was the obvious choice. From where I was standing, and no disrespect to a cricketer who has worked so hard to improve his weak areas, Monty wasn't exactly Don Brad-man with the bat and he was no Jonty Rhodes in the field either.

As for the skipper's knee, Michael had complained of a little soreness during the match, but he gave no indication then that he considered it a serious problem at this stage.

Although I was making a fair fist of distracting myself, some-where deep inside I could feel the anxiety growing in me again and my state of mind was not helped by the thought of leaving Mumbai for the rather quieter and very much smaller Baroda. My experience of touring in the sub-continent before had taught me the bigger the city we were staying in the better for me; more to see, more to do, more to take my mind off home-sickness. What I was not looking forward to was being stuck for large parts of the day, staring at the four walls of my hotel room and not much else.

We arrived in Baroda on the evening of Tuesday 21 February. Within five days I would be flying home, broken and in bits.

By the time I got into my hotel room that night I was completely exhausted and I actually slept like a log, without the help of a pill, which was an encouraging sign. But it turned out to be a false one. From the moment I woke up the following morning, I began to go downhill rapidly.

The first thing that hit me, on the way from the hotel to the ground, was how affected I was by the sight of the beggars. If you haven't experienced these men, women and children of all shapes, sizes and ages, in rags, some of them little more than skeletons with skin, their sad eyes sunk deep into their faces, tapping on the windows of stationary traffic, pleading for coins, all I can say is that it takes a hard spirit to say no. Yet that is what tourists are advised to do as, according to the local authorities, these poor souls are controlled by local gangs who make profit from their misery, and handing over money only keeps this terrible exploitation going. I knew the drill as I had been here before, but here the streets seemed to be lined with them. Watching mothers carrying babies in their arms, pressing them at the car windows, tore my heart to shreds. They made me think of Ellie.

The tears swept over me. I'm pretty sure no one else in the team bus noticed. But no one said anything, even if they did. I managed to get through the day's practice, but I was becoming increasingly detached from what was happening around me.

When we arrived at the ground the next day, for instance, and watched Michael painfully fail a fitness test to establish whether he could play in our final warm-up match prior to the start of the Test series, against the Board President's XI, the news hardly registered at all. When Fletch confirmed to me that I would be taking over as captain, I said okay without a second thought, even though I understood this time a recurrence of Michael's cartilage problem this close to back-to-back Tests meant I was almost certain to be asked to take over for the whole series. On the face of it, I was taking a lot of things in my stride actually; Paul Collingwood's back spasm, the fact that Udal and Simon Jones were down with stomach bugs. Truth is, I was running on pure anxiety-filled adrenaline.

It didn't take long for it to run out. I won the toss and elected to bat first, got to 18, then called Andrew Strauss for a second run that existed only in my overwrought imagination. I was run out by half a century. We were rattled for 238, Kevin Pietersen had gone off with a back strain and by the close on the first day the opposition were a very healthy 93 for one. Or at least I remember someone telling me they were. I had spent the whole of their innings that evening battling to stop myself from breaking down there and then. If anyone had come up to me on the field and said 'Cry' I would have gone.

The next thing I knew for sure was that I was following the doc, Peter Gregory out of the hotel lift towards his room. 'I'm struggling, doc,' I was telling him. 'Something's not right. I need some help.'

I had decided I needed to tell someone how I was feeling and I'd decided to tell the doctor, rather than Vaughan or Fletcher or any of the players or management at this stage, because I felt I needed to be able to talk to someone in confidence. In that old macho way, I didn't want to admit to anyone what the problem might be, least of all my team-mates … least of all my mates. I didn't think I could trust anyone else with what was inside me. But the doc was the doc, patient confidentiality and all that. It was almost like going to a priest.

The moment he let me into his room I broke down. In between the sobs and tears I told him: 'I feel sick. I feel anxious. I feel really nervous, I feel homesick and I'm missing Hayley. I'm missing Ellie and every time I see these kids begging at the side of the road I just want to cry. It busts my heart.'

'What do you want to do?' he asked me. 'Do you want to go home?'

'No,' I said. 'I can't leave the tour,' I insisted.

He could see clearly that I was in a terrible state. He attempted to calm me down by using acupuncture. He took some needles and stuck them in the pressure points, in my thumbs. It didn't really make a great deal of difference. Then he told me he was going to give me something that would ease the immediate situation. He prescribed the tranquillizer diazepam. I took it and went back downstairs to try and eat something. Then I visited Vaughan in his room and told him: 'Look, mate, I don't really understand what's going on but I'm really f***ing struggling.' I can't even recall his response, but maybe by now I wasn't listening, for this was the night the sleeping pills finally stopped working.

It began with me literally pacing up and down the room. I couldn't stop. I couldn't sit down and I couldn't relax. I decided I would try and watch some of the videos of Ellie, but I was gripped by a terrible sense of foreboding and never even got as far as starting up my laptop. I opened my diary, the one I had used so successfully in the past to reinforce positive thoughts, as I had done during the 2005 Ashes, and banish the bad ones, as I had in South Africa in 2004. I scribbled a few things down, 'dig in,' etc. But this time they seemed laughably inadequate.

I'd been through some tough nights before. But what happened between now and the following morning was unlike anything I had ever experienced before.

I started sweating heavily. I started shaking. I felt myself losing control. I was petrified.

I grabbed the packet of sleeping pills and popped one out. Get the tablet down me, I thought, and at least sleep will help me stop this feeling until morning. One tablet, roll over and it would be tomorrow, like so many times before. This time, I took one, nodded off momentarily then woke up with a start. As I came to, I realized the effect of the tablet had worn off almost instantaneously. That wasn't right. That wasn't supposed to happen.

I tried again. Same result. Now I *am* struggling, I thought. If the pills don't work, if the pills can't work, what…

My mind was racing, pulling itself apart in a hundred different directions. I was sweating. And I could hear a loud banging noise – *thump, thump, thump* – like someone banging a big bass drum. I couldn't work out where it was coming from and then I realized. It was my heart. It wouldn't slow down. And it was just so loud. I was terrified it might actually burst.

Then came the pictures in my head, specific, enormous, terrifying, images.

What was happening at home? Was Hayley okay? Was Ellie all right? Oh God, what if something happened to Ellie and she needed my help and I wasn't there? What if she was upset or had been hurt and she was calling for her Daddy and she couldn't find me? What if something really bad had happened? Oh God. I should be there. Oh God, I've got to get back there, now. What the hell am I doing here?

What the hell is happening? When will it stop? Will it stop at all? Am I actually, here and now, in this room, going mad?

During the moments of fitful sleep, those waking thoughts intermingled with terrible, awful dreams and, in my state of drifting in and out of consciousness, I was having difficulty distinguishing between what was real and what I imagined to be real. When I had a terrible thought about what might have happened back home, to Hayley, or Ellie, it would take me ages to force myself to realize it hadn't happened at all. And then another would come and as hard as I tried to push it out of my mind, it would take over. The thoughts were no longer inanimate. They were things, beings, beasts, bastards, and now they attacked in waves, one after another, each worse than the one before. 'Oh God. Please, make it stop. Oh God, please make it stop.' Sometimes, inside the bed with the covers pulled tightly over my head, I would try and hide from the thoughts. Then, sometimes out of bed, almost blind with fear, I tried to run from them. Sometimes, I would stand stock still and imagine I could fight the fear with my bare hands.

Nothing worked. I felt myself fighting for breath and for a single moment's peace. 'God. Make it stop. Please.'

Should I call someone? You're joking. What, let someone see me like this? I can't let anyone see me like this, going half out of my mind. What would I tell them? What could I say to them? What could I say to them to make them understand what was happening to me when I didn't know what the hell was going on myself?

The fear filled up every part of me. It was a physical sensation and it was physically painful. For a moment I wondered whether I had overdosed on the sleeping tablets. The pills must be making me like this, I thought to myself, and maybe once the effects wear off I'll be okay again.

But that thought was quickly replaced first by a creeping feeling, then by an utter certainty that I was suffering something like a brain tumour or that my brain had somehow been damaged by the virus spreading, or even poisoning me. For a moment I was convinced I was actually dying. I was scared out of my wits, but what was left of them told me I was in serious trouble. I didn't just have to get home. I had to get help.

As light and day came that morning of Friday 24 February, and the horrors of the night gradually subsided, I somehow managed to persuade myself, once again, that if I could just get myself through this now, get to the ground and carry on with the game, I might still be all right. Things might still be all right.

But they never were. From the moment I got up the rest of the day was awful again. We were in the field but I didn't have much of a clue as to what was taking place around me. I just wasn't there. I was supposed to be captain, making decisions, working out tactics. All I could think of was how bad I was feeling inside. I dropped an absolute straight-in catch at slip, the kind which, at that stage of my career I was used to taking with my eyes closed, and I suddenly realized all the other players were looking straight at me, as if to say: 'What the hell is wrong with him?'

At the end of the day's play, back in the dressing-room I was all over the shop. I didn't want to sit down because I feared the moment I did that I would collapse, so I dashed about talking to all and sundry. Vaughan said to me, 'Just sit down, chill out, man' and I said, 'Mate, not at the moment. I can't.'

By now people must have known something was seriously wrong. Unbeknown to me the message had reached the management.

That night I asked the doc to come to my room. He tried acupuncture again and again he asked me if I wanted to go home.

I told him: 'Doc, I need help. Something happened to me last night that I don't understand. If it happens again I don't know what I'll do. I don't know if I'll be able to cope. It was so bad I cannot bear the thought of it happening again. I'm serious. I think I must be really, really ill.'

I rang Hayley and, for the first time, I told her the full extent of the problem, how I was feeling, what I had been going through. I couldn't hide the truth from her any longer. 'I can't do this any more,' I told her. 'I don't want to be away. I want to come home.'

'Marcus,' she replied. 'Don't suffer out there on your own. Do what you need to do.'

It was another long night for me, if anything, even worse than the one before. And it was tough for Peter Gregory too. I asked him to stay with me until I fell asleep, to talk to me, to relax me. He tried to coach me through some breathing techniques but that didn't work. Nothing did. I was agitated, jittery and out of control. The poor bloke didn't know what to do.

By the time morning came on Saturday 25 February, I was ready to pack it in. I didn't want to stay in my room. I didn't want to go downstairs. I didn't want to go to the cricket ground and I didn't want to get on the bus. I couldn't face the idea of looking out of the window of the bus and seeing all those kids in rags and fighting for food. I knew that if I did the terrible thoughts I had had about Ellie would come at me again. Nothing else mattered to me at that point except the knowledge that I was gone.

I couldn't see how I was going to get through another day feeling like this. But the next problem was that I also couldn't work out how to tell the management, or Fletch or Vaughan that I had to leave. I knew what I wanted to do, what I had to do. But I just couldn't bring myself to come out and actually say it.

Somehow I hauled what was left of me down to breakfast but I just couldn't face eating. I managed to force down a couple of mouthfuls of porridge and about three sips of water. Still I hadn't told anyone. Still I hadn't actually gone up to anyone and uttered the words: 'I've got to go home.'

I boarded the bus in a kind of trance. Strauss told me later he had never seen anyone looking so ill. I think by then the rest of the guys realized I was on the edge. Surely they must know, by now, I thought to myself. Surely Fletch or someone is going to come to me and say, 'Okay. It's all over.'

Then almost the moment I got on the bus I fell fast asleep, through sheer exhaustion. When we reached the ground I carried on doing what I was supposed to be doing, but I was just hanging on for someone in the management to come over and say: 'That's it, Tres. Enough is enough.'

I clearly recall constantly glancing over towards Fletch as if to somehow communicate to him that I wanted him to come over and end all this, but he never did, and so, busted and bashed in and operating completely on auto-pilot I went in to resume my innings.

I've no idea who I was batting with most of the time or what was actually happening in the game, but instinct must have taken over when the ball came anywhere near me because I went from 4 not out to 35, all the while looking towards the dressing-room to see if Duncan was talking to anyone about me or if he and Phil Neale were looking like they might be planning something.

I never saw the ball that got me out, about half an hour before lunch, but as I walked off I started to go. I knew I was going to crack the moment I walked in through the dressing-room door and I was heading straight for it. I was thinking to myself: 'This is it. I can't hold this back any longer.' I'd known for a couple of days that I had to go home, but it was such a big decision and the ramifications so huge I had tried to fight and fight. Now I just didn't have any fight left in me. I walked in, threw my helmet in my bag and there, in the middle of the dressing-room, I let it all out. Phil Neale and the doc were in there and they called Fletch in from outside. I told them: 'I can't stay here. I want to get out of this place. I've got to go home.' Then I began sobbing uncontrollably.

I rushed outside. I was nervous and uptight and retching and I didn't want to cause any more of a scene in front of the other players. But Fletch came out, grabbed me and sort of pulled me back inside the dressing-room to get me out of sight of the public and the media.

At that point I was a shell. You could have taken all my kit, all my money, taken my life away. I didn't care. I'd lost the will to do anything else but try and be happy and secure. Vaughan signalled to the other players to vacate the dressing-room. And they scattered. When Strauss suggested it might be better for one or two close colleagues to stay with me, Vaughan told him: 'No. Tres is gone. Completely.'

Finally, after what seemed like ages, someone spoke – I can't recall who exactly – and said: 'Right. We're sending you home.' Phil Neale then disappeared to make all the arrangements. The management were desperate to get me away from the ground as soon as possible so as not to alert the press. Within half an hour I was in a cab on the way back to the hotel with Peter Gregory.

I rang Hayley and I told her. 'I'm flying home tonight.' I rang mum and dad. 'Come home and we'll sort all this out,' said mum. I phoned Neil Fairbrother, my advisor and friend, and told him what was happening. He listened and said: 'If you think this is the right thing to do, then do it.'

Then we sat in the doc's room and chatted through what had happened and about the decision I'd made, what was actually going to happen now. Thanks to the concoction of drugs he gave me – more diazepam, the tranquillizer, with a twist of betablocker, I was becoming calmer by the minute and I was enjoying a sense of sheer relief. Feeling slightly better, the crazy thought even occurred to me that I might stay. I was also starting to think about the consequences of going home as regards my career. 'I'll probably lose my sponsored car,' I thought. 'I'll probably lose my contract. Then what will happen to us?' And so the vicious cycle kicked in again, until the doc nipped all that in the bud with a few calming words and another pill.

At the ground the management had somehow succeeded in keeping the news of my departure quiet. Even when we were all out a second time and the Board President's XI went in to knock off the 55 runs required for victory, duly achieved by eight wickets, my absence was explained as being due to a migraine. Then, at the end of the day's play, Duncan announced at the post-match press conference that I had returned home for 'family, personal reasons'. The use of the word 'family' was a slip of the tongue, but, as it turned out, it set a lot of other tongues wagging.

By the time I was ready to leave the hotel for the flight from Baroda to Delhi from where I was catching the night plane home, some of the press boys thought they had the story all sewn up.

Someone had put it about that I had actually been perfectly all right when I came off the field after having been bowled, that I then received a phone call from Hayley in the dressing-room which caused me to break down in tears and pull out of the tour. All night long Fairbrother was fielding calls from increasingly frustrated journalists trying to confirm the story that I had gone home to look after Hayley because of her post-natal depression. Some imaginative types had already put it to him that there must be something sinister in all this for me to have fled as quickly as I did. One demanded to know if a kiss and tell story was about to appear in one of the Sunday tabloids and didn't sound all that convinced when Neil said: 'No chance.'

For me, for the time being at least, all this was someone else's problem. I had received a text message from Strauss telling me: 'You've done the right thing. Go back and get yourself well. We are all thinking of you' and suddenly, there I was at Delhi airport, spirits further raised by the fact that I had been supplied with a first-class ticket for the flight home.

The lady at the counter soon pricked that particular balloon, however.

'Excess baggage, sir.' She smiled. 'That'll be £400, please.'

Chapter 13

A KIND OF HELL

'I was thinking to myself: I've got to make people realize I am really, really hurting here. Talking is not doing any good. The diazepam isn't doing any good. The sleeping pills aren't doing any good. Nothing is working.'

I slept for virtually all of the nine-hour flight home from Delhi to Heathrow. Shortly before the plane was due to land, in the early morning of Sunday 26 February 2006, I was woken by a stewardess asking me whether I fancied anything for breakfast and I suddenly realized I was absolutely starving. I couldn't remember the last time I'd eaten anything you could accurately describe as a meal.

'Any chance of a bacon butty?' I asked, thinking it's not every day you get to fly first-class.

It never touched the sides, so I pressed the button to attract her attention again and said: 'I'm famished. I've not eaten for a week. Can I have another go?'

I decided I was going to take some time over the second one, savour it a bit. I did. It lasted two bites.

Rested and fed and, for the moment, free from the stresses that had hounded me out of India, I was feeling pretty good by the time the plane landed. Met at the top of the gangway, I was led through a small doorway into what I was told was the VIP area where all the A-list celebs go while the rest of us mortals are scrumming down at the baggage carousel. I wondered briefly whether this might be the moment to mention the four hundred quid, but thought better of it. Then, after being brought my bags, I walked through another door to be greeted by David Collier, the chief exec of the ECB.

David drove me round the corner to the Marriott Hotel. Five minutes later I was opening the door of a hotel bedroom provided by the Board, and inside was Hayley.

We hugged.

'You all right?' I asked.

'Yeah, I'm fine,' she said.

'You all right?' she responded.

'Yup. Fine.'

Fine, I had said. I wasn't, of course, and Hayley said later I looked completely glazed, but, whether it was the tranquillizers, the rest, the food, the effect of being away from the place where I had been so dreadful or all of the above, I was at least a hundred times better than I had been during those miserable days prior to leaving the tour.

There were no tears. There was no breakdown. Just a feeling of calmness that the family life I had missed so much would soon come together again.

We didn't talk much about what had happened on the way home. In fact, anyone sitting in the back of the car would have had little or no idea of the crisis I had just been through. As I drove along, the conversation was mainly me asking Hayley about how things had been going, what she had being doing in the past couple of weeks and Ellie. I think I just wanted to get back into normal life before facing what had to be faced.

Neil Fairbrother had arranged for us to disappear down to Bovey Castle Hotel in Devon for a few days with Ellie, just to give us some time away together. Hayley had brought a bag with her and I had my stuff, so the plan was for us to collect Ellie from our house where Hayley's mum and dad were waiting with her.

Just as I pulled into the Shell garage near to the County Ground in Taunton to fill up for the remainder of the trip down to Devon, my phone rang. It was Hayley's parents. A crowd of press and photographers had gathered at our house. A cold shiver ...

I was not ready to face them. In fact, at that exact moment, I would rather have had my eyeballs barbecued. So we changed plans. Hayley asked her folks to collect some clothes for Ellie and take her to their house, a five-minute drive from where we lived. We could then by-pass the waiting media, go straight to their place, collect Ellie and be off.

As I was filling up the tank, my attention was drawn to a man on the opposite side of the forecourt, who appeared to be checking me out. Oh, no. Here we go. A bloody reporter and he'd bloody clocked me.

I studied the man's movements, expecting him to pull out a camera at any moment, or to come towards me firing questions. I even started thinking about what I was going to say. Even when he drove away I still felt he was looking me up and down in his rear-view mirror, probably about to call his mates. I paid for the fuel, got back in the car and started her up.

We'd gone about two hundred yards up Priory Bridge Road and were just about to pass the entrance to Somerset's ground on our left, when I first became aware that there was something not quite right with the car.

Had I left the handbrake on? No. Then what the hell was that bloody racket?

It only took a few seconds for the penny to drop, with a resounding thud. 'Oh, sod it,' I realized. In my state of distraction and paranoia, focusing on that bloke at the garage and convinced he was scrutinizing my every move, I had failed to notice that I was filling my 3L Volkswagen Touareg Turbo Diesel with petrol, to the very top.

What to do? Call the AA? All I could think of was the time it would take for them to arrive, tow the car away, empty the tank etc, time I just didn't want to be wasting like that. And what if that bloke actually was a reporter? Imagine him bringing his mates back to the garage, snapping away while I had to explain what I'd done.

I knew that, under normal circumstances, the idea of trying to drive a diesel-engine car filled with petrol was among the three worst of all time when it comes to motoring. But, having racked our brains, we couldn't think of anything else to do except try, somehow, to complete our journey home, so we did. Talk about flying under the radar. The noise it made when I switched the engine back on was like a dentist's slow drill revving up and you could probably have heard us kangarooing all the way from the centre of town to Hayley's parents.

Finally, after what seemed like an age of cringing embarrassment, at around 11 a.m., we pulled into the little cul-de-sac where they lived. At first we were pleasantly surprised to find that the coast seemed clear, but then I glanced to my right and saw it; a silver Vauxhall Vectra, with its windows down and a great big zoom lens poking out. In an instant the horrible feelings flooded back in.

We got into the house as quickly as we could, but not quick enough. Within minutes the place was swarming with press and photographers. And my discomfort quickly turned to panic.

Looking back, I don't blame the individuals concerned. I've no particular axe to grind. By and large over the years, until this point the press had treated me pretty well. I knew what to expect.

Whether or not people in the public eye deserve the scrutiny that comes with the territory, it is a fact of life and these individuals were doing what they were paid to do; put themselves in awkward situations and ask awkward questions. And the uncertainty inadvertently caused by the ambiguity in what Fletch had said back in Baroda meant there were plenty of them.

It was just then I couldn't face confronting all that now. In fact, at this particular moment I wasn't actually capable of very much at all.

I had barely had time to pick up Ellie and give her a huge cuddle when there was a loud knock at the door.

'Marcus, we'd just like to ask a few questions.'

'Marcus, if you just answer a few questions, then let us take a snap or two, we'll leave you in peace.'

'Marcus, why have you left the tour?'

'Marcus, how is Hayley?'

'Marcus, what about the rumours?'

I was in no condition to talk to anyone, let alone the press. I was sitting in the back of the house, with the curtains closed in broad daylight, shaking like a leaf.

I snapped out of it pretty quickly because we couldn't just stay there and hope they would go away. I had to do something.

First I rang Richard Bevan. It suddenly occurred to me that we needed a means to escape and my getaway car was a non-starter, literally. Bevan had been responsible for arranging the deal by which all the England players were supplied with top of the range VWs, so I rang him first to tell him that I had put petrol into the tank and then to see if he could possibly organize a replacement, straight away. 'Sorry, Marcus,' he told me. 'I can't get anything to you today. But leave the car there and we'll sort it out.'

Then I rang my Somerset colleague and close friend Jason Kerr, who lived nearby, and said: 'Look Jase, I can't explain everything now but I need you to lend me your car for the week. Just bring it over to us at Hayley's mum and dad's place and when we've gone you can go nip round to my house and pick up my other one.' Thankfully, he could tell my need was greater than his.

The next thing on my mind was the question of how we were going to get away from these blokes on the doorstep and just then I had a brainwave. Neil Fairbrother had told me how, after the Ashes-winning celebrations the previous summer, Freddie Flintoff had been tailed more than once by a posse of snappers, and that they had employed a foolproof method of shaking them off. I told Hayley's dad the plan; Hayley, Ellie and I got in Jason's car and John and Sue got in his, driving as close behind me as he dare without hitting me. Then we drove in convoy, nice and easy, bumper to bumper with the press cars following on behind. We drove away from the house and out into the country, down a nar-row lane we both knew and then, when all the press cars were in a line behind us, Hayley rang her mum to give her the signal for John to stop his car right in the middle of the lane, so no one could pass on either side of him, pull on the handbrake and switch off the engine. Instant roadblock. We were away.

We checked into our three-bedroom house at Bovey Castle at around 3.30 p.m., the idea being for me, Hayley and Ellie to have a complete break from everything and everyone; a few days of peace, quiet and isolation for me to try and get myself together.

For about ten minutes, during which time I was sitting on the floor of the main room watching Ellie running around enjoying her-self, it worked. Then, out of the blue, in front of her and Hayley, I felt a massive surge of anxiety overwhelm me, washing over me like a huge wave. It sucked the breath clean out of my lungs.

The next 48 hours were a kind of hell.

First I had to get away from Hayley and Ellie. I was about to col-lapse and didn't want them to see me when it happened. I didn't want the sight of me breaking down in front of them to upset them. Too late. I had started to hyperventilate and fled upstairs. Then I phoned my mum. 'I can't breathe,' I told her. 'Something's really wrong here. I can't stand still, I don't know what's happening. Can you come down now …?'

Mum pleaded with me: 'Marcus, You're going to have to calm down nil with you're going to have a nervous breakdown.'

The phone call lasted about half an hour. I just couldn't calm down or slow down. By the end of it mum said she and dad would be on their way in five minutes, but, living in Bristol, they were still two hours away. Two hours seemed like a lifetime. I needed someone to come right now.

Hayley and I decided it would be better if Ellie wasn't there while I was in this state, and not just for her sake, for the fact is that so much of my emotional turmoil in India had centred around Ellie and now a recurrence of those feelings was just too powerful for me to cope with.

I couldn't bear the thought of her running around, playing happily or trying to, while her dad was rolling around the floor, or rushing about the room, in anguish and in bits. Hayley rang her parents and asked if they could take Ellie for a couple of days. They came straight away.

I just didn't have a clue what was happening to me, or why. All I knew was that I couldn't deal with it, because I didn't really know what it was I was supposed to be dealing with, let alone how. It felt like something – or even someone – was taking over my mind and my body and was trying to destroy me.

By now, with me left gasping for breath as each new wave of anxiety crashed against me, Hayley was obviously as terrified as I was. She suggested we should call a doctor and rang the number of our contact in Bovey Castle. She said she would contact the GP on duty and ask him to come as soon as possible, though we may have to wait a while as it was now well into Sunday evening.

And that is when I started thinking seriously about doing something stupid. About doing myself harm. Or rather, the thing inside me did, the thing busy trying to take me over.

I was thinking to myself: I've got to make people realize I am really, really hurting here. Talking is not doing any good. The diazepam isn't doing any good. The sleeping pills aren't doing any good. Nothing is working. I've got to show people something, some evidence they can actually see, of how ill I really am, so they can put me in a hospital or somewhere where I can be properly looked after.

As so many will be painfully aware, people as ill and confused and as desperate as I felt at this moment can be stricken with thoughts of suicide – the darkest idea of all flashing through an unbalanced and disturbed mind of 'Maybe it would be better for everyone if I wasn't here.' And, tragically, some stay in the feeling.

I don't think I actually thought I would kill myself. I don't remember saying, look, I'm going to do myself in here. I never actually got to a point where I was making plans or thinking how I was going to do it.

But I knew I didn't want to carry on living like this. In fact, I couldn't.

The pain was so strong and the hurt so deep that I had to stop them, but how?

My brain was in frantic, panic-stricken overdrive; sliced into a thousand pieces by sharp thoughts shooting this way and that. I was in a small room, with no light nor windows, and no door. There was no way for anyone to come in and help me and no way for me to get out.

I asked myself: what if I never do get better? How am I going to live the rest of my life feeling like this? Is this how it's going to be from now on, because if it is I'm not lasting a week, I'm really not, because it's like torture, like someone torturing you all day, sticking in a knife and twisting it all day long, and how much of that can you take before you just say, enough? I couldn't have lived like that; every second was like an hour, every hour was like a day and every day seemed like an eternity. All of it was dark, bleak, sad, terrifying and awful. And I couldn't take it any longer. This was not a life. It was a living death and it was just too dreadful to put up with. The feeling inside me was not to do with planning how to end my life or anything like that, it was the certain knowledge that, if how I was feeling now was going to be how it was going to be forever, or even for the foreseeable future, then I simply was not prepared to live like that. Looking back now, I fully understand that far from rational thinking on my part, this train of thought was being driven by the illness, the demon in my head.

All I knew for certain was I wanted people to see, I needed people to know, how much I was hurting.

At around 8 p.m., with mum and dad there and Ellie already gone with Hayley's parents John and Sue, I met the GP in the downstairs room of the house and spoke to him on my own. 'I want to go to hospital,' I told him. 'I really don't feel well. Something's not right. I need them to do tests on me.' I described how the past few days had been and the horrors I had gone through. And I told him I couldn't take much more of it. I needed him to give me something to make me better, now.

The doctor could see how desperate I was. He told me I had been experiencing anxiety attacks and immediately gave me more diazepam to help counteract that. So far, so much the same, and not, I have to say, what I wanted to hear. But then he mentioned something else. He mentioned the word 'depression'. It was the first time since all this began that the word had been used.

Depression? I wasn't ready to accept that idea. Depression? Surely that was for weak people.

He said, in his opinion, I needed to consider other types of medication rather than rely on tranquillizers and sleeping pills. He thought the best for me to try at this stage was escitalopram, normally prescribed for anxiety and depression. He wanted me to start straight away and explained the medication might take up to two weeks or more to begin to kick in and that it might take months before I made real progress towards recovery. Two weeks to kick in? Months to recover? What the hell was he talking about? I wasn't going to last five minutes unless he gave me something to stop all this now.

With no pharmacy open, I would not be able to fetch the new medication until the following morning. So, for the time being, the doctor dosed me up with tranquillizers and left.

I was drugged up to the eyeballs. Everything was a complete blur. I was floating, away with the fairies. I remember saying to Hayley that I wanted to sleep in the same bedroom as my mum that night. I crashed out, woke up after about two hours absolutely drenched in sweat, crashed out again, woke up around 8 a.m. again sopping wet, and wandered round the house like a complete zombie, with my eyes out on stalks. Later mum told me I had been shaking and shivering all night, with my body going at 100mph.

I cannot imagine how painful the experience must have been for Hayley, who was still suffering herself from post-natal depression, or for mum and dad to watch me going through this, literally cracking up in front of their eyes, unable to do anything about it.

The next day I slipped in and out of sleep. I woke up feeling sick, still unable to eat and terribly anxious, but I recall taking my new medication for the first time. The next thing I recall with anything approaching clarity was an item on Sky Sports News, saying that

Simon Jones was coming home from the tour because his knee had flared up again. The news had a strange effect on me. I was relieved, I'm sorry to say, because I knew that it would deflect a little bit of the attention from me and that it might take a little bit of pressure off.

During those days down at Bovey Castle I think I was almost worse than I had been in India. And the result of a combination of not eating and the adrenaline-fuelled agitation was that I lost around a stone in little over a week.

After two nights, I remember Hayley coming to me and saying: 'Look, I just want to be at home. It'll be easier if we're at home in our own place so we can do what we've got to do and we can work everything out.'

I agreed. There wasn't much point being stuck down here delaying what had to be faced. In any case, the idea of a casual break doing the trick had become merely ludicrous. It was clear to both of us that my condition was far more serious, though, in the back of my mind, I was still hanging onto the hope that it might pass as quickly as it came, especially now I was on new drugs.

Initially, when we got home around lunchtime on Tuesday 28 February, we were pleasantly surprised to find a complete absence of reporters and photographers. For me that was a massive relief because I felt if I could just get back in the house without having to deal with that stuff and place myself out of danger's way, then I could address the process of dealing with my problems.

I remember the first day I got back home I enjoyed playing with Ellie in the front room and we sat down to watch TV. *Deal or No Deal* was on and it all felt so normal. For a couple of days I did start to feel a little better. Perhaps the worst was over…

Of course I knew that, sooner or later, the posse would be back and that, whether I liked the idea or not, I was going to have to confront them. The fact of the matter was that now, four days after

I had quit England's Test tour to India in such dramatic fashion, I still hadn't said anything publicly about why. The speculation was mounting and we knew it would only get worse.

Little did we know how much worse.

Chapter 14

THE LIE

*'The interview was all a bit of a blur to be honest,
but what I do know is that once I had started my
journey down the path of blag and bullshit,
there was no turning back. And so the great
lie was born.'*

Reviewing how my life unfolded from this point onwards, and knowing what I now know, I have to say that, given the chance to go back and do it all again, the one thing I would do differently is to be much more honest and open about my problems and do it much, much sooner.

I'm not beating myself up over the fact that I didn't and I wasn't. Not much point in that now. As anyone who has done so knows, it can be a huge and extremely difficult step to actually admit that you might be suffering from what is commonly known as mental illness. Just think of a few of the words which have been used to describe such problems through the ages and even now: mad, crazy, insane, for instance. Who, in their right mind, would want to admit to being any of those? And who in the wrong mind would either?

It is eminently possible, actually, that I never had a real choice in the matter anyway. By the time Hayley and I returned from Bovey

Castle to our home in Taunton on Tuesday 28 February 2006, the illness from which I was suffering was in total control.

In view of that, perhaps there was nothing that could have been done to prevent the forthcoming events from taking place.

I saw my GP back in Taunton within a couple of days of returning from Devon, and found myself explaining in detail what I had been going through. He immediately referred me to a local psychiatrist who made an appointment to see Hayley and me in order to make a detailed assessment. By the time we saw him, the following Monday, 6 March, I was in a slightly better state. There had still been horrendous moments, but they were lessening in frequency, and intensity. I had slept a bit more and eaten a bit more. Maybe the pills were starting to work. Maybe it was because I had been at home with my family in the environment in which I felt safest and not subjecting myself to the stresses of the tour, I was definitely feeling more comfortable and much more composed. In India the ECB had put out a statement confirming that I would not be returning to the sub-continent for the remaining Tests. It read: 'Marcus Trescothick has been ruled out for personal reasons which cannot be revealed at the moment.' So that situation had been locked down – for now, anyway – though nothing was said about the seven-match one-day international series to follow.

I'd had a chat with Michael Vaughan on the phone and been well enough to tell him how bad I had been, *past* tense, and apparently detached, objective and rational enough to tell him I had even contemplated doing something stupid to myself, though I don't think he really had any idea at all how to respond to that piece of information.

When we met the psychiatrist he asked me a question along those lines: 'Have you ever thought about harming yourself?' When I replied 'yes', poor Hayley rushed out of the room in tears.

She hadn't known. I quickly reassured her that I felt such things were in the past now and, as the meeting progressed, I must have managed to persuade the psychiatrist that I was getting better because when, a couple of days later, I read his report, he stated that, although I had experienced a lot of anxiety and stress I 'probably' didn't need to carry on taking the medication.

He wouldn't have said that if he'd seen me at my worst. Unbeknown to either of us the worst was not yet over.

Initially after our meeting I did feel I was at least holding things together. There were occasional moments of anxiety, but there were also good times. Times when playing with Ellie was only a joy, not the trigger for my attacks of separation anxiety; times I felt I might yet be able to get myself right under my own steam, return to playing cricket and carry on as though what had happened was just a terrible but short-lived blip. I started thinking about getting back to the club for pre-season practice. I started doing normal stuff, like going to the gym, thinking normal thoughts. I started thinking ahead. I was wishing myself well and, at that stage I seemed to be winning the battle.

Gradually I also gained enough confidence to start thinking about facing the media for the first time When, on 11 March, the ECB confirmed I had been ruled out for the ODIs, I had put my name to a quote – 'I'm naturally disappointed to be missing the tour of India, but it is my intention to play cricket for Somerset this summer and also to make myself available for England selection for this summer's international programme' – so the lines of communication were partly open. My mood had also improved enough for me to enjoy watching Freddie lead the boys to a brilliant comeback win in the final Test in Mumbai to square the series 1–1, albeit with the help of Johnny Cash and his 'Ring of Fire'. I had been genuinely impressed with Fred's rugged leadership. Despite all our reservations over the years, he had shown he could handle the responsibility. Maybe that was what he needed. And I noted with interest the improved relationship between Fred and Duncan. Winning cures a multitude of ills, it seemed. Not that I minded a bit by now, but any chance I had of ever becoming captain of England on a permanent basis, should Michael eventually succumb to his knee problems, was now gone.

I was aware that, apart from the business at our house on the day of my return and a couple of knocks on the door since then, the press had to a certain extent respected our privacy. I do think the feeling among newspaper editors was that because they believed the problem might have involved Hayley's post-natal depression they approached us and our story with some sympathy and sensitivity. I thought the time had come to say something in response. Furthermore, though the shit-storm was still some way off, certain ridiculous rumours had already begun to circulate about the 'real reason' for my premature return and the kind of people who live their lives for a nod and a wink and a juicy piece of gossip were beginning to let their imagination run loose.

When I first raised the idea of facing the press with Neil and Richard Bevan, they were not overly keen on the idea. We arranged to meet up at The Belfry to have a game of golf and discuss the issue and, during that meeting, they made it clear to me that they were not convinced going public was the right thing to do.

'Are you absolutely certain you want to do this?' Neil asked me. 'Yes,' I said. 'At some point I am going to have to front up and I'd rather do it in a situation where I can talk about what has happened on my own terms, rather than be quizzed on it.'

Once they understood I was determined to go ahead, they insisted that if I was going to talk what I said had to contain at least some of the truth. No need, at this stage, to tell chapter and verse about my illness. In any case I just wasn't ready to do so, mostly because I was still trying to come to terms with understanding the nature of the illness. But, as long as I indicated that personal issues were the real cause of my flight from India, then they had no objections. 'If you are going to say anything at all, you will be far better off in the long run to tell the truth,' was the gist of their advice. And I agreed.

That resolved, the next item on the agenda was how to go about the nuts and bolts of it. One possibility might be to wait until the Somerset press day, scheduled for Tuesday 11 April at the County Ground in Taunton. We also discussed linking up with a television or radio broadcaster to cooperate on a controlled interview for which they might provide me with the questions in advance so that I could prepare and rehearse. Neil mentioned he had been in regular contact during the winter with Barney Francis, the producer of Sky's cricket coverage and that Barney had suggested that when and if I wanted to go public, he would be happy to cooperate. I didn't want to be a ventriloquist's dummy, but I did want to ensure that I didn't end up saying something I shouldn't, or find myself in a stressful situation that might prompt another collapse.

I wasn't certain which option to choose. In due course we contacted the ECB Head of Communications, Colin Gibson, for his input.

Colin was formerly employed by the Football Association as their Head of Communications. Prior to that Colin had been a newspaper journalist of many years' experience, then the sports editor of the *Daily Mail* and *Sunday Telegraph*, and was well versed in the ways of managing the news, good and bad. That expertise had served him well earlier that year, in fact, when Wayne Rooney, at barely 18, had suddenly found himself thrust into the full glare of the media spotlight thanks to his brilliant performances in the Euro 2004 qualifying matches. Wayne was terribly shy and wary of the press, and hated the idea of having to talk at a full-on press conference with the football reporters firing in questions at him left, right and centre. So Colin had arranged for him to go in front of a television interviewer in a controlled situation and then give all the papers the transcript of the interview from which to farm quotes.

Discussions between the parties continued. Colin contacted Barney at Sky and told him what might be on offer. Barney was keen, but, like Neil and Richard, believed the idea only had merit if they could ask me some pretty difficult questions and I answered them honestly.

Barney was told: 'Marcus will be open and frank, but he doesn't want to be grilled.'

Barney insisted: 'We have to ask the question [about why I came home from India], or there is no point in doing it at all.'

'That's absolutely fine,' Barney was told. 'No problem.'

After a couple of further chats between Colin, Neil and Richard, Colin and Neil had a prolonged discussion by phone on Friday 24 March. A day later, on 25 March, Richard emailed me and set out the position so far.

Under the heading 'Media Handling Strategy', he wrote: 'We need to decide whether the Somerset press conference is the best "first" engagement for you.

'While we can appeal to the better nature of the usual familiar circle of cricket writers, there is a chance a news reporter will get involved and publish a negative article.

'We did consider advising whether you should issue a personal statement briefly explaining the personal problems that led to the decision. The fact that you had "personal" problems and are "dealing with family matters" has been well documented.

'I envisage after you have presented yourself to the media, the issues for the most part will go away. However, we will need to be sure the facts stay private.

'We will allow Sky a very controlled interview with only pre-agreed questions. It will probably take you an hour to put you through your paces and get word perfect.'

On 26 March Colin sent an email to Neil and Richard, copied to ECB Chief Executive David Collier, confirming his thoughts.

Richard,

Had a long chat with Neil on Friday and my view has not changed.

1) the Somerset press day will be too random and too difficult to control. We can't have a situation where someone asks questions and then either Marcus or a combination of the three of us steps in to say no comment.

It would just make the matter worse.

2) I believe the controlled interview option, either TV or radio with a full transcript and pix being made available would be the best option.

3) I am not sure that Marcus needs to go to the Somerset press day at all. If he does he will be the only player anyone wants to talk to and could be faced with either a large press conf or a stream of one-on-ones. All this would b v taxing and we would not know if Marcus was up to it until the event was over.

4) If we take the television/radio route (this is what we did with Rooney at the FA) then Marcus can say he has said all he has to say on the matter if any journalist tries to raise it again.

This, though, is your decision and I can only offer advice but it did work brilliantly with Rooney pre Euro 2004.

My view is that, if you accept my suggestion, (sic) should take place on Sky and on April 10th – the day before the Somerset press day. Filming can be either at Taunton or a nearby country house hotel.

We can select the interviewer and monitor the questions.

Best wishes

I discussed these suggestions with Neil and Richard and we all agreed that we should proceed accordingly.

I have to say, in relation to what happened next, my mood at this time was subject to change. I was still fighting to stay well and, for the most part, I believed I was making progress. But there were bad moments and bad days. Through all that, however, my overriding feeling was that I needed to get some kind of holding message out there.

In due course the details of the interview with Sky TV were finalized. I had asked for it to be conducted by Ian Ward, who had recently retired from professional cricket after a long career with Surrey and Sussex and a rather briefer one with England, and who had been a friend ever since we roomed together on an England A tour to New Zealand in the late nineties.

The arrangement was that Sky would send Ward and a camera crew to the Holiday Inn Hotel in Taunton and the interview would take place on Sunday 9 April for editing on Monday 10 April. Sky would then broadcast a brief 'teaser' on that day, featuring the most newsworthy section, trailing the fact that the full interview would be screened on Wednesday 12 April during the break between innings in the sixth and final one-day international between England and India in Jamshedpur, the day after the Somerset press day at Taunton on Tuesday 11 April.

It had also been agreed between Colin and Barney that Sky would make available a full transcript of the interview for release at the same time it was to be broadcast.

Obviously it was crucial that all of the above was kept strictly confidential. Even more obviously the key question was going to be: 'Why did you come back from India?'.

After we had all discussed the various options and possible forms of words, Richard sent an email to Neil and Colin on the morning of Friday 7 April, proposing the following response, as a guideline:

'Having picked up a virus and also some personal issues to resolve, I decided to return home. It was a difficult step but, with the support of team management, the break has provided me with the breathing space to get back on an even keel, I'm now fully refreshed and will make myself available for County and England selection.' Richard invited Colin and Neil to respond with their thoughts.

In a reply which he might have had cause to ponder later, Colin wrote: 'The key to all this is telling the truth or saying nothing, but not making any misleading statements. If you are happy this fits the criteria then great.'

To which Richard replied: 'Could not agree more.'

When I looked at the guideline response above I was clear in my own mind. When Ward got round to asking me the question, Richard's suggestion would form the basis of my answer. I was not going to go into great detail about my problems. But I was going to say: 'Yes, there is a problem and I'm doing my best to deal with it. As for 'getting it word perfect' I was still pretty confident that, provided I had some time to look at the questions, I could wing it.

*   *   *

On the afternoon of Friday 7 April Barney Francis, then the head of Sky's cricket department, sent a list of questions to Colin, who sent them on to Neil and Richard, who sent them on to me.

1. *Firstly, how are you?*
2. *How long have you been back in training?*
3. *Are you fit and ready for the new season?*
4. *When will you play your first game?*
5. *It has obviously been a tough winter. Are your problems behind you now, or are there still 'issues'?*
6. *Why did you decide to leave India?*
7. *How did Duncan Fletcher take the news?*

8. *Some people would say you have let your country down – is that fair?*
9. *Will you be opening the batting for England against Sri Lanka at Lord's next month?*
10. *How impressed were you with Alasdair (sic) Cook and Owais Shah?*
11. *Surely you feel you deserve a bit of loyalty though – you played 69 Test matches and are arguably England's best batsman.*
12. *What about the captaincy, has Andrew Flintoff overtaken you now in the pecking order?*
13. *England have a very tough schedule this winter – are you prepared to tour again?*
14. *Does that include the Champions Trophy in October?*
15. *Will the World Cup be your last England trip?*
16. *What ambitions do you have left in the game – an Ashes hundred?'*

I probably stopped reading after question no.6. Get past that and I would be in the clear, for now. What could possibly go wrong?

* * *

I hadn't exactly been punching the air at the prospect of opening up the discussion about my health and state of mind to the general public. But all my instincts said that the process of finally 'coming out' had to start somewhere and it may as well start here.

Yet, as the time approached for me to do the interview, my mood began to change for the worse. A slight shiver kicked in; it wasn't the full-on spine-freezer, but it was uncomfortable enough. From the moment I rose on the morning of the Sky interview, a familiar sense of foreboding settled over me like a heavy coat on a sweltering day.

Oh God. Am I doing the right thing? Is this the right thing to say? Personal issues? How will people take that? Will they think something is up between Hayley and me? There had already been whispers. Even on the night I had come back from India Neil had fielded questions about a kiss-and-tell story. What if they think personal issues means that? Or what if they see through the words to the real truth? What if they put the clues together and somehow discovered that I had been suffering from these huge anxiety attacks? What if they already knew about me crying my eyes out in my room, about having to have Peter Gregory sit with me all night long? What if they had somehow found out about my meetings with the GP or, god forbid, the psychiatrist? What if they knew I had been on anti-depressants? What if they had somehow found out that I had thoughts about harming myself, or worse. What would they be thinking then? How would the world perceive me? Mental illness … personal issues … Would they think I was crazy? Would they think I was mad? Maybe I am mad? Oh God. This isn't right. Oh God, this is not right.

By the time I left home for the interview that Sunday afternoon I was crapping myself. I wasn't absolutely sure what I was going to do, except I had definitely decided I did not want to answer question no.6 in the way we had agreed. It wasn't that I wanted to deliberately mislead anyone. I was just so scared of what was going on and how people might perceive me. Whereas the rational, stable Marcus had been keen to get a message out in the open, the ill Marcus now recoiled at the very thought. My head was spinning. I didn't know how I was going to handle the rest of what was supposed to happen. At one point the thought flashed through my mind 'How bad would things be if I actually tried to pull out?'

Oh God, I can't do that. What will everyone think of me? Oh God…

Neither Neil nor Richard was present at the Holiday Inn that afternoon. If they had been things might have turned out differently. Neither had been particularly keen to go ahead with the process in the first place and, if I had told them what I was about to tell Colin, my guess is that they would have quietly explained to the Sky boys that the interview would have to be postponed; that, with regret I was just not quite up to it right now. (A recurrence of the virus, perhaps?) But the last they heard was that everything was going according to plan and they were both comfortable that Colin's presence would ensure it would be carried out. During their final discussions with Colin, Richard and Neil suggested it might be better if they did attend, but he had reassured them: 'Not necessary. I'll handle it' and, as I was an ECB employee, they felt it entirely appropriate that the matter should be overseen by a representative of my ECB employers.

When I arrived, the Sky crew was all set up and ready. Oh God, what do I do?

I spoke with Ward and, though I was sure he would spot my nervousness, he later told someone I had been chatty and in good form; I must have been a better actor than I thought. As soon as Colin arrived I asked him if I could have a quick word in private and we went off to the restaurant.

'Look,' I said, 'I'm sorry, but I'm really quite nervous about having to talk about these "personal issues". I've thought about it and I just wish I didn't have to say those words.'

We talked through the whole business, the pros and cons. All the time I was thinking to myself: 'How the hell am I going to get out of this?'. As I saw it, as we had all gone too far to call off the interview altogether, I had two choices and both of them were bad.

In my current state I had convinced myself that if I went ahead and talked about personal issues, everyone watching and reading would think I was mad. But if I went ahead and didn't talk about the personal issues, the worst they could think was that I was an idiot.

Again I asked Colin: 'Do I really need to say that line about personal issues? Is it really the best thing to do? I'm really worried about saying it'.

And Colin said: 'Look. If you don't want to say it, just don't say it.'

A Get Out Of Jail Free card? It felt more like the governor's eleventh-hour reprieve. And I grabbed it with both hands. There was no discussion about the possible repercussions. Nothing about what might happen afterwards, or as a result. And I gave no thought whatsoever to how the other questions might appear once I had failed to give the agreed answer to no.6. I appreciate that everyone involved was operating under difficult circumstances, but allowing me to go ahead with the interview, once I had made up my mind to deviate from the agreed form of words, was a big mistake. I ended up paying a very high price indeed.

The interview was all a bit of a blur to be honest, but what I do know is that once I had started my journey down the path of blag and bullshit, there was no turning back. And so the great lie was born.

Ian Ward: So why did you leave India – was it to spend more time with your family?

Marcus Trescothick: The main reason was I picked up a bug...

And so on.

I felt not the slightest pang of doubt as I sailed through the rest of the interview, making a monkey of the truth as I went. Afterwards I did feel slightly guilty towards Ward. But my main concern was for myself. For me doing what I had done was all about survival. By now, I didn't really give a damn about what sort of fallout there might be. I was off. I had got away with it. All I felt was relief and that, I can assure you, was enough.

On his way home Ward was contacted by Barney Francis, asking him how the interview had gone: 'Well, err, I'm not sure,' said Ward.

'What did Marcus say when you asked him why he had come home from India?' Barney pressed him.

'Well, he said he had a virus …'

The next day, in the Sky studios, Barney, Ian and his production team watched the tape. Barney realized that I had ducked the question, though, at that stage, he had no idea why. He decided to go ahead and broadcast that section of the interview on Sky Sports News anyway.

That afternoon Neil took the first of as flurry of calls from reporters. By the time I rang Neil, at around 4 p.m., I was feeling okay. The feeling didn't last.

'How has it all gone down?' I asked him.

'Well, mate. Not particularly well, because you didn't say what we had agreed you would say.'

Shiver…

'F**k. Who's said what?' I asked him.

'Derek Pringle's been on the phone and had a go, basically kicking up a stink about it. What happened?'

The blood drained out of me.

The irreversible process had begun.

The next day, Tuesday 11 April, the day of the Somerset press launch, Pringle led the charge in the *Daily Telegraph*: 'The enduring mystery of why Marcus Trescothick left England's tour of India in a hurry just before the first Test appeared to have been solved yesterday, or was it?

'Speaking in what looked and sounded like a stage-managed interview on Sky Sports News yesterday, Trescothick revealed that his sudden departure was due to a combination of a virus and the creeping fatigue of six years of constant cricket. So why keep something so anodyne from journalists? A question not yet satis-factorily answered by Trescothick or his employers at the England and Wales Cricket Board.'

If I had had a virus, Pringle asked, 'Why was it not mentioned in the daily bulletin given by the team doctor?'

I met Colin in the Castle Hotel in Taunton for a coffee. I don't recall whether we spoke about the interview, possibly not because by now we were concerning ourselves with the club's press day ahead. When the media pitched up, a few of them were still under the impression that I might be available for interview, even though anyone who had contacted the club had already been told a firm 'no'. Obviously interest was higher now because of what had been broadcast the day before on Sky and they thought they had better have a go at getting me to talk, whatever the club had said.

One or two asked Richard Latham, my ghostwriter for columns for the *Bristol Evening Post,* to approach me. I did pose for Richard for a new photo to accompany the columns out of sight of the rest of the assembled media, but I bluffed that I wasn't sure what the form was.

Speaking to the club afterwards, what they found odd, and somewhat annoying, was that Colin appeared to take a back seat as proceedings unfolded, leaving them to deal with the increas-ingly frustrated press guys without his help.

For my part, I was surprised that a couple of reporters actually claimed they were told they would have the chance to speak to me, as I had genuinely assumed Colin, or someone, would have told them I was not talking and was only going to be posing for photos. I was also under the impression they had been informed of the arrangements for the following day, when Sky would be run-ning the interview at the pre-arranged time and everyone would be supplied with a full transcript. I could sense the mood among the reporters and, while not exactly aggressive, one or two appeared pretty agitated. Once the team group photo had been taken, in front of the pavilion, I clocked a local BBC Television reporter called Clinton Rogers, telling his cameraman to start filming, then he chased after me calling out a load of stupid questions. It was left to my good mate Darren Veness, the Somerset physio who was a nightclub bouncer in his former life, to make it plain their attention was not wanted. Where was Colin at that moment?

That night in London, at the traditional eve-of-season dinner to celebrate the publication of *Wisden*, the cricketer's bible, Bevan was telephoned by an irate ECB official, shouting and swearing and demanding to know 'What the f**k is wrong with Marcus Trescothick?' The ECB had been contacted by several members of the press wanting an explanation for the discrepancy between the initial reason given for my departure from India by Duncan and the nonsense I had come up with in the Sky interview. Already someone in a high place had gained the distinct impression that Richard and possibly Neil were to blame for the cock-up, an erroneous belief that was to have further repercussions later. Richard kept him at bay for the time being.

If the press day was not a happy experience for me, the next day, Wednesday 12 April, turned out to be an utter disaster.

It started badly, when, in *The Times*, Ivo Tennant complained about the lack of access to me at Taunton the day before. 'It is unprecedented,' he wrote, 'for an England cricketer to appear with an ECB minder and not even exchange pleasantries with reporters, some of whom, down the years, have shared his favourite bangers with him.' That was about the high point.

*　　*　　*

I didn't watch the Sky interview broadcast, as arranged, between innings in England's sixth ODI against India in Jamshedpur. Truth is, I didn't actually watch it for another two years, until I forced myself to do so for the purposes of writing this book.

This is how it went. Stand by for a masterpiece of misinformation.

Ian Ward Well Marcus, great to see you, thanks for talking to us. First things first, how are you?

Marcus Trescothick: I'm good – it's nice to be back up and enjoying things again. It's going pretty well really. The sun's out, it's great, Taunton's looking magnificent, so I'm itching to get back into it.

IW – Back in training then?

MT – Yeah, I've been going for about three weeks of gym work, just working hard and getting my fitness up to the levels they need to be. Cricketwise, I've done a couple of nets, nothing too drastic just yet. But as I said, I'm gagging to get back into it, I'm picking my bats up and getting ready.

IW – When's the first game?

MT – The first championship match is on the 18th at Bristol, so hopefully that will be nice, it'll probably be quite cold, it generally is that time of year but you get over that pretty quick so it should be good.

IW – Good to see some familiar faces at Taunton?

MT – Yeah, it's always good. The guys have been in Cape Town, so luckily enough I've just had the time to continue resting and enjoying spending time with my family.

IW – It's been a tough year for you – are your problems behind you, or do you still have a few issues to sort out?

MT – No, very much behind me – I just needed a break pretty much. Playing six years of solid international cricket just takes it toll after a while and you get to certain stages of your career and you know there's reasons why, what you need to do and just be with your family, take a bit of time out, recharge the batteries and then go again and obviously move on, play a good standard of cricket and hopefully play internationals again.

IW – So why did you leave India – was it to spend more time with your family?

MT – The main reason was I picked up a bug when I was out there, the second part of Bombay when we were there at the end of that trip, and it really hit me hard. I wasn't sleeping and I couldn't shake it off really and when we moved on to Baroda, it just didn't get any better. I couldn't eat too much, I wasn't really drinking and it really took its toll on me and it got to the point when I said look, I'm pretty fatigued here. I was struggling to concentrate on my cricket, as much as I can do obviously leading up to a big Test match and prepare myself in the right way. So I spoke to the people that I needed to and decided that the right thing to do was to come home.

IW – So from that period in Bombay when you picked that bug up, did you keep Michael Vaughan and Duncan Fletcher in constant updates as to how you were feeling or did it build up for a while?

MT – It sort of just took its toll. I don't think it was a case of me having to inform them that I wasn't well – we played warm-up matches and I stayed involved in those. I was in constant communication with the doctor Peter Gregory out there, just sort of letting him know how I was going. He was obviously keeping a constant eye in terms of how I was feeling just to make sure everything was alright. When I finally made the decision, I spoke to Duncan, they were thoroughly supportive and accepted what I needed to do and supported me all the way through it.

IW – I was going to ask about that. How was the support you received?

MT – Yeah, good – I haven't been in contact too much since I've come back. They need to concentrate on the cricket but at the time when I was there I obviously got a lot of support from the boys, who obviously knew what I was going through, and obviously the management, whoever really found out about what was happening, they were fully supportive. We're lucky with the envi̶r̶o̶n̶m̶e̶n̶t̶ ̶t̶h̶a̶t̶ ̶w̶e̶ ̶h̶a̶v̶e̶. We're able to make decisions like that and get support from the team.

IW – There's an awful lot of cricket coming up – the whole international programme for everyone around the world is now massive. Is there a chance this will happen again?

MT – Who knows? The virus is a funny one – it's stuck with me for such a long time, up till about three weeks ago I was getting relapses if I trained too hard or came back too quick. I really thought I could hit the gym hard, then it seemed to knock me back for a couple of days so if I picked up another virus I wouldn't think it would affect me in any different way. I think having this time to really recharge my batteries and really have a rest, it made me realize again why I play the game and what I love about the game and giving me that enthusiasm. We play so much. We spend 300 nights of the year out of our own house, either travelling the world or in hotels preparing for games in England so I think there's times when you do need to have a rest and that was definitely the one.

IW – The ECB management are very much concerned with player well-being, their home-lives, births of children etc. There needs to be that understanding in terms of the amount of cricket you guys play.

MT – I think we have that understanding which is great. We spoke many a time as an internal management group – the players, Duncan, some of the assistant coaches, about up and coming tours, how we approach it and the right we have to spend as much time with our families as possible. We do play so well in England because we have so much time with families, you have your normal life with you. Unfortunately the two tours – Pakistan and India, which are tough tours, the hardest to go on – it's not easy to take your families to that part of the world and you spend a long time away from home. You need your comforts and your security to be able to perform at a good level.

IW – So you are prepared to tour again?

MT – Oh, for sure. It's just an ideal opportunity for me to have a rest. I've played six years of non-stop cricket for England travelling around the world and before that A tours (as you know we went on those together) and Under-19's so for 12 years it's been non-stop cricket. I'm making myself available for Somerset at the start of the year and hopefully things will then flow from that.

IW – So will you be opening the batting against Sri Lanka at Lord's next month?

MT – I hope so. I would love to be given the opportunity again. My main priority at the moment is to get in the nets, get working hard, play well for Somerset at the start of the year, then it's up to other people to decide if I'm to get back in the team.

IW – You mention those tours and the toll it takes. You've got the Champions Trophy back in India, then the Ashes, an enormously long and mentally tough tour, and then the World Cup. Assuming you are selected for those, will you take the family with you? Will that help?

MT – It will definitely help me for sure and as much as you can take them on that sort of trip then yeah they'll be there for a lot. When you go to Australia generally they are there a lot. It's a lovely country, you get great apartments, great hotel rooms and you can lead a normal life. Obviously you are away from a certain amount of family but immediate family are always quite close. It's the same for the World Cup. The West Indies is a brilliant place, probably the best tour I've done was two years ago. Everybody is looking at these situations all the time and making sure we've got it right and everybody's happy.

IW – Difficult for them as well, a wife and a young baby travelling around in hotels?

MT – Yeah, it is tough. I don't think we ever really appreciate that enough. We are lucky that we can do that at the moment but that may change in a few years.

IW – England have struggled a bit in India, certainly the one-dayers. Have you been watching?

MT – Yeah, I'm glued to the TV! I'm obviously a die-hard cricket fan – I've been watching most days. We knew it would be tough. It's a really hard place. The guys have done well, obviously with injuries it's not gone quite the way we wanted it to.

IW – Some would say by leaving the tour you've let England down. How would you respond to that?

MT – I don't think so, to be honest. I think people will realize. I've had a lot of support, players and management and I think that says a lot for me. I know I've made the right decision. I'm sure I've made the right decision. It's just unfortunate with the timing, obviously with everyone else going down as well it's just highlighted it a bit more.

IW – Surely after 69 Tests you deserve a bit of loyalty from the selectors?

MT – I don't know if loyalty is the right way to put it to be honest. I think one of the reasons England have been so good over the last few years is that we've been consistent with selection. We've been a good side, players deserve the right to play, they've done well. It's great for the young lads coming through pushing the guys in the team. They've done well. When they do that the only thing that's going to get better is the team. We'll see what happens, I just have to concentrate on what I have to do. I'd be delighted to get picked again.

IW – Let's talk about some of the young lads you've mentioned – Alastair Cook and Owais Shah particularly in the Test matches. How impressed have you been with them?

MT – Delighted. Cooky has been threatening. He got his double hundred against Australia; we've known for some time, the team and management group that he's close. When he got that hundred in his first Test, a great moment for any cricketer, I got in contact with him. He's a good lad and a friend. Same for Owais – he played really well in an opportunity when it was tough, under pressure, it's great to see someone come in under that pressure and do so well for the team.

IW – Continuity of selection is important. Could you see yourself batting in the middle order?

MT – Not for me to say. If they come to me with a suggestion, it's their decision at the end of the day. From my point of view, I've played well opening the batting but it doesn't mean to say that's where I'll stay all my career. That's just something for Michael and Duncan to work out.

IW – How do you think Flintoff has done?

MT – He's done really well. He's enjoyed the way he's led the team. I spoke to Freddie about the captaincy. He's happy to take it on. I think his role as an all-rounder, batting, bowling and being captain, it may take its toll after a while.

IW – That is obviously a danger. He's obviously gone past you in the pecking order in terms of being the next England Captain. Does that concern you?

MT – (laughs) I don't think it's too much of an issue to be honest. I've captained my country and hopefully done a decent job. I've enjoyed it when I've done it, great opportunity for me, but we're looking forward to getting Michael back really. He is our captain. He is our leader and led us to the great victory against Australia. We need everybody back.

IW – Is it something you covet, the captaincy, or is it a case of you've done it and you need to concentrate on yourself?

MT – Hard to say. I'm quite involved already. I've been unofficial vice captain for a while, being quite closely linked to decisions on the pitch and off the pitch. It's all left to the captain and the coach. I always think about the game quite intensely anyway, whether I'm standing at slip or whatever, working things out.

IW – The euphoria after the Ashes was quite remarkable. I guess that took you and the players by surprise?

MT – We could see it coming. It escalated after every win and we were 2–1 up going into the last Test. We knew we were on the verge of something huge, something we'd dine out on for the rest of our careers. To play under that amount of pressure, which is great for us, the buzz, excitement, it was just good fun. The parade after made it all sink in, what we'd achieved.

IW – Did you get a chance to let it all sink in, to sit down and understand what you had done before you had to move on to a very difficult winter?

MT – Not as much as we'd like to. It was just another series at the end of the day, probably the best one we'll ever play in. You've got to keep improving. The next important Test was Pakistan, we had to keep driving forward. In years to come I think that's when we'll realize what we achieved. Maybe once we've finished playing – DVD's, books etc!

IW – If you weren't able to put that all to bed, did that contribute to your problems this winter?

MT – I wouldn't have thought so. We've all played at the highest level for quite a number of years. The pressure and the strain is great, that's why you play. It's so demanding, every day you play Test cricket it's just something you have to deal with.

IW – What about your long term England plans?

MT – I don't think they've really changed. Just continue to play well as long as I can really. I've not set a date or a time when it is going to be my last trip or last game. I'm hitting my peak at the moment, I just need to work hard, need to keep going and enjoy the success that we're having.

IW – Are you statistically minded? 100 Tests have a nice ring about it?

MT – It does have a nice ring about it but it's not the be all and end all to me. I just love playing for England and Somerset, as long as I'm good enough to play then I will do.

IW – Looking ahead to the Ashes, when do you and the players start thinking about that first Test at the Gabba?

MT – We can't get into it too quick. Big summer ahead against Sri Lanka and Pakistan, we can't get too far ahead of ourselves. Our ground work will be done this summer leading up to the euphoria of a major contest.

IW – Thanks.

When news of the interview and its full contents reached Duncan in India, he went absolutely ballistic, because what I had said went completely against what he had told the press on that day in Baroda. Virus? What happened to the 'personal, family reasons' he had announced? He felt he was going to get it in the neck for appearing to lie to the press and he was, understandably, cross. I couldn't blame him, though he might have felt differently if he had had a clearer understanding of my illness. Mind you, I was still some way off understanding it myself at this stage.

Any objective analysis of the interview would have taken very little time to understand this simple truth. Had I given the agreed answer to question no.6 the rest of the interview would have made some sense. It would not have been the whole story but it might have given the media something to be going along with until I was ready to tell all.

Once I did not, however, most of the rest was utter nonsense. If my troubles were all down to a bug, for example, why on earth would Ward then ask me – 'How was the support you received?'

What sort of support do you usually receive when you have a virus? People calling out: 'Mate, best of luck with the virus?' or 'about that bug. I just want to let you know we are all thinking of you.' Laughable. And what about this little exchange?

'IW – There's an awful lot of cricket coming up – the whole international programme for everyone around the world is now massive. Is there a chance this will happen again?

MT – Who knows? The virus is a funny one –'

Poor Wardy. To think I had sat there with a straight face. And to think Colin Gibson had sat there and allowed this sorry farce to play itself to its ghastly conclusion. By then I was past caring, but, sitting in that room watching and hearing my responses go from bad to worse, couldn't he see how damaging this could turn out to be?

As I said, only recently did I pluck up enough courage to watch the whole interview on DVD. The look of utter terror that flashes across my face as Ward is asking question no.6 says it all. My eyes disappear into the back of my head and my eyebrows go inwards and downwards like Mr Spock on *Star Trek*. It looks as though someone has inserted something particularly unpleasant where the sun doesn't shine.

Of course, I know now that saying what I said was about the worst thing I could have possibly have done, for all kinds of reasons.

For myself, for my chances of making a full and permanent recovery, my bullshitting just missed the point. If I wanted to get better I had to face what it was that had made me ill, not run from it, but I only found out much later that running away was what I did and why.

From the perspective of my relationship with Fleet St, though this was secondary in my thoughts at the time, my actions were catastrophic. In the sports pages, the mood was summed up by my first Test opener partner Mike Atherton, who wrote in the *Sunday Telegraph* that the line about the virus 'was so utterly implausible that ridicule is the only response'.

I lost count of the number of times I read the words 'cover-up'.

As for the attitude of those whose job it is to fill the other pages, it changed completely.

Up to that point it was felt I had benefited from a degree of sympathy from the press, that, generally, they had been sensitive about the whole issue of me coming back from India.

They hadn't been looking for a kiss-and-tell type of story but the issue of at least one, maybe two people having a tough time of it, so they had kept a respectful distance and hadn't chased us as they might have done.

What the editors had expected in return, once I did go public, was that I didn't try to spin them a line, that I told the truth and was honest.

The result of my shambolic attempt to pull the wool over their eyes and everyone else's was that the newspapers were now convinced there must be something more to this story than they'd originally thought and that is when they removed the gloves.

The rumours about Hayley and me that had been bubbling under for some time were now vigorously pursued by certain sections of the press. And the reaction of the general public towards me was hard to take. Whether it was my own paranoia, I don't know, but I became convinced that everyone in the world had seen the interview, known I had lied, or at least been extremely economical with the truth, had read the newspapers and was now thinking to themselves: 'There's that Marcus Trescothick, that cricket player who made a tit of himself on the telly. What's the real story? What is he hiding?' It's always the lie that gets you in the end.

I rang Richard Bevan's home on the morning of 13 April. His wife Suzanne answered. I was in such distress that it took her several seconds to recognize my voice.

When Richard came to the phone he was shocked by what he heard.

'Richard,' I said. 'I need help, now.'

Chapter 15

THE WAY BACK

'I had taken a massive step in the right direction, one that, cruelly and tragically, so many sufferers find themselves simply unable to take. I had reached the start.'

Until the time I first met with and spoke to my counsellor from Performance Healthcare, the depth of my understanding of the condition known as depression was on a par with my knowledge of the dark side of the moon.

Sure, I knew I might have it, because the GP who had attended me down at Bovey Castle on the day of my return from India had said so, and had put me on anti-depressants. The problem was I didn't really have a clue what 'it' actually was and I certainly didn't want to believe he was right. For me to admit to suffering from depression was a matter of shame and embarrassment, provoking feelings of inadequacy and fear of what people might think of me. Hence my performance over the Sky TV interview.

Until I learned the hard way, from first-hand experience just what the illness entails, how it works and what the effects can be, I had been one of those whose attitude to depression bordered on the sceptical. If someone complained of being depressed my initial reaction would be the words: 'Cheer up', swiftly followed by 'Pull yourself together'.

As for me, what the hell did I have to be depressed about? We'd just won the Ashes, life was going pretty well. I had a family, we'd just bought a new house in the countryside and I was earning good money. What did I have to worry about? I had always been some-one who coped.

If anyone out there reading this is currently experiencing any-thing like what I have so far described, or recognizes something in my words that strikes a chord with them, then my plea to them, for what it is worth, is this: understand that what I was suffering from was a physical illness, that you are not alone, that how you are feel-ing is not a sign of weakness or failure and nothing whatsoever to be ashamed of.

Depression doesn't care who it attacks. If it wants you, you can-not beat it off with a CV or a bank balance.

And trust me, there is nothing brave about suffering in silence. The sooner you seek advice, help and support for what you are going through the better your chances of getting your life back as soon as possible. Or, at the very least, to stop feeling so bad.

On the morning of Thursday 13 April 2006, the day I rang Richard Bevan in despair, I was, literally, in a state of hopelessness. The Sky interview had been an unmitigated disaster and I hadn't slept in the three nights since the Monday 10 April when the 'virus' line was first broadcast. The feelings of fear and panic I had been fighting on and off for the past week were busy tearing me to shreds. I was becoming increasingly paranoid and my behaviour at home was becoming more and more odd and more and more frenetic. Hayley said that I was jumpy, irritable, nervous and miserable.

Every time the phone rang it was like someone had plugged me into the electric socket. I was forever peering out of the window, thinking I had spotted someone moving about in the garden, a photographer, maybe, a reporter, whoever. I just felt under so much pressure all the time, working myself into a frenzy, worrying about the slightest little thing and at the same time panicking that I was doing so. What if this or what if that? And worst of all, what if I never get any better? What if I have to spend the rest of my life like this? The feeling was so powerful and I had no way of switching it off.

By the time I picked up the phone to call Richard I was a gibbering, burbling, blubbing wreck. I could barely speak and when I did he could hardly make out what I was saying.

In his capacity as Chief Executive of the Professional Cricketers' Association, Richard had instigated a tie-up with an organization called Performance Healthcare, specializing in confidential advice, information and help for those experiencing personal problems. Every county club was supplied with a helpline which any player could contact at any time in complete confidence. Within minutes of finishing our call, Richard contacted one of the directors of Performance Healthcare and asked them to send someone to see me as soon as possible. Within minutes one of their cognitive behaviour therapists, who lived in the West Country, about an hour away, rang to speak to me. The following day he came to my house.

The guy in question wishes to remain anonymous. For the purposes of the narrative I'll call him Chris.

The first time we met, Chris just asked me to talk, to tell him how I felt and what I had been through. Tearful, exhausted and battered, I told him the whole story of what I had been going through while he settled down to take notes. Occasionally he would ask me to clarify something I had said, or whether he had understood me correctly, but other than that he hardly interrupted. So I told him how I felt, my symptoms, my fears, the story of what had happened to Hayley's dad in Pakistan, and about me not coming home to support her when I should have done, about my guilt over that, and how I had had huge doubts over whether I should have gone to India at all. I told him about Hayley's post-natal depression; about how I should have read the signs better and stayed at home. I told him about what had happened there and what happened after I got back. I told him about the terrible moments of anxiety I had had about being separated from Hayley and Ellie, the dreams that had haunted me, the terrible irrational fears. I told him about the sleepless nights, the night spent ticking off the hours one-by-one until morning, and then realizing morning was no better than the night had been.

Somehow, and from somewhere, the thought occurred to me to take him back to my childhood, to that week I had spent away from home on a school trip in Torquay and how I had cried my eyes out day after day. About how close I had been to coming home from the 2004 tour to South Africa, how I had always found touring and being away from home hard to cope with until the cricket took over. I told him about the unnatural dreariness of living in hotel rooms day after day at home and especially abroad. I told him how much I missed the comfort of a familiar environment, how much I missed just being able to be anonymous. I tried to explain as best I could about the ghastly day-merging-into-day grind of international cricket and how the enjoyment and even the joy I had always felt about playing the game, ever since I first picked up a bat in my garden in Keynsham through to the wonderful events of the previous summer's Ashes series, had all but disappeared for me now and how I felt I might never get it back. I told him how I felt ten feet tall batting against some of the most fearsome quick bowling imaginable but couldn't face the prospect of a camera being pointed in my direction or a reporter camped outside my house or another day in a five-star prison staring at four walls and a TV. And I told him how ashamed I felt about making such a fuss, about how ridiculous it must sound that I could not cope with a room-service lifestyle and ever-increasing earning potential as a modern Test cricketer when countless numbers of people would gladly pay money to do what I did for a living. And how crazy it must seem to others with real, genuine life-altering diseases, cancer or Alzheimer's or whatever, to the recently bereaved or to those wearing themselves out caring for the ill or afflicted relatives, or members of the armed forces putting their lives on the line in dreadful conditions every day, or those poor desperate kids in India who had nothing but the rags in which they stood, that I was being such a baby. And how I worried what others must think about me if I admitted to all of the above. And how fearful I was about the future and how I was ever going to feel better. And how much I currently despised myself for all of the above.

As I was in the process of spewing this out, I became aware of Chris's voice. I realized I could hear him saying things like: 'Yes, of course' and 'that's a classic sign', and, occasionally, finishing my sentences. And suddenly things didn't seem quite so catastrophically bad. He knew what I was talking about. He'd heard it before and if he'd heard it before I was not the only one. Even in my state of confusion that was absolutely huge.

It wasn't just what Chris was saying, but the way he said it that appeared to have this dramatic effect. I don't know exactly what it was, the manner, the tone, the voice, the calm assurance; whatever it was, it was almost like someone putting their arm around you saying: 'Look. I'm going to take care of you. I'm going to look after you. I'm going to make you better.' That was the thing I gripped onto and I didn't let go until I had finally let out all the things I had been bottling up inside me for so long.

In that one session, there and then, I had begun the process of coming back, of coming back to me.

Some of what Chris told me was not what I wanted to hear. When you are suffering like I was, the last thing you want to be told is 'this is not going to be easy ... there is no quick cure' because what you actually want to hear is 'I've got this magic pill and when you take it you will be well again.' And when he spoke of seeing progress over six to nine months, he may as well have said six to nine years.

But, as well as the relief of finally opening up to someone, the most important thing that I gained from the meeting was the beginning of a realization and understanding of what the illness was and, crucially, that IT WAS NOT MY FAULT.

I was not feeling like this and acting like this and behaving like this because I was weak, feeble, pathetic and not up to it. Nor was I mad. I was feeling like this because a physical illness called depression was making me feel like this.

What is more, not only was I not alone, but the illness of which I was displaying textbook symptoms was far more common than I could possibly have imagined.

Chris began explaining to me, in a way I found able to understand, why he thought it had happened to me.

'You are exhausted,' he said. 'You can see your body is saying that's enough. It needs a rest. You need to give it some time away from the fighting and the battling.

'Why has it happened? Maybe because you've had six years of constant playing, training and travelling with England, six years of the pressure of doing what you do at the highest level, of being subjected to the minutest scrutiny. And the exhaustion you are suffering from has led to you being physically depressed.'

And over the course of several sessions thereafter he then also explained about the anxiety attacks. He explained about the theory of 'fight, flight or freeze'.

The human beings we have evolved into, he explained, are behaviourally programmed to react to danger in three different ways. Going back to pre-history, when the greatest physical danger to man lay in facing the sabre-tooth tiger and other predators, early man and woman would be divided into three types according to instinct; those who fought, those who fled and those who froze.

Modern man retains those base instincts, deep in the subconscious. And when suffering from anxiety linked to depression he reverts to them. It didn't take me too long to work out which category I fell into.

To help me better understand all of this, Chris also recommended a book called *Depressive Illness – The Curse of the Strong*, by Dr Tim Cantopher, a member of the Royal College of Psychiatrists since 1983. First, Chris asked me to consider the book's subtitle and then a few of the names of those who have also suffered: Oliver Cromwell, Abraham Lincoln, Isaac Newton, Edgar Allen Poe, Ludwig van Beethoven, Vincent Van Gogh, Winston Churchill, Evelyn Waugh and Ernest Hemingway. Not that I, a cricket-ball-hitter from Bristol, am comparing myself to anyone on that list. To fellow sufferers who have sought help, no doubt some of what follows is all too familiar. I'm no doctor, so it would be irresponsible of me to talk or write like one. Every single case is different, every single case more or less severe than the next and every single case will respond differently to different forms of treatment. And some cases, sadly, do not respond successfully. All I know is what I went through.

But I do believe it is reasonable for me to try and explain the illness in relation to how it affected me and, in that context, I offer a selection of short, paraphrased extracts from the book in order to help put the illness into words.

'If you really want to help, try to understand that the sufferer of this illness is going through torment of a pretty awful kind. Among the descriptions of the experience that have impressed me are "it's like falling down a well with no bottom; the blackness surrounds you and the tiny circle of light gets ever smaller till it disappears".

'Depressive illness is not a psychological or emotional state and is not a mental illness. It is not a form of madness. It is a physical illness.

'Depressive Illness, or at least the commonest form, which is that caused by stress, nearly always happens to one type of person. He or she will have the following characteristics; (moral) strength, reliability, diligence, strong conscience, strong sense of responsibility, a tendency to focus on the needs of others before one's own, sensitivity, vulnerability to criticism, self-esteem dependent on the evaluation of others.

'This person is the sort to whom you would turn if you had a problem to sort out upon which your house depended, a safe pair of hands you can trust with your life, though often somewhat taken for granted. People are usually very surprised when he gets ill, indeed he is the last person you would expect to have a breakdown.

'But it isn't so surprising when you consider that depressive illness is a physical condition. Think about it; give a set of stresses to someone who is weak, cynical or lazy and he will quickly give up. So he will never get stressed enough to become ill. A strong person, on the other hand, will react to these pressures by trying to overcome them. After all, he has overcome every challenge he has faced in the past through diligence and effort. So he keeps going, absorbing more and more until, inevitably, symptoms emerge. At this point most people would say, "Hang on, this is ridiculous. I'm doing too much." So they pull back from the brink before it is too late. But the sensitive person, without a very solid sense of self-esteem, can't stop struggling, because he fears other people being disappointed in him. Even more than this he fears being disappointed in himself. So he keeps going, on and on and on, until suddenly: *BANG!* The fuse blows.'

Chris listened as I talked and I listened as he talked and eventually he told me that I was a classic example, almost a model of someone suffering from a 'depressive illness of mild to moderate severity with marked anxiety features'. He saw this as the culmination of stresses that had been building up for some years and he called the gastro-intestinal infection I suffered in India the straw that broke the camel's back.

He told me that best practice in cases like mine was to go in with a combination of medications to try and help stabilize things and give help to the kind of talking therapies which he specialized in. He prescribed an anti-depressant intended, he said to my dismay, to be taken for six to nine months.

The road to recovery would be long and anything but straight. As you will read I would stagger and stumble and fall again and again as future events demonstrated and, at the time of writing, I am fully aware I have not reached the end of it yet. But at least, on that April afternoon, I had taken a massive step in the right direction, one that, cruelly and tragically, so many sufferers find themselves simply unable to take. I had reached the start.

Chapter 16

PULP THAT FICTION

*'... all of those [rumours] you are about to read are
total and utter fiction, except, of course,
for the one about my past life as
Miss Fifi Sauvage ...'*

Hayley and I shared more torrid times in the next few weeks;
the next two years to be precise. The first thing we shared,
though, was pills. Though my therapist Chris had wasted no time
in recommending that I went back on anti-depressants during the
meeting at our house of Friday 14 April, I would not be able to see
my GP for him to authorize the prescription until the following
Monday. When Hayley suggested I could share hers, which she
had been taking for a couple of months now for PND, it so happened that her Citalapram was just what the doctor had ordered.

I was not due to see Chris again face-to-face until the following
week. In the meantime I knew the one thing I simply had to do was
try and get back into cricket. I wasn't sure when or how and I was
very uncertain over whether I should play in Somerset's pre-
season practice match against a local select XI the next day, Saturday
15 April. Aside from my concerns over whether any media guys
would turn up to quiz me over recent events and matters arising

from the Sky interview, I had no idea at all whether I would actually be physically able to play a game of cricket.

Everyone at the club was brilliantly supportive, as, in fact, they were from the start of my problems. I was never put under the slightest pressure by anyone. They left everything up to me to gauge how I was feeling and what I believed was right for me at any given time. They never bombarded me with advice or suggestions or questions. In fact, looking back now I couldn't have wished for better employers or friends. But the decisions I was making at this time had to be mine and mine alone.

I rang Chris that morning and asked for guidance.

'If you feel like going out and picking up a bat,' he said, 'do it.'

Before the start of play Peter Hayter had rung me to ask if he and another Sunday paper cricket writer, Simon Wilde of the *Sunday Times*, could have a word at some stage during the day. I said yes, but only on condition that we would be talking about the future and not the past. The moment I put the phone down I started getting that uneasy feeling again. What had I done? Was I ready? Then I began thinking through the process. Peter and I went back six years, to the very start of my England career. He had ghost-written my columns for the *Mail on Sunday* in my early days and we had always got on well; better, in fact, once we stopped doing the columns for the paper. I didn't know Simon that well, but I felt that if I could get through this experience then that would at least be a start.

Stepping onto a cricket field for the first time since I fled from the pitch in Baroda was a weird experience. There was hardly anyone at the ground, but I was convinced that the eyes of everyone who was there were trained on me. My innings of 74 was pretty bizarre, as well, as my concentration fluctuated between being completely focused and totally distracted by the prospect of

talking to Hayter and Wilde afterwards. I almost felt like I was playing in my sleep.

When Peter rang me again, after an agreed period of time had
elapsed following my dismissal, I clenched myself and invited them
round to the back of the pavilion. And not long afterwards, I found
myself giving my first interview to representatives of the written
press since I left India back in February.

We chatted for about ten minutes, with Hayley and Ellie standing nearby. I thought I put on a terrific show. Peter next day
described me in his article as looking 'trim and relaxed', which just
shows you can fool some of the people all of the time, and I gave
them some pretty decent lines.

'I don't want to keep dwelling on the issue of why I left India,' I
said. 'That is in the past and I need to move on and hope everyone
can move on with me.

'As long as my form is okay I will be available for everything England want me for over the next 12 months and beyond: all the
series, all the tours, the Ashes, the 2007 World Cup, everything.
Physically I am fine and everything else is clear, and the feeling that
I've really got to work my nuts off to get back in the Test team has
given me a drive and enthusiasm I haven't had for a couple of
years.'

Right, then.

As the pair of them walked away I complimented myself on
another job well done. Even though I had begun the process of
facing up to my illness, thanks to Chris, I was still a million miles
from being able to do so in public. Again my intention was not to
deceive or mislead, but I did feel that speaking to Hayter and
Wilde and telling them what I wanted them to hear would at the
very least buy me some more precious time. And maybe they
weren't the only ones I was trying to convince. I did want to send
out a clear positive message, to the Board, to Duncan and to

Michael or whoever would end up leading the side in the upcoming Tests against Sri Lanka.

Peter later told me he felt something was wrong but couldn't put his finger on what exactly. He reckoned he might have seen something in Hayley's eyes that said: 'Don't believe him', but put the thought to one side.

As for me, I rang Chris again the day after. The next hurdle was slap bang in front of me, a four-day championship game against Gloucestershire at Bristol, starting on 18 April. Despite what I had said in the Sunday papers, I was cacking myself again. It was all well and good going out and having a hit in a one-day game against local club, minor counties and 2nd XI players but was I really up for a full-on game of first-class cricket? I couldn't answer that. After discussion with Chris I decided I simply had to have a go and see what happened, whatever the consequences, and Hayley agreed to come with me, at least for the first day and night, to offer support. Neil Fairbrother also thought this would be a good opportunity for us to catch up face-to-face for a debriefing following the Sky interview.

Underlying my thinking was that if I didn't play, an even bigger story would be created and I might be back to square one, at best.

Truth is, I did want to get back into the swing of normal things, to show face and say, 'Look. See. I'm playing again. I'm batting again. I'm all right. I'm really all right', even if that might actually have been little more than wishful thinking. As I have said, I was hoping against hope that Chris's help and treatment might get me back on my feet quickly, and if it did, there was still a chance that I might never have to publicly admit to my illness. No matter how fragile I might be feeling inside, if I could continue to behave as if everything was normal, sooner or later everything might actually be normal and no one would be any the wiser.

Fat chance, in the event, because, having crawled to the top of the slope, the big dipper was about to start another downward journey.

Gloucestershire hammered us in three days at Bristol by an innings and seven runs. I scored 12 and 4, was out lbw twice to Jon Lewis and, though I did manage one sharpish slip catch, I also managed to dropped Craig Spearman twice on the way to his hundred.

They were the highlights.

The first incidental event turned out in the end to be no more than a blip. When we made for the dressing-rooms at the end of the first session on day one, a familiar figure greeted us. Erica Hayward, a young trainee physiotherapist, had done a couple of spells of work experience at Somerset in previous seasons and was later taken on as an assistant to Darren Veness. Based in Bristol, she had popped down to the ground to say hello and a few of us gave her a friendly hug and a kiss as we left the field. Unbeknown to me, a photographer decided to make himself busy.

Later, during a rain break, one or two of the press guys approached and asked if they could have a few words. Buoyed by my successful return to the pages of the national papers, I agreed, and the session, again with a few very familiar faces, like Mike Dickson of the *Daily Mail* and Dave Kidd from the *Sun*, went well. Again I insisted I wasn't going to go into detail about my own situation but I managed to put down a few pointers about the issue of burnout, which had, after all, been one of the major causes of my problems. As the reporters were leaving, Dickson pulled me to one side and said: 'Mate, I'm sure it's nothing serious but our picture desk have been sent a photograph of you from here with a girl they are describing as a "mystery blonde". If you let me know who she is, I will nip any nonsense in the bud.'

I laughed nervously and told Dickson the story. It was a load of nothing, of course, but, as the day progressed I started to wonder exactly how the photos might be presented. I told Hayley what I thought might be coming and she told me not to worry. The next day's *Daily Mail* duly appeared and, across a double-page spread they published not one picture, but three. Funnily enough, there didn't seem to be any pictures at all of any of the four or five other players who had also given Erica an affectionate welcome. And the picture caption was not exactly helpful either, reading, as it did: 'Marcus Trescothick, welcomed back into the bosom of his Somerset family …' Hilarious.

To be fair, I had been half-expecting something like this from the moment I realized there might be a negative press reaction to the Sky interview. In fact, though I was pretty irritated about how they presented the photos, Dickson's piece, quoting me about the dangers of burnout, was fair enough.

Hayley had been home for a couple of hours when, at lunchtime on Wednesday 19 April, the buzzer connecting the communications panel in our kitchen to the security gates at the end of our drive rang.

'Who is it?' Hayley asked, through the speaker.

'Hello, Hayley,' a woman's voice answered.

'I'm a freelance reporter from the South West News Service,' she continued, 'and I …'

'No, thanks,' Hayley interrupted. 'Sorry, but we have nothing to say at the moment.'

'Yes, but can you listen to what I have to say?'

'Go on, then,' said Hayley.

'Well, I've had information saying that the reason Marcus came home from India is that you are having an affair with Steffan Jones …'

Hayley wasn't listening any more.

'Yeah, yeah, whatever,' she said and switched the speaker off.

Obviously the story was utter tosh. Steffan, one of my best mates, married to Alex, Hayley's best friend since their schooldays, having an affair with Hayley? Total and utter rubbish.

Hayley was in a quandary, however. She knew how fragile my state of mind was at that time and had seen how aggravated I had been the night before about the prospect of those photos appearing in the *Daily Mail*. She reckoned this latest nonsense was the last thing I needed to hear or have to deal with, but she felt she had to do something.

She decided to try and ring Neil Fairbrother. She made a couple of attempts to reach him on his mobile but couldn't get through. Next she rang Jason Kerr. There followed five minutes of pure cloak and dagger.

'Jase,' Hayley said. 'Don't let on it's me speaking, but are you anywhere near Neil Fairbrother?'

'Yeah,' Jason replied. 'He's talking to Marcus as a matter of fact. What's up?'

'Well, I can't tell you now, but can you do me a favour? When Neil is away from Marcus can you ask him to ring me, urgently?'

In due course Neil called and Hayley explained everything that had happened. She told him she hadn't spoken to me and, for the moment, didn't want me to know in case the incident upset me. She assured Neil the allegation was a total and utter fabrication and that she was sure this reporter had just been trying it on to see what response she got.

Neil told her there was nothing to worry about and that he would get on the case. He then rang Richard Bevan, who contacted Gerrard Tyrell, from Harbottle & Lewis, the PCA's solicitors.

Gerrard got in touch with the South West News Service and asked them what the position was. He was told that one of the national papers was all set to run the story, at which point Gerrard politely informed them that it was utterly untrue and that, if they printed a word of it, they would be sued for defamation. The story was 'spiked'.

When Neil rang Hayley to tell her the good news, she thanked him, then breathed a sigh of relief that she hadn't had to involve me and decided that, as it was all resolved satisfactorily, there was no point in risking me getting upset for no good reason. I got home on the evening of Friday 21 April and when Chris arrived for our next face-to-face meeting the next day, neither he nor I were any the wiser.

Chris noted that I was feeling far more at ease. I told him I felt I had coped reasonably well with the game in Bristol and was looking forward to playing the following day, in a Cheltenham & Gloucester 50-over match at Canterbury against Kent.

Travelling down that night, I was aware that I was beginning to experience a strange feeling. I couldn't put my finger on exactly what it was, but it was like a memory of something I hadn't felt for a long, long time. And then I realized what it was. I was feeling good.

By the time I woke up the next morning, Sunday 23 April after an uninterrupted night's sleep, I was feeling fantastic.

Initially I didn't really care why. All I knew was that it was gone. That bastard monster which had been eating me up from inside for so long had f***ed off. I was touching wood all over the place, but the sheer joy of being free of it, even if it turned out to be only temporary, was impossible to resist and fantastic to experience.

For the moment, almost miraculously, all the dread and fear and anxiety appeared to have vanished. I even found myself trying to remember the sensation of feeling bad so that I could make sure I was beyond it, like when you pinch yourself after something wonderful has happened just to make sure you aren't dreaming.

All those times when I just couldn't see a way forward, all those black moments of mental and physical agony, all those attacks of anxiety about Hayley and Ellie that had left me half-dead with worry, all those bleak thoughts. Gone, for the moment. Could they possibly be gone for good?

I started to rationalize how I felt. I reasoned it all out; a combination of the medication coming to really kick in, appreciating that, though I had made a mess of the Sky interview, so far there had been no discernible reaction – apart from the photos of me and Erica, the actual press reporting had been positive – and feeling I could at last see how my recovery could progress from here, it all added up. I was okay. Not totally cured, obviously, and certainly not taking anything for granted, but okay. Doesn't sound much, does it? It was just about the most brilliant feeling I had ever experienced.

It told me, no matter what happened from now on, and how long it took, I *could* be well again.

They couldn't bowl at me that day. I was lucky to get a life on 43, when Darren Stevens shelled a simple return catch, but after that I mashed it everywhere. I reached my hundred in 103 balls, shared an opening stand of 177 with Matt Wood, and finished on 158 from 135 balls, with 20 fours and three sixes. It was Ellie's second birthday, cause for a double celebration.

By the time we completed victory by 112 runs in a rain-shortened match, I felt like a million dollars and the innings wasn't just good for my own peace of mind. With the first of two Tests against Sri Lanka due to start at Lord's on Thursday 11 May and the England squad to be picked and announced the previous Sunday 7 May, clearly Duncan and the selectors, David Graveney and Geoff Miller needed some evidence that I would be worth picking for the upcoming international season.

They were aware at this stage of the background to my departure from India, and that I was undergoing ongoing treatment, but none of them had a clue about the detail of what I had gone through, or even that I was currently on medication. Indeed, that piece of news was kept from them all summer.

But they had heard what I had said and read about making myself available again and wanting to play. Now, seeing that I was playing a good game as well as talking one, and especially as Michael Vaughan was still absent with his knee problems, as long as nothing went wrong in the next fortnight they had no reason not to pick me.

I had a slight wobble one evening during our next match against Worcestershire at New Road, when, after making a duck in our first innings, a reporter approached me and raised the question of whether I would be available to captain England at Lord's. Christ! That was a bolt from the blue. But there was some logic to the inquiry. I had skippered the side in Michael's absence in Pakistan and I was all set to do so in India before I broke down. Fred had done really well and led a great fightback against Tendulkar & Co. to come away with a highly creditable 1–1 draw, but there was a strong feeling within the camp that he might be better off concentrating on his batting and bowling, rather than taking on the responsibility of captaincy as well.

'Let me just play, first. Everything else can look after itself,' I said, or words to that effect.

On Friday 28 April, after having polished off Worcestershire with a day to spare, by 227 runs, the lads were ready for a team night out in Worcester. I still wasn't quite up to that, I was keen to get home and enjoy being with Hayley and Ellie, so I made my excuses. I hitched a lift as far as Weston Super Mare with Brian Rose, who lives in the town, then Hayley came to collect me from there.

On the way home, she said she had something to tell me, and that I probably wouldn't like it.

Unbeknown to me, for the past week Hayley had been grappling with whether to spill the beans about being approached by
the reporter from the local agency, and why. As time passed she
had become more and more certain that it would be unfair to keep
it from me, that I had a right to know and should be told. Now,
sensing I was in a much stronger state of health and more able to
cope with the news, she drew a deep breath and proceeded to tell
me what had happened.

Her instincts had warned her I would not be happy and they
were right. In fact I was angry. Of course, I knew the story was nonsense and was only someone asking the question that had formed
the basis of the absurd rumours that had previously been circulating. But I was angry that Hayley hadn't told me before. 'Hayley, if
anything like that happens again, don't keep it to yourself. You
must tell me,' I urged her. 'We've got to get through this stuff
together and the sooner you tell me about it the quicker I can sort
it out.'

In fact I was more angry that the reporter had tried it on, angry
with how she had tried to tease a 'confession' from Hayley over
such utter nonsense and angry that we had to go through this kind
of crap at all. What bloody right did these people have to try and
come into our lives and try to f**k us up? And with my anger some
of my anxiety came back. How much more would we have to put
up with?

Well, loads, is the answer. Indeed, if this was the start of increasingly wild speculation over some people's ideas of why I had come
home from India, with which Hayley and I and those closest to us
subsequently had to contend, it certainly wasn't going to end there.

Some stories were very hurtful, one, in particular, just awful,
some were laughable, and some just plain crazy. But from time to
time certain people have managed to convince themselves
absolutely without question that one or all of them were fact.

I can state categorically, however, that all of those you are about to read are total and utter fiction, except, of course, for the one about my past life as Miss Fifi Sauvage, the Bangkok-based night-club chanteuse and internationally-acclaimed horse impersonator...

So here are a selection of those other rumours, in no particular order and all as ridiculous as each other:

Aside from Hayley having an affair with Steffan, there was also her affair with Jason Kerr. And Kevin Shine, formerly of Somerset, who succeeded Troy Cooley as the new England fast bowling coach. And Michael Vaughan. And Kevin Pietersen.

And if you want proof, here it is, straight from the pages of *The Corridor*, a so-called 'cricket-blog'.

Robin wrote: 'That is a lie ... The truth is that Pietersen slept with his wife and now marcus (*sic*) finds it impossible to share the dressing-room with him.'

Woody wrote: 'I reckon I have the real truth right here and it comes from a friend of mine who works in a barbers. One day Darren Gough strolled in for a haircut and announced tht (*sic*) the real reason Tres isn't playing for England is because Michael Vaughan has slept with his wife. Thts (*sic*) genuine word from inside of the england (*sic*) team itself, Goughy does not lie.'

Anonymous wrote: 'I shouldn't come on here and say this but tresco's mrs was sh***ing Kevin Shine. Shine was coach at sommerset (*sic*) and got to know resco's (*sic*) and when he was away with England Shine used to get friendly.'

And he also added: 'This is all what I have heard and is not necessarily true just saying what ive (*sic*) been told.'

So there you have it, and a warm thank you to 'Anonymous' for clearing up the mystery and to the rest of your mates for your concern and respect.

As I say, I understand that, to a certain extent, I laid us open to an increase in speculation and hearsay when I bailed out of telling some part of the truth in the Sky TV interview. Had I done so, I'm fairly sure none of what subsequently passed for investigative news reporting among the media, and idle rumour-mongering among the internet blogging fraternity, would have happened. But only fairly, because both of those are part of the reality of the world in which we live.

While I understand what happened, that does not mean I can ever accept it or what we were put through as a result. While both of us are able to look back at some of this stuff and chuckle, I can assure you it was no laughing matter at the time.

Once Hayley had finished telling me her story I rang Chris and asked to see him the next day. Chris said he understood why I was so anxious but he soon managed to calm me down again.

'What is the worst that can happen?' he asked me. 'What can they actually print, apart from lies? And because they can't print anything apart from lies, they can't print anything at all.'

It worked. The incident had affected me quite badly but, being in better health than I had been, I was much more able to put something like this in its place, or to one side, and not let it totally dominate my thoughts, though God only knows what might have happened if the incident had happened when I was in the depths.

By the time I turned up at Northampton on Wednesday 3 May, my sense of well-being had been at least partly restored and I was ready to go again.

The job in hand was to make some runs for the club and keep my name in the minds of the selectors. I hit 154 out of our first innings 258 on a turning pitch, fortuitously in front of Geoff 'Dusty' Miller, who was there to check on my form and 'fitness'. Though we were eventually thumped by an innings, he had seen enough. I spoke to him that evening in person, then Graveney on the phone. They were happy if I was. The next day a familiar name flashed up on my mobile phone.

Duncan never mentioned India or Baroda, or my early departure from the tour or the Sky interview and, like Grav and Dusty and 99 per cent of the people I was mixing with, he still had no real idea about my illness or that I was on medication to help me through the early stages of recovery.

All I remember him actually saying was, 'Are you sure you're all right to play?'

'Yes,' I replied. 'I'm all right.'

Chapter 17

WHAT'S
THE STORY?

*'The moment he spotted me looking at him,
Duncan quickly closed the paper shut. I walked
in and said: "Right, what's the story?"
Duncan picked up the paper, the News of
the World, handed it to me and said:
"You'd better read this."'*

There were no qualms on my part. When I turned up at Lord's on Monday 8 May 2006 to meet the rest of the England squad and start preparations for the first Test against Sri Lanka starting on the Thursday, not only was I ready, I was really ready.

There were a few butterflies, little nervy flushes about catching up with the guys again for the first time since I'd broken down in front of some of them in Baroda; the national media would have to be faced, one or two no doubt, preparing to scrutinize me more closely than usual; the step-up in class from county to Test cricket would have to be made; and all in front of a capacity crowd at a cricket ground that had always made the hair on the back of my neck stand to attention. There were also the Sri Lankan bowlers to worry about: Chaminda Vaas and Murali, keen to make his mark in his first Test at Lord's.

But the true measure of how I was feeling was that I was anticipating all of the above as challenges to be relished, not feared. And another arrived that Monday evening in London, when we all turned out in best bib and tucker to celebrate the achievements of the past year at the traditional pre-Test dinner hosted by the team sponsors Vodafone at the Saatchi gallery, on the south bank of the Thames.

The mood was lively and upbeat and friendly. No one probed too hard and, in any case, fielding questions in this sociable environment was good practice for what might have to be faced in the coming days. Actually most of those present were far more interested in re-living their favourite moments from the 2005 Ashes and applauding the 1–1 draw in India and were far too polite to raise even the 2–0 defeat in Pakistan, let alone my troubles, or the Sky interview.

Lord MacLaurin, still chairman of Vodafone, though he had stood down as ECB chairman some time before, said Grace before the meal. 'Our final thanks before we eat,' said his lordship, 'for the ball you placed, beneath Glenn's feet,' a reminder of possibly the pivotal moment of the entire Ashes contest, when McGrath turned his ankle an hour before the start of the second Test at Edgbaston.

When the time came for the awards, Fred, now officially installed as captain for the series against Sri Lanka in Michael's continuing absence, was, deservedly, Player of the Year, and there was an award for the Ashes highlight, the moment when Steve Harmison had Mike Kasprowicz caught by Geraint Jones at Edgbaston and we were back from the near-dead. Nasser Hussain received a special achievement award for his part in helping Duncan lay the foundations for our success and I collected a silver award, given to England players for individual performances, for my century in Multan. How long ago did that seem now?

The next day at the ground, being back in the swing among players with whom I had shared so much, Strauss and Geraint and Fred, KP and Hoggard and Collingwood, just felt right. This *was* where I was supposed to be. And it was such a relief to me to be thinking almost exclusively about cricket; about how we should bat against Murali, how to try and spot his 'doosra' and the rest of his repertoire. And once we had spotted them, how to play them. It was also interesting to see how Cook, Liam Plunkett and Monty Panesar were fitting into the set-up, in place of Vaughan, Simon Jones and Giles. Then there was Saj Mahmood, of Lancashire, who had been brought in to make his debut in place of Harmison, still recovering from a shin problem that had forced him home early from India. Capable of bowling really fast, inswinging yorkers like Simon had done the previous summer, I've rarely seen a newcomer treated with quite so much respect by the batsmen, though the fact that one of his cousins happened to be the boxer Amir Khan might have had something to do with that.

From the moment I settled into my usual spot in the dressing-room I felt, well, at home. I could never get enough of that place, still can't. The sense of history, the shadows and the ghosts of those who had sat here, changed here, won and lost here, all connected by the sheer raw thrill of playing for England at Lord's. Every single one, at some time or another, would have sucked that last gulp of air into their lungs before walking out to play a Lord's Test for the first time. Some would have known what it felt like to score a century or take wickets or be involved in a great victory and walk out onto the balcony to share the feeling with those who could only dream of it. Just looking at the batting and bowling honours' boards on the walls, seeing my name among those who had scored hundreds or took five wickets in an innings, sent a spark through me. No disrespect intended but I couldn't give a monkey's that the name of the opponents against whom I had made my first and so far only Test ton here happened to be Bangladesh. It felt that way the first time I saw it and every time since.

And now I was back in that place to which not long before I feared I might never return as an England player, joining in the banter, or rather finding myself, very happily, the target for most of it, as usual.

I don't know whether the lads had spoken together in advance about how they should behave in my company. Some here had witnessed first-hand my collapse in India, and as I had spoken with Vaughan and others, one or two of them must have been aware of the severity of my illness, but they seemed determined to behave now as though nothing had happened that day in Baroda.

They may have felt the subject was just off-limits, especially as even those who had some knowledge of the severity of my symptoms and the nature of my depressive illness and anxiety attacks would also have been aware that quite a few within the camp, including Duncan and the selectors, still had no real idea. Neither the coach, nor Graveney, nor Miller, for instance, was aware that I was currently on medication and would be for the rest of the summer, nor would they find out for several months, nor why I was. Indeed I myself was still only in the very early stages of recovery and of fully understanding the illness.

Just as my sense of well-being persuaded me that the worst was over and that no more need be said, I got the distinct impression that the very fact that I was there, had made some runs for Somerset and appeared well in myself, encouraged all concerned to crack on as normal, unless something untoward happened. And, in any case, they must have been pretty uncertain as to the prescribed form of mickey-taking for someone who had spent the last three months barking at the moon.

There were no jarring moments, no sudden silences when I entered the room as people watched in case I started crying my eyes out again and, actually, no ice-breakers either. Maybe most people just reckoned I was okay now and it was time to put the past away. That was fine by me.

Hayley, who had been with me all week with Ellie, went so far as to remark on how normal everyone and everything seemed to be.

On the first morning of the match I prepared, as usual, I netted, an usual, I went through my routines, as usual. What *was* different was my desire to soak up every bit of the experience.

The events of the past three months had taught me to take absolutely nothing for granted, ever again. So, even though I fully expected to be back in contention for the England side for as long as my fitness and form justified it, and wanted to bat for them forever, when I walked out to the wicket with Strauss, after Fred had won the toss and decided to bat, I did make extra sure of taking a second look.

And when Vaas, running in from the Pavilion End, sent down the first ball of the rest of my England career, it was a good job I was on full alert. It took no time at all to realize that, on a green-tinged surface, the ball was zipping around all over the place. Vaas, the tall left-armer, had never been exactly lightning, but his ability to move the ball in the air and off the seam at medium pace more than made up for that. Now, almost every delivery was asking a question and neither Strauss nor I had many answers. In the end, we weren't good enough to get a touch and Vaas, at first exasperated, ended up just standing there laughing. Clearly the Sri Lankan bowlers weren't interested in helping me ease my way back.

As the pitch dried out and batting became easier, I started to find some rhythm and timing but I was so absolutely stone dead lbw to Murali's doosra on 28 that I almost didn't bother to wait for the signal of the umpire, Rudi Koertzen, to send me on my way. Incredibly the slowest but deadliest finger in cricket stayed down, as it did once more when, on 85, Murali did me again. Bang in line both times. I decided the time had come to play him with my bat, finally unfurling the slog-sweep, once bashing him into the grandstand for six. By now I was in gear, never exactly fluent but knowing that unless I did something daft a century was within my grasp. And when, after tea, I swept him to bring up my second Test hundred for England at Lord's, I had it.

I accepted Alastair Cook's handshake – he himself was on his way to making 89 in his first Test at Lord's. Helmet off, arms up, I looked first towards our balcony, then to Hayley, and quietly cursed myself that I hadn't thought to do it the other way around. Then I let the roar wash over me like a warm shower. To my ears, it was the sound of 28,000 England cricket supporters saying: 'It's all right, Marcus. Whatever you've been through, whatever your problems, as far as we are concerned, it's all right.'

When I was out for 106, out of 312 for three not long before the close of play, the reception I received all the way back to the dressing-room, and inside it, was fantastic. Walking back to a standing ovation at this special place was a sublime moment. Not so long before, when my depressive illness was at its most powerful, my future had appeared so bleak to me as to be almost impossible to bear. And now this. How do you think I felt?

I was good and ready to face the press. 'It was time to move on,' I told them. 'It was time to get things rolling, get back in an England shirt and enjoy playing cricket again. I used the time away to take stock, sit back, then move on.' That would do for now.

That night in the hotel, I celebrated by sitting out in the corridor watching Ellie, who had just started to walk, pick up a little football, throw it, walk after it and repeat the action over and over again. Isn't this great?

Ellie, Hayley and I were together and happy, and, as far as the cricket had gone, I had managed to prove to myself that I could still do my job and I could still enjoy playing international cricket again and I had managed to prove to everyone else that I was still worth picking by scoring a Test hundred when it mattered.

I was well aware it was my fourteenth. I had no idea it would turn out to be my last.

The following day, KP completed a gorgeous 158, equalling his Ashes-winning Test best at The Oval. And he included in it, for the first time, the switch-hit to put Murali over the ropes for six. It was an audacious shot, but, to him, not at all reckless, especially as we had made well over 400 when he played it. With no fielders in the deep on the off-side, his power and strong wrists meant that, as long as he got a fair bit of the ball, it was bound to land safe, and if he got all of it, cheerio. Tactically, anything that would make Murali think twice about where he was pitching the ball had to be a good thing. It was also a clear statement that, at his best, Kevin was capable of playing a different game to the rest of us. The effect had been such that, when he was out leg-before to Murali two balls later, no one seemed to mind too much at all.

After we had declared at 551 for six, we bowled Sri Lanka out for 192 in their first innings, asked them to follow-on and, though not complacent, pretty confident we would be able to finish the task. Had we caught all our our catches, we would have done so, comfortably. But we didn't. Second time around the very talented Mahela Jayawardene ground out 119 in six hours but we still had a fair squeak when Kulasekara offered a chance to Cooky on 14, at 449 for eight, with them just 90 ahead overall seven overs after lunch on the final day and with plenty of time left. It went down, Kulasekara and Vaas put on 105 in 189 minutes and they finished safe at 537 for nine. Fred got more and more frustrated and ended up bowling 51 overs in the innings. Faced with the growing stubbornness of the Sri Lankan resistance, it was almost as though, as captain, he believed it was his personal responsibility to bowl Sri Lanka out and the longer they survived the harder he tried, but the pitch, now flat, and their batsmen thwarted all his superhuman efforts.

I found it strange that, instead of highlighting our seven dropped catches, most of the post-mortem was about Fred. According to Mike Walters of the *Daily Mirror*, writing in the *2007 Wisden*: 'England's failure to grasp a yawning opportunity to draw first blood in the series put Flintoff's captaincy under the microscope and began a nationwide debate on whether his genial manner and his workload permitted the ruthlessness required to convert superiority into Test victories.' Indeed, once the debate had been raised it followed Fred all the way through the summer and beyond, to the end of the next Ashes series.

Generally speaking I did have my doubts over whether it was reasonable to expect Fred to continue to prosper as the best all-round cricketer in the world and carry the captaincy as well. Maybe he did overbowl himself and underbowl Monty in that second innings – and in the end, how much of a toll did that take on his troublesome ankle? Maybe another captain would have handled Fred differently. But Michael Vaughan was not averse to using him in long spells himself, as at The Oval the previous September, when that suited the needs of the side. To me, the reality of our failure to win this match was far more simple; we shelled seven chances. But with our Ashes tour down under now less than six months away, the uncertainty growing over Vaughan's future meant the issue of who would lead us on tour in his absence was starting to exercise a few minds within the England camp. And soon they would have to start thinking even harder.

Still, my return had been a success for me personally, and when I met Chris again on 19 May for a debrief, my spirits were high. Hayley and I spoke about how things had progressed in the month since we had first met. Hayley told Chris she thought I was much improved, if not totally back to my old self, because I was still sensitive to things like the phone ringing at home or cars passing by our house. But I was happy to tell him I was off the sleeping pills now and I saw this as another big step forward.

Little did I know that I was about to take another step backwards.

In the second Test at Edgbaston that started on Thursday 25 May, as we had done in the first innings at Lord's we bowled Sri Lanka out cheaply after they slumped to bat, all out for 141. I batted okay, making 37, and KP again batted brilliantly, getting out his switch hit a second time, again hitting it for six, then, amazingly, in a carbon copy of his dismissal at Lord's, falling to Murali two balls after playing it, and again lbw.

But we owed our total of 295 and a substantial lead all to him and, by the end of the second day, Sri Lanka already looked cooked, though Michael Vandoort's 105, and the rain that fell on the Saturday, extended the game into a fourth day.

When I arrived at the ground on the Sunday, I soon got the impression that something was up. No one actually said anything, it was just a vibe. Before play resumed I happened to be outside the dressing-room, looking in through a window in the partition wall, and my attention was drawn to Duncan and Andy Walpole deep in discussion. Andy had his back to me, but I could see Duncan standing with his hands on the desk in front of him reading a newspaper article. The moment he spotted me looking at him, Duncan quickly closed the paper shut.

I walked in and said: 'Right, what's happened?'

Duncan picked up the paper, the *News of the World*, handed it to me and said: 'You'd better read this.'

Under the headline: 'Revealed: Tresco's COVER-UP', was the following piece by David Norrie, their cricket correspondent:

'The *News of the World* today exposes a remarkable cover-up surrounding England cricketer Marcus Trescothick – and reveals the man who masterminded the bizarre plot.

'I have seen documentary evidence that proves Richard Bevan, Chief Executive of the Professional Cricketers' Association, hatched a desperate plan to try and explain why Trescothick suddenly walked out on England's India tour this winter.

'Tresco's departure was clouded in mystery and triggered rumours about his home life.

'Even England coach Duncan Fletcher admitted he was going home for "personal, family reasons". But Fletcher was made to look foolish when Trescothick appeared on television in April claiming illness was the reason for his flight home.

'It infuriated the England camp, who were unaware he was apparently suffering from an ailment. But I can now reveal Trescothick's TV statement was a cover-up.

'The blame was unfairly pointed at the ECB, especially Head of Communications Colin Gibson, and Trescothick's agent, ISM's Neil Fairbrother.

'But I have seen evidence that proves the Trescothick fiasco was orchestrated by Bevan – an English cricket powerbroker, dealing with central contracts, sponsorship and other issues.

'And it was Bevan who set up Trescothick's interview with Sky which resulted in the removal of any reference to his "personal problem" at home.

'Bevan's cover-up began with the England vice-captain due to attend a press conference at Somerset. On 25 March under a headline "Media Handling Strategy", Bevan wrote: "We need to decide whether the Somerset press conference is the best 'first' engagement with the media for you.

'"While we can appeal to the better nature of our usual familiar circle of cricket writers, there is a chance a news reporter will get involved and publish a negative article.

'"We did consider advising whether you should issue a personal statement briefly explaining the personal problems that led to the decision (to leave India).

'"The fact that you had 'personal problems' and are 'dealing with family matters' has been well documented.

'"I envisage after you have presented yourself to the media, the issues for the most part will go away.

'"However, we will need to be sure the facts stay private.

'"We will allow Sky a very controlled interview with only pre-agreed questions. It will probably take an hour to put you through your paces and get word perfect."

'Up to a couple of days before the interview, the planned explanation was: "Having picked up a virus and also some personal issues to resolve, I decided to return home."

'But when Tresco was questioned on TV by Ian Ward, who had been requested by Bevan, the England man said: "The main reason was I picked up a bug while I was out there and it really hit me hard."

'Now the ECB are seeking explanations.'

They certainly were, though primarily as to how and why sensitive and possibly damaging personal information about me had been leaked to the *News of the World*.

Most of the detail contained in the article was incorrect. Or rather, whoever Norrie had got his information from had either been misinformed or had presented a version specifically designed to identify Richard Bevan as the man who 'masterminded the bizarre plot', and erroneously lay all the blame for what happened at his door. Anyone in possession of all the facts as I laid them out in an earlier chapter of this book would have come to a completely different conclusion. The idea that the England camp had been 'unaware he was apparently suffering from an ailment' was interesting. News of stomach bugs travels pretty fast on tour and I doubt that my two days in quarantine in my hotel room, one away from the ground when a match was going on, went completely unnoticed. And Ian Ward had not been requested by Bevan, but by me.

However the central plank of the story, that it had been arranged and agreed in advance that I would say the words 'personal issues to be resolved' in the Sky interview and then ended up not saying them after all, was indisputably right.

The effect of that piece of information appearing in print was that, at a stroke, whatever sense of well-being and normality I had been enjoying over the past fortnight was severely undermined.

My first reaction was a mixture of mild panic and paranoia; the fear that my personal life and problems would be back on the agenda and back in the public domain, when I had been hoping against hope that I would be able to deal with them on my own, in my own time and in private.

It didn't take long for some of those other familiar, unwelcome feelings to return as well. Would everyone be looking at me now? And what would they be thinking? Who actually knew about my illness and my traumas and my breakdown? Who knew about the medication? What would I have to do now, or to say, to deal with all this again?

Obviously there was no way I would have to give a press conference to react to the article, but what if I scored runs in the second innings and I was therefore put up by Andrew Walpole to speak to the media afterwards? They were bound to ask me questions about the article. Cover-up, it had said, and plot. There are no words in the entire English language more likely to prick up the ears of reporters. And the *News of the World* article had contained those words and more. Was I going to have to go through all the questions again? And what the hell was I going to say this time?

It would be fatuous to blame my second innings duck on the effect of reading the paper that morning and I certainly did not get out for nothing on purpose in order to avoid facing the media that night.

One thing is certain: if the person responsible for leaking the story thought doing so was more important than the possible effect on me of their actions, they cannot have had a very high regard for me or my well-being.

What definitely helped now was that, on that Sunday morning, there was a match to be closed out and a victory to be savoured. We duly reached our target of 78, no thanks to me, of course, to win by six wickets and take a 1–0 lead.

The following day I noticed with relief that there was hardly a mention of the *News of the World* story in the Monday papers, and as we soon found ourselves on the road to Nottingham to prepare for the third Test, due to start on Friday 2 June, there was no time to dwell on the matter further, for the time being anyway.

To me, though, I had had a lucky escape. Had I been in a more fragile state at the time the *News of the World* article appeared, who knows how damaging it might have turned out to be?

Later, I did ask Richard Bevan to see if he could find out more. How had the leak come about? Who had been in the know and who might have been prepared to give Norrie this kind of stuff and why? Was the whole thing the result of an accident or a misunderstanding? Or did the wrong email fall just into the wrong hands at the wrong time?

It was not until later that I was told a story that confirmed the leak was no accident.

Prior to Norrie being supplied with certain emails, another senior cricket correspondent from a daily paper had also been offered the same information.

On that occasion the informant was politely told that unless he was prepared to put his name to a quote to back up the story, the paper was not interested.

Chapter 18

COMING CLEAN

'As the discussion progressed you could see the colour drain out of Duncan's cheeks. Up to this moment I truly believe he hadn't really had a clue about what had been wrong with me.'

As the summer of 2006 progressed, most of the attention of the cricket-loving public, and within the England camp, revolved around the issue of who would be leading us on our defence of the Ashes down under that winter.

Sadly, Michael Vaughan didn't seem to be making much progress at all. Every time we saw him being put through his paces he was either limping faster or limping slower but always limping and it was obviously getting him down. I know he was extremely worried that he might never be able to play again for anyone, let alone England and that, after what we had all achieved in 2005, was a very bitter prospect. It came as no surprise when a change of medical staff recommended a change of approach. Nick Pierce joined the ECB, eventually to replace Peter Gregory. Vaughan went under the knife for micro-surgery, which, while ruling him out of contention for now, enabled him to make his Test comeback a year later.

Andrew Flintoff was in harness for the whole of the Test series against Sri Lanka and, after his fine effort in India, appeared to be the odds-on favourite for the job.

But for him, and us, events took a turn for the worse in the third Test at Trent Bridge in early June. On a dry pitch ideally suited to his arts and crafts, Murali finally got the better of KP and the rest of us, taking eleven for 132 in the match, including eight for 70 in the second innings, featuring a magical spell of eight for 26 from 17.3 overs, to earn his side victory and a 1–1 series draw. Furthermore, towards the end of their second innings it was becoming more and more evident that Fred was starting to struggle with his ankle. It was announced almost immediately after the match that he would miss the rest of the international season, the one-dayers against Sri Lanka followed by Tests and one-dayers against Pakistan, to undergo a second operation. It was also announced that Andrew Strauss would take his place as captain. Unsurprisingly, my name had not warranted a mention, either in the press or within the management.

I enjoyed some success in the one-day stuff in mid-summer, making my first and so far only hundred against Ireland on 13 June, and 72 in the Twenty20 match with Sri Lanka at the Rose Bowl. The less said about our five-match one-day series with Sri Lanka the better, as they hammered us 5–0. In every one of the five games one of their batsmen scored a century. Jayawardene got two in a row in Durham and Manchester and in the last match, at Headingley, after I got our first ton of the series, 121 out of 321 for seven, they reached 324 for two in 37.3 overs to win by eight wickets with an unbelievable 75 balls to spare. This time both their openers Upul Tharanga and Sanath Jayasuriya reached three figures in a one-day international record opening stand of 286 in 32 overs, with Steve Harmison going for 97 from his ten overs, the most runs taken off an England bowler in one-day cricket. He didn't bowl that badly.

Anything straight they smashed for six over mid-wicket and any-thing wide they smashed for six over point. It was a massacre. If Sri Lanka had batted first and kept up their scoring rate of 8.64 per over for the full 50, they would have scored 432, the third-highest total in one-day history. With less than a year until the 2007 World Cup you might say we had a spot of work to do on our one-day game.

Poor Strauss didn't know what had hit him. Even so, when Duncan began asking my opinion as to who should lead the side in Australia if Michael couldn't, I had no hesitation in recommending him ahead of Fred.

To me it was clear-cut. 'You've got to go with Strauss,' I told him, 'because Fred is the key to us winning the series and if you make him captain the pressure on him will be massive.

'If we are going to win in Australia,' I explained, 'or at least draw, everyone is going to have to play out of their skins, but Fred is going to have to play an absolute blinder with the bat and with the ball. To me, he will not be able to bat like he did in 2005, or bowl like he did, if he is captain as well. It will be far too much for him.'

I had no doubt whatsoever that Fred could be an absolute inspiration to the side as a player. I'd seen it happen. His over at Edgbaston the previous year when he got out Justin Langer and Ricky Ponting was a case in point. It was the best I have ever seen. For those six balls it wasn't England against Australia, it was Fred against Australia, and Fred won. That incredible ability to change the course of a match was too precious to risk.

I also had my doubts as to whether Fred's individual way of going about things would necessarily be the best example for the rest of the players to follow. In Vaughan we had had a captain who led from the front off the field as well as on it, someone who, at every training session was prepared to say, 'Right, lads, let's do more, let's push this further', and, with all due respect to a great cricketer and friend, that is not Fred's way. Fred is very much his own man and always did his thing the way it suited him. There was no way he would train as hard as Strauss, for example. Clearly he has put in an unbelievable amount of work to get himself back to fitness not once, but four times, following ankle surgery and each time would have been tougher than the last. But he was never going to be the one driving us forward saying 'Let's get down to the gym', and, in my opinion, while working on improving skills is always the priority, sometimes those arduous physical sessions are far more valuable than Fred ever believed them to be.

By the same token, Duncan always had his difficulties with Fred. Forgetting his much-publicised comments about Fred's social habits for the moment, theirs was at best a marriage of convenience. Duncan thought Fred was a great bowler and a good batsman, but he thought his approach and attitude left a lot to be desired.

I got the distinct impression that Duncan agreed with my assessment, in fact I'm pretty sure he wouldn't have asked me for my views if he thought they might not match his own. So, when the decision over the captaincy was announced at the end of the summer, knowing Fred and knowing Duncan and knowing the way they regarded each other, I must confess I was very surprised at Fred's appointment. And I was just as intrigued to read later in Duncan's autobiography that, with David Graveney backing Fred and Dusty Miller in favour of Strauss, he made up his mind to go with Fred after watching a motivational video at Loughborough where we were having our end of season fitness assessments. That just didn't sound like Duncan at all.

Between this point and then, however, I had other issues to confront. I was determined to be fit and ready for the Ashes tour and to me that meant fit, ready, off the medication and cured. I had a notion, though this may not have been entirely accurate, that, as time went on the medication had begun to have an unwanted side-effect. I was more grateful than I can express that it had helped me as much as it had. Make no bones about it, the pills were nothing less than a lifeline. But I started to get the feeling that they might be taking the edge off my reactions. Obviously, the whole point of the medication is that it has a calming effect, but throughout that summer I was prone to lethargy and some days I felt I actually had to force myself to get going.

I had a couple of chats with Chris and I explained my concerns. I told him how vital I thought it was that I should be completely off the medication by the time we left for Australia. If I could go there 'clean' it would mean a lot. It would mean I was well.

Chris was a little wary, told me there and then that I shouldn't even contemplate coming off straight away, as a relapse was possible and a second wave of depression can often be more severe than the first. He advised caution, informing me that six months was considered the absolute minimum time-frame for this form of treatment. He did agree that we could consider reducing the medication in stages and set a provisional target for me to stop taking the pills by mid-October. At this time, still only a handful of people knew I was taking them at all.

The next thing I wanted to talk to him about was the upcoming ICC Champions Trophy tournament in India, also in October, prior to the start of the tour to Australia in November. Though I was feeling very confident I could cope with the Ashes trip, Tests, one-dayers and everything, India was another prospect.

I cannot say my thinking was entirely rational or even in a straight line, but the memories of what had happened there in February and what took place subsequently were still strong and still awful; I had already started to have flashbacks of the separation anxiety I had suffered in Mumbai and Baroda and the terrible dreams I had had about Hayley and Ellie and I was concerned that returning to the place where they had overwhelmed me might trigger a recurrence. If that happened, from England's point of view, I would have no chance of making the Ashes tour and, on a personal level, what guarantee did I have that I could survive a second all-out war with the illness? Chris listened and agreed. Nothing what .... with this fantastic beguiling country or its wonderful people, but, for the time being at least, it would probably be better for my health if I stayed away from India.

Fortunately, Pakistan proved easier to beat than Sri Lanka. The four-match series started with a high-scoring draw at Lord's, in which KP and I were the only two of our top six not to score hundreds. Ian Bell's not out 100 was England's 100th century at Lord's.

Then, at Old Trafford, Harmison absolutely blitzed them in their first innings, taking six for 19 in thirteen overs as we bowled them out for 119. The pitch was quick and bouncy and Harmison was utterly terrifying, and that was standing 40 yards away at slip, so God knows what it must have been like to bat against him. You got the feeling quite a few of the Pakistan batsmen weren't overkeen on hanging around too long to find out, and who could blame them? At his best and quickest and straightest Harmison was not only bloody hard to play, he was just scary. And when he bowled like that he was comfortably first-choice among batsmen the world over as the fast bowler you would least want to face, which made it so frustrating for everyone, him included, that he could not do it more often.

Cook and Bell followed up their centuries at Lord's with one each here, then Harmison and Monty took five wickets apiece in their second innings to win us the game by an innings and 120 runs.

At Headingley, Bell got his third hundred in successive Tests and, though Pakistan batted better here, Monty and Saj Mahmood bowled them out for 155 and we won by 167 runs to go 2–0 up in the series.

It was just as well for me that the other batters had been in such good form because, apart from a 50 at Headingley, I hadn't been able to buy a run. Maybe my growing concern about the prospect of having to return to India was one of the factors in my loss of form. Maybe I was right about the effect of the pills after all.

*   *   *

With the Test series secured and one final match at The Oval to play, I decided I needed to bring the matter of my availability for the winter tours to a head. Duncan had already heard a whisper that I might be having second thoughts about going to India and he was apparently concerned that I seemed to want to pick and choose my tours, something he was rightly dead against. He and I had discussed the issue several times through the years and I was in complete agreement with his position. We could not have play- ers dictating where they wanted to play and where they didn't. To him, and to me, the Martini principle applied; if you were an Eng- land player you were an England player anytime, any place, any- where, not where and when it suited you.

He was about to arrange a meeting with me to discuss it, when David Graveney intervened and advised him that he should talk to my counsellor from Performance Healthcare. Duncan and David agreed to travel to Taunton for a meeting at my house on the morning of Friday 11 August, in the week between the third and final Tests, to discuss the issue, and, for the first time, to meet and talk with Chris.

It was an off-the-record, informal discussion. It lasted about an hour and, for Duncan in particular, it was an illuminating experience.

I started by explaining that I did not want to go to India for the Champions Trophy because I did not feel I was ready to return to the place where my illness had first flared up so painfully; and I feared going there might make me unwell again. Generally, I was doing okay, I assured Duncan and David, but I felt going to India might put my progress and recovery at risk. I did stress, however, that if I did not go to India I believed I would be fine and ready for Australia.

Duncan reiterated his position and it sounded non-negotiable. He simply did not believe it was right for players to pick and choose and, at this point I wasn't sure whether he was ready to be persuaded.

'I understand completely,' I told him, 'but I am asking for a bit of special help here, some allowance. I'm not saying I don't want to go to India because I don't fancy it. I'm saying I don't want to go because I think it will make me ill.'

Then Chris decided the time had come to place all the cards on the table. Carefully, and in detail, he started to explain the whole start-to-finish story of how I had been so catastrophically affected by depressive illness, the history of what had happened in India, my breakdown, my return, my collapse at Bovey Castle, my partial recovery and my setbacks, from Multan to now and all in between.

As I listened to Chris talk, I watched Duncan's face. It was clearly all news to him. This was the first time he had heard any of the details about my illness, about my anxiety attacks and about the fact that I had been on anti-depressants all summer. Chris also explained how the illness worked, its causes and symptoms and how best to try and stop it recurring.

He explained about the Limbic System – the set of brain struc- tures that control emotion, behaviour and long-term memory – and he discussed the 'flight, fright or freeze' principle, how ancient humans were programmed to react to imminent danger in one of these three ways, and how my programming made me predis- posed to flight.

As the discussion progressed you could see the colour drain out of Duncan's cheeks. Up to this moment I truly believe he hadn't really had a clue about what had been wrong with me. What little David Graveney had known he had been sworn to secrecy over. But I don't think even he was aware of the full picture, or the full extent of my symptoms.

Duncan's response was interesting: 'I just didn't realize it was that bad,' he said. 'I've never had the illness explained to me in these terms before. I was pretty naïve.'

Chris then explained that why, in his professional medical opinion, going to India, where I had first succumbed to the full force of the illness, might trigger further problems.

'Marcus has regained his confidence to a level where he can play Test cricket,' said Chris. 'But the chances are if he were to go to India he would end up feeling overwhelmingly anxious, suffer a setback and that might well jeopardize his recovery.'

He made it clear, on the other hand, that if I didn't go to the Champions Trophy he could all but guarantee I would be ready and available for the whole of the Ashes tour.

It took some time for Duncan and David to digest what they had been told, which was hardly surprising as almost all of it had come completely out of the blue. By the time the meeting broke up, however, they had accepted everything Chris had said. Duncan even went so far as to raise other instances of players disappearing from the game for reasons that weren't apparent at the time but which now appeared to him to make perfect sense.

To my great relief it was agreed all round that the best course of action was for me to miss the Champions Trophy in India in October and travel to Australia in early November. In the meantime, I would complete the summer's Test series at The Oval, then play in the Twenty20 and five-match one-day series against Pakistan.

There was no tearing hurry to make the decision public. As the squads for all the winter commitments were not due to be announced for a further month, on Tuesday 12 September, two days after the fifth and final one-day match against Pakistan at Edgbaston, there was plenty of time for a statement to be prepared explaining why I was not considered for selection, which Chris would help I draft, and it could be released on the day the squads were announced. This time, however, it would reveal the real reasons.

Chris stayed for a while after David and Duncan had left. He had decided that, while the right decision had been made for now, and he was sure I would be okay for the Ashes, it would be vital to my chances of making a complete recovery in the long term if I could actually face the trauma of what had happened in India and get it out of my system. If I didn't, he warned, it might sit inside me, smouldering, and return to burn me later. He asked me to write down what I had felt in Mumbai and Baroda, to leave nothing out, no matter how personal or painful the content might be.

It took me a few days to write because the memories were so vivid and so upsetting. When I was writing about these experiences, it was almost as though I was re-living them. I felt the same shiver down my back and I ended up crying and writing at the same time. I only read it a couple of times because each time I did everything I had written about seemed so vivid and so real. Later, when I was doing a spring clean, I came across it again. Reading it was such a harrowing experience that I took the notepad down to the bins and ripped it to shreds.

Travelling to London for the final Test of the series a few days after the meeting, I was looking forward to completing the job I had started back in May, to get back into the England side and to prove I was worth my place. A third victory was the target, of course, but a nice and easy batting draw would be good enough.

Then, if I got through the one-dayers as I was sure I could, I would be able to concentrate on getting myself fully well and ready for Australia without any distractions and, once there, I would be able and ready to throw myself into our efforts to retain the Ashes.

Nice idea. Shame about how things turned out.

*   *   *

For the first three days of the fourth and final Test at The Oval we were totally dominated by Pakistan, who, on a belting pitch, finally turned up. Mohammad Asif and Umar Gul were excellent and we were not. They bowled us out for 173. Then, thanks to openers Mohammad Hafeez and Imran Farhat, who both made 90s and Mohammad Yousuf, who scored 128, they reached 504 all out and a lead of 331. On the Sunday morning, I failed again in the second innings, though I was in just about long enough to get involved in some ridiculous sledging with their short leg fielder Faisal Iqbal, nephew of the great Pakistan hero Javed Miandad.

Sledging very rarely bothered me, but I certainly wasn't one of those who enjoy being targeted because it keeps me fired up. What I did know was that if I started to answer back, then my attention wasn't where it should have been. Faisal Iqbal had a well-earned reputation for his verbals but he wasn't even sledging me directly at first, more coming up with general stuff. I just turned to him and said, 'Mate, why don't you shut the f**k up?' That set him off and he started giving me heaps. 'Trescothick,' he said under the helmet, 'you're playing your last couple of Tests. When you get to Australia Brett Lee is going to kill you.' It was pretty standard fare and, in normal circumstances, I wouldn't have given it a moment's notice, but something went inside me and I gave him a real volley.

'Listen, mate,' I told him. 'You're only playing because your uncle's bloody Javed Miandad. What are you averaging? Twenty-five? You ain't going to make a Test career out of that.'

Inevitably, two balls later I nicked one to Kamran Akmal and, of course, Faisal gave me a right send-off as I dragged myself away. What did I say at the very start of the book about the perfect way to end an England career? Trescothick c Kamran Akmal b Mohammad Asif 4, sledged to death by a chirpy short-leg, was not exactly what I had in mind for what turned out to be my final Test innings.

Strauss made our first half of the match and put on a century for the second wicket with Cook. By now most of the problems were being posed by Danish Kaneria's leg-spin rather than the pace bowlers who had been so effective in the first innings. But Cook and KP were looking comfortable, as they put on another ton. And then, from nowhere, Umar Gul produced a fantastic inswinging yorker to have Cook plumb lbw. KP then tickled an edge to the keeper off Shahid Nazir and we were 277 for four. The ball had started to reverse-swing and pose huge problems for the incoming batsmen Ian Bell and Paul Collingwood. There was nothing untoward in that. Reverse-swing had been our great weapon against Australia the previous summer, after all, and it is not necessary to tamper with the ball to make it happen, only to look after it properly. I got out the binoculars for a closer look.

I concentrated on Mohammad Asif because he was taking charge of shining the ball at mid-off, which was my job in our team. The next few minutes were pretty comical as I tried to watch him through the glasses without being spotted myself. If Asif glanced up at our balcony I immediately dropped the bins down on my lap so he could not see me looking at him, though I think he clocked me eventually. Before I knew they had the cameras on me, Sky then broadcast pictures of me bird-watching.

Then we noticed that the umpire Darrell Hair was starting to take as much interest in the ball as we were.

Just after 2.30 on that fateful afternoon of Sunday 20 August, when Trevor Jesty, the fourth umpire, ran out to the middle with a box of balls, most people in the ground or watching on the box, must have surmised that the ball was about to be replaced because it had gone out of shape. Inside the dressing-room, however, it was a different story. We sensed immediately that something was going to kick off. As Hair and his fellow umpire Billy Doctrove from the West Indies, first showed the ball to Inzy, their skipper, but then offered the choice of a replacement ball to the batsmen, Paul Collingwood, our suspicions were confirmed. Umpires only offer the choice of a new ball to the batsmen for one reason, that they think the one currently being used has been tampered with. Put bluntly, they had decided Pakistan had been cheating.

Uh-oh.

Afterwards, reports suggested that we had started the ball rolling when Duncan had gone in to see the match referee Mike Procter before the start of play. One word. Cobblers.

Strangely, nothing much else happened for a while. Inzy had obviously been unsettled by the incident but he didn't seem to make much of a fuss on the field when Darrell tapped his left shoulder with his right hand, the signal that he was awarding five penalty runs to England and, after that, the game seemed to continue as though everything had been perfectly normal. Even when Bell and Colly came back into our dressing-room at about 3.45, after play stopped for bad light and an early tea, and talked us through what had happened, there was no inkling of what was about to take place.

At about 4.45, the dressing-room bell went to signal that the umpires had decided the light was okay to continue and it was time for the match to resume. Only it never did.

The umpires went out and, as per protocol, the batsmen, Bell and Colly waited until the fielding side went out before going back to the middle. And waited. And waited. And waited. There was no sign of them, in fact we could actually see their dressing-room door next to ours firmly shut. What we didn't know for sure, but some of us had already begun guessing, was that the full implications of being punished for ball-tampering had now dawned on them. We learned later that they saw this as a slur on the integrity of the Pakistan nation, they believed they had been found guilty without a fair trial and were determined to make their anger known. Meanwhile, having paid good money to watch cricket and there being none to watch, the crowd were starting to get more restless and considerably more vocal.

With no fielding side actually on the field, Hair and Doctrove came back indoors. Ten minutes later, after inviting Bell and Colly to join them, they all trooped back on again and, when they reached the middle this time, Hair removed the bails, his signal that the match was over. The umpires had decided that by refusing to continue Pakistan had forfeited the match and awarded it to England.

The match may have been over, but no one was leaving. The crowd were by now in a state of utter confusion, and things did not look a whole lot clearer from where we were sitting.

Meanwhile the management were going about quietly reminding us how we should be seen to be behaving, though most of us were just in vague shock. Duncan and Phil Neale and others stressed to us that, however events played out from here, it was vital that we acted responsibly so as not to risk inflaming an already volatile situation. The cameras were going to be on us constantly looking for reaction shots, so no one should be seen to be laughing or joking around. Keep your heads down and out of sight was the order of the day.

Just after five o'clock the ECB chairman David Morgan arrived from thin air and went into the Pakistan dressing-room. Morgan was a consummate politician who did some of his best work in the shadows and later was elected ICC chairman. If anyone could sort things out now it would be him.

Five minutes later someone emerged from their dressing-room with a thumbs-up. Morgan came into our dressing-room and said the game was back on. Then, to loud booing from the crowd, Inzy took his lads back out. Two minutes later, this time with no umpires in sight, they came back in again to even louder boos. All of which KP recorded on his video camera, presumably unseen by the management.

The Pakistan Board chairman Shaharyar Khan then explained that, while they had originally refused to take the field in order to make a short protest at the accusation of cheating, his team was now happy to resume play, but there was no more action for the day, at least not on the field, though some of the beer-snakes the crowd were putting together to keep themselves amused were mightily impressive. How many plastic pint 'glasses' do you need to make a 40 ft snake? A lot.

Just before 6.15, to even more boos, it was announced that play had been abandoned, but only for the day.

Talks continued well into the night, with both teams ready to start again, but now the umpires wouldn't budge. As they saw things, they had followed the letter of the laws of the game first by penalizing the Pakistan team for ball-tampering and then, after Pakistan had refused to continue the game, by awarding it to us. They were in charge and they wouldn't be persuaded to compromise.

We returned to our hotel, the City Grange and, later, when the official announcement was made that the game was over, a surreal atmosphere descended as we did our best to try and 'celebrate' our win with a few beers. Richard Bevan came up with the suggestion that we should donate our win bonus, around £60,000, to charity and we readily agreed, but the difference between that night and our night of nights a year earlier could not have been more marked. The following morning we realized someone had forgotten to book the open-topped bus.

The fall-out from the first forfeited match in 129 years of Test cricket was mind-boggling and went on for months, during which time an ICC enquiry, led by chief referee Ranjan Madugalle, cleared Inzy of ball tampering but banned him for four one-dayers for bringing the game into disrepute by refusing to resume the match. The ICC revealed Hair had demanded $500,000 for loss of earnings to quit cricket, then stood him down for the Champions Trophy because of 'concerns over his safety and security' and finally sacked him from officiating in full ICC international matches. He was eventually brought back in 2008.

At the time, Darrell appeared to pay the price for doing what he saw as his job. Even so, I can't help wondering if all the controversy and bad publicity for the game could have been avoided, let alone how much of the rain-forest might have been saved, had he had a quiet word with Inzy as soon as his suspicions were raised and warned him what action he might take.

For a few days it looked as though our one-day series with Pakistan might be cancelled. But everyone calmed down sufficiently for it to go ahead, starting with a Twenty20 match in Bristol on 28 August.

I wasn't in the greatest nick, but I did manage to make 53, my last half-century in international cricket, though we were comfortably second best. Indeed, it might have been argued that, as I wasn't going to India, England should have omitted me from the five-match ODI series in order to give my replacement a chance to bed into the side. But Duncan and David said their priority was to win the matches immediately in front of them and let the future look after itself and, after the 5–0 hammering handed out to us by Sri Lanka, you could see their point. In any case, I was still very much part of their plans for the one-dayers in Australia and the World Cup, so the less disruption to the side the better.

By the time we pitched up in Cardiff for the first match, Chris had begun drafting his contribution to the statement to be released to coincide with the announcement that I would not be going to the Champions Trophy and I felt ready for the truth to be told at last, if a little uncertain as to how people might react. Part of me still wondered whether I could carry on hiding, but we had to have a good reason to tell the public why I wasn't going to India and, in any case, my concern about having to admit to my illness and the fact that I had misled the public back in April was overridden by the feeling that I had simply had enough of bullshitting and lying and having to remember what I told 'A' and what I said to 'B' to keep those lies alive.

I was definitely feeling better and more able to understand the process of my illness, how it worked and what it was, and I was much more comfortable with the idea that people could handle the truth without thinking too badly of me. It was time to confirm what some people already knew and most must have guessed by now. It was time to come clean.

But the time had to brought forward unexpectedly when, after a rain-ruined match in Wales and a Duckworth–Lewis defeat at Lord's, we arrived at the Rose Bowl for the third match, a day–night match under lights on Tuesday 5 September.

First things first, or rather last things first.

I took guard brilliantly. My eye-to-eye contact with the bowler Shoaib Akhtar was impressive. My looking around to see where I could take one off the mark and at the gaps and open spaces to hit over or through the field could not be faulted. And my walking back to the dressing-room was exemplary. It was the one ball I faced that was the problem. I missed it. It was a decent ball at a decent pace and I just missed it. It could have happened at any stage in my career. It just so happened this was my last innings for England. That's all folks.

I had no way of knowing, but the press box was buzzing with rumours. Though the timing of the announcement was still a week away, the *Sun* had got hold of the story that I was not going to India for the Champions Trophy and were preparing to print it the next day. After close of play, I was approached by James Avery, our media relations man for one-day cricket. He was looking a bit sheepish. And then he told me why. The *Sun* had been tipped off that I was not going to India and they were going to run the story the next day. In the circumstances, James explained, it was probably best to bring the announcement forward and arrangements to do so the next day were already in hand.

I had given up trying to work out how these leaks happen and I was pretty much past caring. It wasn't great news, but I did feel a tinge of relief that the issue was finally going to be put to bed, and soon.

I walked down the pavilion steps to be met by a posse of about 15 reporters. 'Hi, lads,' I said. 'What's up?'

'Sorry, Marcus,' someone piped up. 'We think the *Sun* have been tipped off that you are pulling out of the Champions Trophy. Can you confirm that's correct?'

I didn't, in so many words. But I was a bit miffed that someone had leaked the information in the first place and I decided to give them a firm steer in the right direction. 'I can't confirm anything at the moment,' I told them, 'but there is a statement coming out tomorrow and you'll have to wait for that.'

The next morning they all ran the story and, in due course, the ECB statement was released:

'Following specialist medical advice received by the England selectors,' it read, 'opening batsman Marcus Trescothick will not be named in the 14-man squad for October's ICC Champions Trophy in India.

'The selectors have been pleased to learn that the treatment Marcus has been receiving throughout the summer has resulted in very positive progress and that he is expected to be fit to resume playing for England prior to the Ashes Tour.

'A spokesman for Performance Healthcare, the specialists treating Trescothick said: "After his return from the tour of India in March, Marcus sought specialist help for his ongoing symptoms. In addition to the deleterious effects of the acquired gastrointestinal infection on his health, it later became evident that he was also suffering from an underlying stress-related illness.

"He has been receiving specialist treatment, which has allowed him to resume his position in the England team. However, we believe it would be premature for him to tour India in October. Rest is an important part of his treatment and he will need recovery time before the Ashes tour of Australia which begins in November."'

Not only was I relieved that the truth was out, I was also relieved initially that Duncan and the selectors decided to bring in Ed Joyce to replace me, not only because it gave me some breathing space, but also because my form was wobbling. The feeling didn't last long, however. I stayed around to do twelfth-man duties for the last two matches and we won them to draw the series 2–2, but I've rarely felt so dejected because I was not part of anything that was going on.

I'd enjoyed being a big part of all our success during the past six years and I recall thinking to myself that I never, ever wanted to feel like the odd man out again. It felt like it was someone else's team.

Chapter 19

THE FIGHT IS OVER

'I sat on the couch, facing the wall, with my head in my hands, just crying my eyes out ... As I placed the navy blue cap with the three lions in my bag I stopped for a moment, turned to Mark and said: "This is probably the last time I'm ever going to wear this".'

If things had turned out differently, or rather very differently, our Ashes rematch with Australia over the winter of 2006–07 could have been a classic.

Injuries happen, of course, but I have often wondered what we might have achieved if the 11 players who played in the first four Ashes Tests of the 2005 summer, plus Paul Collingwood, drafted in for Simon Jones for the fifth, had been able to stay on the field and in form in the intervening 14 months, and beyond.

Trescothick, Strauss, Vaughan (captain), Bell, Pietersen, Flintoff, G. Jones (wkt), Giles, Hoggard, Harmison, S. Jones. No disrespect to the players who came in to replace those injured, but I would have loved to have seen how that XI might have developed with another 13 Tests' worth of experience under its belt – three in Pakistan, three in India, three against Sri Lanka and four more against

Pakistan. I'm sure such feelings were in the forefront of the minds of the management and selectors not only when it came to choosing the squad for the five-Test series, but also for the first Test in Brisbane on Thursday 23 November.

Injured players? Try a hospital ward full of them. Michael Vaughan had not played since the Pakistan tour, nor had Simon Jones, nor Ashley Giles. Harmison had missed the first series of the summer against Sri Lanka and Fred's ankle had forced him to miss the second series against Pakistan. And then there was me.

When we drenched The Oval in champagne that incredible September evening, then fought through industrial strength hangovers at Trafalgar Square the next day, we weren't just celebrating beating Australia, we were basking in the feeling that we were about to become the best side in the world. Every single one of us felt that this was only the start of what we were destined to achieve as a team. It would never have crossed our minds that it was, in fact, the end.

Five seriously injured players and one seriously ill out of eleven, in little over a year. Whatever happened to the law of averages? And I'm certain the tension within the side caused by the uncertainty created by such a turnover was worth at least another player to us, possibly two. I was only in Australia for ten days, as it turned out, and for some of those I wasn't exactly in the best frame of mind for serious analysis, but from our build-up and what I did see before the illness returned to slaughter me again, I saw enough to know what was about to happen with or without me. I knew from the start that the environment within the camp wasn't right and I could sense the feeling that everyone else knew it as well. For all kinds of reasons we were not the team we had been and that meant the next three months were going to be very hard work indeed.

Australia is a demanding and challenging place to play at the best of times but, from the moment we arrived, it seemed like everyone wanted to fight us. Even the hotel staff and the restaurant waiters would say things like 'You know you're going to get your arses kicked, don't you?' For players like the captain Ricky Ponting and my good friend Justin Langer, winning the Ashes back looked like their mission in life, while Shane Warne and Glenn McGrath merely saw this as the perfect way to end their fantastic careers. It had really hurt the Australian public that we had beaten their champions in 2005 after they had dominated us for so long. They didn't just want revenge, they wanted an annihilation. The atmosphere couldn't have been more belligerent if the Aussie government had declared war on the England cricket team and issued a national call to arms. Any chance to make life uncomfortable for the Poms must be taken, and that extended to the home media who were all over us like a rash. Our own press had been writing up this rematch almost from the moment the last series ended and the intensity of the hype was almost painful. What is more, while we didn't believe they were hoping for us to fail, the very fact that the level of expectation was so high meant that if things started to go wrong, we would cop it massively.

We'd known what to expect, and some of it was done with a smile. But I've never ever experienced such open and unbridled hostility and, as a group, I just don't think we had the togetherness required to deal with it. As for me, I felt under pressure from the start.

From a purely cricketing perspective I had been nervous about the prospect of what awaited us down under. I kept comparing now with then. Then we had been strong, solid, with no weak links. We had had Duncan and Vaughan at the top, with a core of experienced players underneath. There had been a collective belief in the team structure, everyone knew their part in it and there were no gaps. This time there were gaps. Everyone could see it. The guys were too quiet and too nervous. We weren't training as hard, nor would we talk so openly in team meetings. The feeling 'We can beat these blokes' that had sustained us last time, even after they had won the first Test at Lord's, was gradually and inevitably replaced by the feeling 'We *cannot* beat these blokes'.

Maybe that is where we needed and missed Vaughan most. I'm not suggesting his presence would have made a huge difference to the final outcome, but his absence certainly did. His knack of seeing the signs on and off the park, the behind-the-scenes chats that would lift you when you needed to be lifted, the right word at the right time, the little bit of inspiration he offered when you needed it most, and the ability to delegate so that everyone was sure of his role in the set-up. Most of all we missed his ability to get the best out of Fred.

So when Australia began to take control and our level of performance dropped we never had the belief or the drive to raise it again.

As things turned out and as I had feared, Fred was simply unable to do everything he needed to do as a batsman and bowler if we were to stand any chance while carrying the burden of trying to lead an increasingly dispirited side. No one could have done. He tried his Superman-sized heart out but sometimes you need more than the ability to run faster than a speeding bullet or leap tall buildings with a single bound. In the end his sense of disappointment and isolation eventually caused him to try to kill his sorrows in his own way. When he fell off a pedalo into the Caribbean Sea a few months later, the issue erupted spectacularly into the public domain. And, as well as me actually leaving before the series began, certain other players seemed to be overpowered when it mattered most. The upshot was Australia, still the best side in the world, totally overpowered us from the moment poor Harmy sent down the widest opening delivery in Ashes history at the Gabba, the cue for headlines like 'Wide they bother?' And if confirmation were needed that the cause was hopeless, it came when they won the second Test, in Adelaide, after our first innings 551 for six dec. should have made defeat impossible. The tears streaming down Fred's cheeks as he tried valiantly to bowl them out in their second innings run chase said it all. His resistance was broken and so was ours. By the end, the principle of 'getting in their space' that had informed so much of our thinking in 2005 just seemed a faint and faintly pathetic memory. We lost 5–0 and we were lucky to get nil.

As the tour unravelled, so the blame game started. Was it a mistake to take Trescothick in the first place? Had Duncan become too powerful in selection? Did Fred get enough support? Why did they make Fred captain and not Strauss? Why did they insist on sticking to the 2005 side? Why didn't they pick Monty Panesar ahead of Giles from the start, or Saj Mahmood ahead of Harmison? Was Harmison fit? Didn't they realize he wouldn't be able to handle the pressure? Why was the bowling coach Troy Cooley, so vital in getting world-class performances out of our Ashes-winning pace quartet, allowed to go back and work for his native country? Why did they go back to Geraint Jones as keeper when Chris Read had replaced him the previous summer? Why did they appoint Jones to the management committee when he might have to have a say in his own selection? Why did they think it was a good idea for Vaughan to continue his rehab in Australia when Fred was trying to run the side and the presence of the 'real' captain was bound to cast a shadow? Who were 'they' anyway? Who was actually in charge? And whose fault was it?

The ECB, in their wisdom, and their embarrassment at having their ears bent by numerous travelling England supporters complaining that they had not paid out all that money and come all that way to be so humiliated, reacted by announcing SOMETHING MUST BE DONE. Unbeknown to Duncan or any of us, they set up a committee to decide what had gone wrong. Under a former golf administrator named Ken Schofield, a load of blokes who had never won the Ashes for England sat in judgement on a coach, a group of selectors, a management team and players who had. They came up with the Schofield Report some months later, in which they seemed to completely ignore 2005 and the terrible disruption caused by injuries to key players since then, and blame almost everything on Duncan, including global warming and deforestation. Immediately after the end of the World Cup in West Indies, Duncan was sacked. David Graveney lasted until the end of the year.

Most of which, of course, passed me by, except the first of those questions.

Was it a mistake for me to go? I didn't think so at the time, nor did Chris, nor did the selectors. Were we right, or wrong? Or were we right at first but subsequently proved wrong?

In hindsight, had I been the only absentee from the Ashes winning team, everyone might have been more inclined, myself included, for me to take a full winter off, to continue my recovery at home in a non-pressure situation. Medicine is an inexact science, of course, and no doctor alive can tell you with utter certainty how long someone suffering from depressive illness will actually need not just to get back on his feet but to be fully well. It looks as though I needed longer than I thought I did. But the Ashes seemed so important to everyone, and, without Vaughan, I just felt I had to make the tour if I possibly could. Maybe I had read one too many references to how indispensable I was to our chances of retaining the Ashes.

What is certain is that nothing more could have been done to make it possible for me to at least try. At one point I even went so far as to enlist the services of a hypnotist, though I very quickly wished I hadn't.

*   *   *

My sessions with Chris continued through September and October 2006. With the flight for Sydney leaving on Friday 3 November, we spoke about the potential pitfalls and problems I would encounter in Australia, about how I might be the target for some special treatment from the crowds or even the opposition, especially as one of the drawbacks of going public about my illness was that the Aussies now know about it as well, and what Steve Waugh had termed 'mental disintegration' had always been one of their major weapons.

I had also discussed these issues with Steve Bull, our team psychologist and the new team doctor Nick Pierce and, though I did have some concerns, I felt strong enough to handle anything they might use to try and put me off my stroke.

Generally I was now making good progress and, reducing the medication incrementally, I was on course to quit taking the pills altogether by my target date of 8 October and I did, which I took as a real tangible sign that if not completely cured, I was well on the road to recovery. And when I gave an interview to the *Daily Mirror* the following week, I was ready to say so.

'The constant treadmill of playing, training and being away from home non-stop took its toll,' I told the paper, 'But now the buzz is back, the energy is back. I'm fit and raring to go. I want to get on the plane now. I want to get going and feel the bat in my hands again.

'There are lots of people who have experienced the things I've been experiencing – but not all of them open the batting for England and have to try and put on a brave face in public. But … an extended break has given me both the chance to take stock and the boost I needed to kick on again.'

Doing well in the Ashes and World Cup would be 'perfect therapy'. Was I trying to persuade myself or was this what I truly believed? Perhaps a bit of both.

*   *   *

In the remaining fortnight prior to departure I threw myself into the normal pre-tour preparations, all my training and all my practice. Any slight fears I had about being separated from home seemed under control because Hayley and Ellie were due to come out to Australia very early on in the tour and stay throughout.

Originally we had tried to persuade Duncan that the wives, girlfriends and families should be allowed to come with us from the start, but he was dead against it. In fact his initial response was that they shouldn't arrive in Australia until after the first two Tests had been played, a month into the tour. Eventually he agreed to a compromise, that they could come out from the start of the Test series, in Brisbane, but that they should arrive there three days before we did to enable them to get over jet lag and so not disturb our sleep patterns too much when they arrived.

As far as I was concerned, though I was starting to get a little edgy, I was further encouraged that there were no really strong indications that anything was amiss, no shivers; but even now Hayley was not so sure. She never said so at the time because she didn't want to upset me or risk planting a seed of doubt in my mind, but later she told me: 'You weren't yourself. I knew you weren't right before you went. I'm actually surprised you did go.'

In hindsight, what happened next should probably have given me a clue. I got a call from my mum and dad telling me that they had had a letter from a hypnotist who told them he was convinced he could cure me completely and quickly.

I was more than happy with the way my treatment had been going, but, believe me, when you have been through what I had, you are prepared to listen to anyone and anything. I'd heard cases of a hypnotist washing out your brain, curing people in two sessions, saying 'There you go, you're fixed'. If he really could do that for me, surely it was worth trying, so I asked Chris what he thought and, though he couldn't quite hide the scepticism in his voice, he said he didn't have a problem with it.

Mum and dad passed on the letter and what struck me first and foremost was that this guy said he had worked with Paul McKenna.

It sounds a bit daft now, of course, and looking back, deep down I must have been so desperate for a cure, wherever it came from, that I was susceptible to such wishful thinking, but mention of McKenna's name made me think 'Now we're talking.' I'd seen on TV what that guy could do, taking people back in their mind to their childhood and reprogramming them as chickens so that they ran around the stage squawking and flapping their wings. Something inside me said if this guy could do what McKenna could do, maybe he could reprogramme me to go back to the time before I was ill and all would be well again. So I decided to do some research and checked him out on the internet. It all looked fine, so I rang him.

I explained I was going away in a couple of weeks and asked him when we could meet.

'What are you doing now?' he asked. 'Not much,' I replied, a little taken aback that he appeared to be available at such short notice. 'I'm just walking round town.'

'I'll come down now,' he said, and I agreed.

I tried to imagine what might be about to happen.

'You're getting sleepy,' he would say, then once I had drifted off, he would reset my thought-patterns like rebooting a computer and away I'd go. I also tried to paint a mental picture of what he might look like. If he was as good as he said he was, people would be willing to pay whatever he asked to be cured. So he must be rolling in it, I thought. And then he turned up at my house in a green Vauxhall Corsa with a 1.2-litre engine.

The session lasted about an hour and a half. First, he talked me through a process whereby if I started to feel bad I should tap myself on the hands and the wrists and that would make me feel better. People swore by this method, he said. I'm sure they did.

The next thing that happened was that he asked me if we had a full length mirror in the house. Before I could stop myself I said: 'Yes. It's in the bedroom' and before I knew it he was following me upstairs.

It was too late. I had to go through with it now.

He made me stand in front of the mirror. I was to look myself straight in the eye, he instructed, and repeat after him whatever he said.

'I do love myself,' he said.

'I do love myself', I said.

'I'm really happy with myself,' he said.

'I'm really happy with myself,' I said.

'I am a good batsman,' he said.

'I am a good batsman,' I said.

Then he asked me to say things about my cricket, that I'd played for England for this long and that I'd scored that number of runs etc.

By now I may have been saying: 'I have scored 14 Test hundreds', but what I was actually thinking was 'What the f**k *am* I doing?'

Then, when he told me his rates, I felt even worse.

'I normally charge £700 per session,' he informed me, 'but I'll take £500.'

I walked downstairs thinking to myself: 'What on earth have I just done?'

I bade him farewell, told him I'd send him a cheque, which I did, and spent the rest of the day in shock. I was gutted. I'd wanted a miracle cure, to be taken to a better place. And all I got was taken for five hundred quid.

* * *

Hayley and I left Ellie with her folks the day before I was due on the plane down under and spent the night at a hotel near Heathrow. When we parted on Saturday 3 November I felt fine. We would only be apart for two weeks. Surely I could manage two weeks. I lasted nine days.

For the first couple I felt okay. Leaving home, Hayley and Ellie had been less painful than I had anticipated and it helped that, after dropping a couple of sleeping tablets to get through the never-ending flight, we were straight down to business.

Our first engagement, on Monday 6 November was a media day at the Sydney Cricket Ground. At the start of most tours there is an arrangement whereby all the home media, radio, TV and newspapers are offered the chance to interview individuals players at some length either one-on-ones or in groups. I hadn't exactly been counting down the hours for this one, but I had met with Colin Gibson and Andrew Walpole in advance, we had discussed what might be asked and how I should answer and once it started I got into the swing pretty quickly. When it came to my turn to present myself to a fair-sized gathering of English and Aussie journalists, I was ready for the inevitable questions about dealing with sledging etc. and events in India and thereafter

'I'm pretty sure something will be said along the way,' I told them, 'but I have to accept that is going to be part of the tour. If I thought to myself that nothing was going to happen, went into a Test match and suddenly got hit by a barrage of everything I didn't want to hear, it would probably catch me by surprise. But I am expecting the worst.'

I also spoke in some detail about my illness and why I had not been more open about it sooner.

'I didn't want to show people anything was wrong,' I explained. 'You just want to carry on and go about your job. You feel like a bit of a failure, if you like. You feel like you're giving in to something, and the term stress-related illness has got a bit of a stigma attached to it. To give in and finally come out and say what had happened was, for me, the best thing I could do.'

Walpole told me afterwards that he thought I seemed very composed and relaxed and that after listening in to the first ten minutes or so of my press conference he was so confident that I was okay that he moved on to deal with requests to speak to other players. He also said that several Aussie journalists had told him how impressed they were at how I handled myself. Little did they, or anyone else know, I had been absolutely cacking myself and that, already, after just three days, my mood had already begun to change for the worse.

I tried to fight it, I tried to summon up all my strength and, at first, genuinely believed that once I had got past the no-sleep disorientation of jet lag and the usual early-tour discomfort, I might still be okay. And, at least attempting to draw on past experience and learn from past mistakes, I decided I should try and confide in those closest to me.

I first talked to Strauss, on the face of it mainly to emphasize how much I was looking forward to Hayley and Ellie coming out at the start of the following week. We planned a solid weights session in the gym one afternoon and I realized I just wasn't into it. Did he suspect? I suspect so.

Then, on Thursday 9 November, on the way to Canberra for our next appointment, a one-day match on the Friday against the Australian Prime Minister's XI, I spoke to Giles.

'Mate, I'm struggling,' I told him. 'I'm not sleeping and I'm starting to get a bit anxious. Can you just keep an eye on me?' Ash was surprised. Of course he would do what he could, he said, but he hadn't noticed anything wrong.

Sharing my concerns didn't really work. I'm sure Strauss and Giles were happy to try and help. The problem was that, deep down, I knew the last thing they needed as they started to prepare for the hardest job in their entire careers was having to try to help me from going off the rails again.

On the field, setting the trend for later events, we were hammered by 166 runs. They scored 347 for five from 50 overs and we were dismissed for 181 with 68 balls remaining. I made two.

By now I feared another breakdown was only a matter of time.

The next day, Saturday 11 November, the day before our first proper match of the tour, against New South Wales, was due to start at the SCG, I left the hotel with Strauss, Giles, Harmison and a few more of the lads to get some lunch.

Shiver.

I spotted the photographer straight away. *Shiver.* As soon as he emerged from the shadows opposite he started snapping. He followed us all the way into the city centre, snapping away and each time I heard the motor drive on his camera, *shiver, shiver, shiver.*

I sat there at lunch not saying a word. Later we went to see U2 in concert at the Telstra Dome and it completely passed me by. If anyone asked me what was wrong, I put it down to tiredness, but I don't think I was kidding anyone. All I was actually doing was hanging on.

I asked to see Nick Pierce and when he realised the state I was in, he immediately suggested I go back on medication. This was a deep and bitter blow. Just as, to me, coming off the medication the previous month meant I was getting better, Nick recommending I should start taking the pills again meant exactly the opposite. But by then I simply had no choice. I still insisted that I thought I would be able to get through this and that I wanted to carry on trying and carry on fighting. And if I could arrange for Hayley and Ellie to come out as soon as possible I might still be all right to carry on.

He didn't really say much in response to that, but I'm sure he knew he needed to put certain people in the picture, and not only about my request for a change in the girls' travel plans.

The remaining 72 hours of my tour are something of a blur. My mood was still swinging wildly, between something approaching despair and spells when I would get a bit of energy from somewhere and things wouldn't seem so awful. One minute it was: 'I can get through these problems and I will', the next it was 'F***ing hell, I can't do this.' And all the what-ifs came flooding over me again.

I had spoken to Hayley by now, told her I was becoming anxious and asked if it would be possible for her to come out with Ellie earlier than originally planned, and straight into Adelaide, our next port of call. I spoke to the management about this and the discussions were ongoing, though Duncan was clearly not over-keen.

I didn't really know whether I was coming or going by that stage and the effect was obvious when, after NSW won the toss and batted the following morning, I was called into action for the first time. Simon Katich edged a ball off Fred and I dropped the kind of catch that I would normally have taken with my eyes closed. Perhaps my eyes were closed. Watching this unfold, Strauss immediately feared the worst. Somehow, I continued to hold the symptoms in check for the rest of that day, and even, amazingly, managed to hold on to three other catches.

I spent another restless, fitful night, my mood still fluctuating wildly and the following day I played my last innings for England. It was a scrappy non-event, ended when I dragged one on from Brett Lee. When I got back to the dressing-room I asked Nick if he would come and sit with me for a chat. My last hope, I believed, was to get Hayley and Ellie out there now. He said he would see what could be done.

That evening I saw Nick again and told him things had got worse. Whatever I had said earlier about bringing my family out as soon as possible, he must have known at this point that my tour was almost certainly over. By the end of the next day, it was.

I didn't sleep a wink. The separation anxiety had kicked in and was starting to fill my senses again. I tried to stay calm, to rationalize my situation, to regulate my breathing, to do all the things Chris and I had discussed back home should the need arise. But inside the battle began in earnest and the emotions were just too strong. I couldn't believe it. I really thought I had cracked it. Maybe I had and that would turn out to be a small relapse. Yes, that was it. I could fight it and this time I would win. The girls would be here in a few days and everything would settle down again and I would be all right. This time I would be all right. Who was I kidding? I'd tried to fight it before and it had nearly killed me. And now I've let everyone down again. I said I was all right and I wasn't. I said all that stuff about being prepared for the worst and I told Duncan and David Graveney and Chris and Nick I could handle this. And now this. What's happening at home? Is Hayley all right? And Ellie? My beautiful little girl, was she okay? And was she crying and calling for me and asking Hayley why I wasn't there? And what if I had to come home? And what if my career was over? And what if I really could never be well again? And what if I had to go away? And what if I had to go to hospital? And what if my contract was cancelled? And what if? And what if? And what if? And on and on and here I go again and oh God, MAKE IT STOP…

Early on that final day of my final match for England, Tuesday 14 November, Fred came off the pitch for a break and was called into a meeting with Duncan, Matthew Maynard, the assistant coach, and Nick. Fred had sensed I wasn't right but had no real idea of the severity of the problem. During the meeting they discussed how I was, and what should be done about it. Fred was supportive of the idea that Hayley and Ellie should be sent for, but Duncan was clear in his own mind that things had gone too far and wanted to take firm and positive action. After some persuading they accepted Duncan's decision, that I should be sent home immediately after the match. Duncan, suffering from a migraine, went to lie down on the physio's couch. There he was pondering how best to tell me when Nick came in around mid-afternoon and told him: 'It's Tres, Duncan. Can we clear the room?'

All day long in the field the feelings had been growing more and more intense. And then, as though someone flicked a switch, I knew it was over. I asked the umpire if I could go off for a leak and I never came back. As I started to walk back to the pavilion the tears began to well up. With each step the understanding grew within me that what was about to happen would put my career in dire jeopardy. I knew that I would be letting down a great number of people, friends, family, colleagues and I knew that I no longer had any say in the matter. The illness had come back, the bastard had returned, and the shadow cast by its black wings had consumed me again. The fight was over. I had no fight left.

The moment I got back in the dressing-room I broke down completely. Nick, having asked Duncan to vacate the physio's room, took me in there and we were joined by Mark Saxby, our masseur and Nigel Stockhill also came in. I sat on the couch, facing the wall, with my head in my hands, just crying my eyes out. They tried to comfort me but I was inconsolable, I was weak and pathetic and letting everyone down.

All the same feelings of irrational fear, despair and panic that had taken over my whole being that day in Baroda, came back in wave after bloody great wave. I didn't want to admit to having failed. But I had to get rid of all these feelings or I was going to go and throw myself off the top of the pavilion. It took about 20 minutes for me to calm down enough and to stop crying long enough to even speak.

As I started to come round I wondered about phoning Hayley but I didn't want to disturb her as it was still the middle of the night. That's what mums are for. Nick left me for a moment so I could ring mum in private.

I told her what had happened and said: 'I can't do this any more. I'm really struggling. I'm coming home.'

She said, 'Of course you must.'

'You know what this might mean, mum?'

'Don't give it another thought. Get yourself home. Don't worry about anything else. Your well-being is all that matters, nothing else.'

'That's it,' I told Nick when he came back into the room. 'I'm sorry. I've got to go home.'

At least I saved Duncan a job he was apparently dreading.

When the rest of the lads came in for tea, they were asked to keep out of the physio's room, where I was trying, not very successfully, to compose myself. They weren't told what had happened though quite a few had a fairly shrewd idea. Once they'd gone back out I was able to go back into the main dressing-room area to pack. I'm not entirely sure Liam Plunkett got the message at all. As I sat in my space packing up my kit bag, with Mark Saxby beside me, 'Pudsey' carried on wheeling away on an exercise bike right next to us without a care in the world.

Perhaps the saddest moment of all came when I picked up my England cap to put it in my bag. The thought of what I was doing and of what it might mean hit me like a kick in the guts. All the fantastic feelings, all the great highs and all the hard work, the sheer joy of playing cricket for England, which had helped me get through the tough times so often before, in all probability I would never experience any of them again. As I placed the navy blue cap with the three lions in my bag I stopped for a moment, turned to Mark and said: 'This is probably the last time I'm ever going to wear this.'

He couldn't think of anything to say. I just felt empty. The moment seemed so final.

Before I left for the hotel and the flight home, I sought out Duncan to say goodbye. 'I'm sorry I've let you down,' I told him.

'Don't worry about it,' he said, and that was that.

At the close of play Duncan got all the team together and said: 'You all know that Tres has gone home. I think we should all spare a thought for him now and remember he has been an absolute legend for England.' When I found that out later, I was moved.

Mark Garraway, our team analyst who I knew well from our days at Somerset, was deputed to fly back with me as far as Dubai. Poor sod. Actually, almost as soon as the plane took off I started to feel a lot better and a lot more relaxed. After all, the hard work had been done.

Then, later on the evening of Tuesday 14 November, Andrew Walpole put out the following statement on behalf of the ECB:

'England have announced that Marcus Trescothick is to return home to the UK from the team's Ashes tour of Australia.

'The Somerset batsman has suffered a recurrence of the stress-related illness which led to him coming back early from England's tour of India earlier this year.

'Trescothick ... will play no further part in the Ashes Tests.'

Back home Hayley had been sitting in the hairdressers when she took a call from Medha Laud, our brilliant team-fixer at Lord's. Still acting on earlier instructions, Medha had told Hayley that arrangements had been made for her and Ellie to fly out that night from Heathrow and that she should get packed and ready to be collected within the next couple of hours.

The next time her phone rang, it was me calling from Sydney airport.

'Hello, love,' I said. 'I'm coming home.'

Chapter 20

'I WISH YOU HADN'T SAID THAT'

'David Graveney said: "The selectors have been acutely conscious that it would be counter-productive to try and rush Marcus back into international action before he was ready." At the time I wondered whether Peter Moores actually appreciated that as well.'

The first thing that Hayley and I did when we arrived home on the morning of Wednesday 15 November 2006 was burst out laughing.

We'd met at the airport a few hours earlier and in the car we discussed what had happened in Australia and what we needed to do now. We knew there would be photographers waiting for us when we got home and this time, though I wasn't thinking of inviting them in for a knees-up, I was determined I wouldn't hide away from them. I would step out of the car for a few moments to give them the pictures they wanted and maybe they would leave us alone, at least for a while.

When we turned the corner into our road we were met by the sight of two police cars creating a gangway for us to drive through. And when the automatic gates were opened from inside the house by Hayley's dad, John, and we sped up the drive like visiting royalty, Hayley looked at me and I looked at her and we both collapsed in a fit of giggles. It was just the release of tension we both needed.

I got out, took my time getting into the house to wait for shutters to click, walked into the house and picked up my 18-month-old daughter. I was home, I had my baby in my arms and I was happy.

Around the same time some other photos of me were appearing on front pages in Australia and the Bristol area, only the me in question wasn't me at all, but some poor innocent bystander who bore no more than a passing resemblance. The procedure to get me out of Heathrow through a back door quickly and unnoticed had worked so well that the best the snappers on the airport shift could manage were a set of photos of a knackered-looking South African-born, but Sydney-based IT executive, named Justin O'Sullivan. When they wired them back to Australia they were splashed under huge headlines reading stuff like: 'Ashes Star's Private Hell'. Over here the early editions of our local paper, the Bristol Evening Post, also ran with them, printing a few thousand copies before someone who actually knew what I looked like saw them and, in time-honoured fashion, called out 'stop the presses'.

The next day, a rather bemused Justin O'Sullivan was inundated with texts and emails from friends and family asking him what he had done wrong.

Our next adventure with the newspaper industry was another matter entirely. A few days later a female reporter managed to talk her way into the warden-assisted secure accommodation housing in Bristol where my 80-year-old grandmother Lilian lived, persuaded her to let her in for a cosy chat and started asking whether her grandson had a history of mental illness. As you can imagine the incident left my nan extremely upset. I know the press has a job to do and sometimes it is a dirty one, but this was beyond all reasonable, ethical and moral limits. They say we get the press we deserve. Nan didn't deserve this. I only hope those involved manage to sleep at night.

By the time I saw Chris, on Thursday 16 November at the County Ground, I was feeling pretty well again. In fact, I told him: 'I can't believe I feel so good. I just feel so relieved to be back here'. Chris told me he didn't think this episode was the same as the first in India, that, as far as he was concerned I had been clinically well when I left for Australia but had suffered what he called an acute stress reaction. He did not, therefore, anticipate me going back to square one again and, when I came off the pills straight away and suffered no setback, he was proved correct.

We talked through what had happened and confronted the question also being debated in the newspapers of why the comeback had gone so horribly wrong. In the end we reached the conclusion that we had possibly been tricked by my progress prior to departure, playing a full season of Test and international cricket, then coming off the pills, into thinking I was ready when I was only nearly ready. What Chris did say was that the circumstances of my return to work were highly unusual among sufferers of this type of illness. Whereas, in other walks of life recovering patients might return to work for a couple of hours a day, for a day or two, then gradually build up over a period of time to the point where it might be possible to return to 'normal' work schedules, in my line of work it was all or nothing. You can't say, well I'll just turn up for a couple of hours then go home, or, do you mind if I only bat for half an hour today? You either play cricket or you don't, and I did, at the highest level in a pressurized environment, watched by up to 30,000 spectators and millions of television viewers, scrutinizing my performance. So, despite the fact that we had planned for every eventuality in Australia, despite all the discussions we had had and all the plans we put in place, maybe I just tried to run before I could walk. I decided there and then never to make that mistake again. Memories of the result were still too fresh in my mind. If I was ever again going to attempt a return to international cricket it would have to be on the basis that I was 100 per cent, completely and totally well. Not only did I owe that to myself, I owed it to England and to my team-mates.

Not long afterwards Nick Pierce suggested it might be beneficial if another specialist was brought on board. Chris agreed that the more help I received the better now and I went with him and Nick to meet the new man.

Within five minutes of our conversation starting he looked me straight in the eye and asked simply: 'Do you want to get back to playing for England?'

My response was illuminating. 'Yeah, I do, I think.' I stuttered. 'No, yeah, I really do'.

'That doesn't sound very convincing,' he said.

'Well, I don't want to play for England if it's going to make me feel s**t again,' I said.

I should have said: 'If all that playing for England overseas entails – going away from home, being separated from family and friends – is going to make me feel s**t again' but I think the penny dropped fairly quickly. No matter what work we did from then on, unless I could find a way past that barrier, my England career would be finished. I tried hard to beat it and I never actually gave up until events at Dubai airport in March 2008 left me with no other option. But the fact is I never did get past that barrier, even when, during the summer of 2007, I thought I was well enough to make myself available for the preliminary 30-man squad for the Twenty20 World Cup in South Africa at the end of it.

My sessions with Chris and the new man were very helpful inasmuch as I learnt more detail about how the illness actually works, the science of it, if you like. Being a bit of a statto, I found it quite fascinating to learn, for instance, that the brain contains around 10 gazillion cells (around 10,000,000,000, to be more precise), that there are about 4 million miles of nerve fibres, the wires connecting the brain cells together in each brain, or roughly eight round trips to the moon. And that the brain works by one cell deciding to send a message to another to make something happen, by an electrical impulse using one of 80 known transmitters. What happens when someone falls under depression is that, whether through stress, exhaustion or a multitude of other reasons, a chemical imbalance occurs, reducing the efficiency and amount of transmitters that help the messages get through and the whole system breaks down. In the case of depression the transmitter that staves it off is called Seratonin. When the medication works, it helps to stabilize the level of Seratonin to the required level. Information about the Limbic System and the theory of 'fight, flight or freeze' was explained again in more detail. You can put your notebooks away now.

The start of the county season coincided with England's desperate performances in the World Cup, on and off the field. I tried to view all of England's trials and tribulations as an objective observer only, but something inside me could not escape the feeling that I should have been there and would have been under 'normal' circumstances. The feeling was made worse whenever Nasser Hussain on TV or Michael Vaughan, in press conferences, talked about how much I was missed.

Though I understood how hard it would be for England to pick me again, I knew full well that, after the winter they had had without me, any sign of form on my part would encourage media speculation concering my future, and, of course, that is what happened.

At the start of May, with England, now under new coach Peter Moores but with Michael back as full-time Test captain, preparing to take on West Indies in a four-Test series, I hit my highest-ever first-class score, 284 against Northants at Northampton. I batted for 379 balls over 501 minutes, hit four sixes and 36 fours and the Trescothick issue was raised for the first time. I bumped into Andrew Strauss when we travelled to Lord's to play Middlesex at the start of June. He was between Tests and not playing for the county and, knowing he had been struggling a bit with his form, it seemed the most natural thing in the world to watch him have a net and pass on my thoughts afterwards. To me it looked as though he was trying to alter the technique that had made him the player he was, but he also looked a bit worn out and, without being too heavy handed, I did pass on some thoughts about burnout and its effects, a subject about which by now I had become a world expert.

At the start of June I hit 182 out of our 675 for five declared against Leicestershire at Taunton, and the Trescothick issue was raised again. I scored 715 runs in my first 11 championship innings, and, though I made a duck on my final innings prior to the start of the domestic Twenty20 Cup, five catches at slip in Gloucestershire's first innings on Thursday 14 June indicated I was seeing the ball okay in the field as well. And now the Trescothick issue was not only being debated in the media.

On 14 June I met with Chris and Nick Pierce and my new therapist, who made it clear he wanted me to think about taking my recovery to the next level. He was quite bullish about what needed to happen now and so, in fairness, was I. He wanted me to kick on now and think seriously about coming back. I didn't want to rush things and I really needed to be certain about my commitment to playing international cricket again, bearing in mind how the last attempt had ended, but the Twenty20 World Cup, due to be played in South Africa in September, was raised. Could this be an achievable target, a way back?

David Graveney and the other selectors had left the ball in my court. When I was ready, I should call them and we would take it from there. But England were required to announce their preliminary squad of 30 players for the Twenty20 World Cup by Wednesday 11 July and time was flying by.

On one level, if I was going to come back at all, this looked like a real opportunity. Lasting only a couple of weeks, in a place where I had had success with the bat before, without too much travelling or playing, this looked and I felt like it might just fit the bill.

The following week I gave my first interview since my return from Australia, to the *Mail on Sunday*.

'Of course, I'd love to be playing for England again,' I said, 'and watching them this summer has sometimes been painful for me. I've seen every Test on TV and it's been, "God, I miss this. I miss this a lot".

'When the first Test started at Lord's I was twitchy because I was thinking I wanted to be there. If you had asked me the day before the match "can you play?" I'd have said yes. But just because I want to do it doesn't make it the right thing to do. I understand the big dilemma; can the selectors take the risk of picking me to go abroad on tour? Can they invest in me again after what happened? That is out of my hands. Clearly, if I want to continue my career I have to undertake another tour, whether it be a Test tour, one day or Twenty20.

'I'm not ready yet. But I'm getting closer and I'm not giving up hope.'

The reference to Twenty20 was deliberate.

The next weekend, prior to discussions to finalise the 30-man preliminary squad, Graveney rang me. Making myself available for the 30 didn't necessarily mean I had to make myself available, or indeed that I would be picked, for the final 15 due to be named some time hence. But if I had said no now, I would have ruled myself out completely and both I and the selectors wanted to keep all options open. I talked through the pros and cons with Graveney, told him how keen

I was to get back but that I could not give any guarantees. If he was prepared to accept me making myself available for the Twenty20 World Cup, on that basis I would be happy to say yes. The issue of what might happen further down the line, England's one-day and Test tours to Sri Lanka and New Zealand, was never raised.

On Wednesday 11 July, Graveney announced: 'We have decided to name Marcus in the provisional squad in order to give us more flexibility should it be decided that Marcus is ready to return to international cricket before the tournament takes place.

'We will not be placing undue pressure on him to make a return to international cricket without first carefully considering all the issues involved.'

Then, when I faced the Northants bowlers for the second time that season, at Taunton the following Friday, 13 July, another century, 146 out of 459, was taken by many to signify I was ready to grab the lifeline England had thrown me.

Over the next few days I became more and more comfortable with the prospect to the point where I was actually becoming excited by it. The chance to play for England again so soon after what had happened in Australia, was more than I could have hoped for. I consulted Chris and Hayley and the consensus was two weeks in South Africa might be exactly what I needed. This really could be the road back. And then I received a phone call from Peter Moores that told me the road was closed.

Peter was his usual enthusiastic, positive self. He was delighted that I had made myself available for the Twenty20, he said. And then he said: 'It would be great for the team to see you committing to the one-day series in Sri Lanka as well.'

Almost before the words were cold, *shiver*. The barrier went up inside my head. Oh f**k, I thought to myself. Oh f**k. I wish you hadn't said that.

The Sri Lankan one-day series was scheduled to follow on straight after the trip to South Africa. So what would have been a short, sharp two-week trip suddenly turned into five weeks away from home. I would leave England on the weekend of 8 September and return on Monday 14 October. Not a chance in hell.

Moores never exactly issued an ultimatum. He didn't say: 'I want you to play in the Twenty20 World Cup but only if you make yourself available for the one-dayers in Sri Lanka after that.' But, looking back at our conversation, it is clear to me that that was what he wanted. Others around me have said Moores should have proceeded more carefully; in terms of my immediate future plans it is hard to argue with that. I can understand his position, basically it was the same as Duncan's – no picking and choosing – but surely he could have helped me just to try and have a go at doing the Twenty20 without nudging me further about what might happen afterwards.

Later events suggest I might not have made it onto the plane for Cape Town anyway. But I might have done and, if the tournament had gone well for me, maybe I would have been ready to take the next step, and the next.

Knowing all that I do now, I seriously doubt whether I would ever have been able to make it back to playing in all forms of international cricket. But a one-day specialist? Possibly? Would that have been acceptable to England? Possibly not.

All I knew then was the moment Moores extended the conversation beyond the Twenty20 World Cup to the one-dayers in Sri Lanka was the moment that kicked me off again.

I kept my responses noncommittal, just to buy some time before I could work out where all this left me. After the conversation was over, I sat there trying to take in what had just happened and consider if there was any way I might actually be able to do what Moores had suggested he wanted me to do. And, bit by bit, the initial sense of unease turned into a full-blown crisis. Five weeks away, leaving Hayley, now pregnant again, and Ellie and home. One sleepless night later, grappling with the idea of fighting the challenge, and my mind was made up. I wasn't going anywhere.

The next thing I did was speak to the guys at Somerset; Brian Rose, Justin Langer and first-team coach Andy Hurry. I told them what Moores had said and what it meant. 'I don't want to do it,' I said. 'I don't want to leave my family for five weeks. I can't put myself through the pain again.'

Justin was extremely sympathetic. He said that even he had actually packed up playing for Australia when being away from home became too tough and that, in his experience, it gets to everyone in the end.

I discussed the options with Brian and we decided the best thing to do was to get what had to be done out of the way without delay. No point in dragging things out or waiting until they cut the 30 to 15. I didn't want to mess England around. So I rang Nick Pierce and told him that I was going to withdraw my availability. The next day I drove up to the National Cricket Centre in Loughborough, met with Nick, David Graveney, Moores and John Carr and sealed it.

There was no animosity, no hard feelings. 'I'm just not ready to do it,' I told them, and as I did so, I felt disappointed, but relieved.

They told me they understood, that if I felt ready again I should let them know and we could all take it from there.

The following day, Wednesday 25 July 2007, the ECB put out a statement saying that I had declared myself unavailable for the World Twenty20.

'Whilst I have been making good progress ... I am now clear I should take more time to complete my recovery. I still have ambitions to play for England.'

David Graveney said: 'The selectors have been acutely conscious that it would be counter-productive to try and rush Marcus back into international action before he was ready.' At the time I wondered whether Peter Moores actually appreciated that. Later, however, while Peter was coaching England in India in 2008, I received a letter from him which softened my opinion. He told me he had read my comments in the book and expressed his regret that I felt his approach may have been too heavy handed. He assured me that the last thing he wanted to do was put me under pressure, and I appreciated the gesture from someone regarded by most people in the game as a very decent bloke.

Did I think that was it for me? Did I think that was my last chance gone? I never said never again because playing for England meant too much to me, and, on occasions I really believed I would be able to write a different ending to the story, especially when getting such a massive kick out of helping Somerset win Division Two of the championship and gain promotion to Division One of the Pro40 League – some massive nights and massive dents on my black credit card, to boot.

But when Hayley produced Millie, a sister to Ellie in January 2008, I cannot in all conscience say that I was sparing too many thoughts for Paul Collingwood and the chaps about to embark on five one-day internationals and three Tests in New Zealand.

And when I failed to embark Virgin Airways Flight VS400 to Dubai on Saturday 14 March, those who thought it was all over knew it was now.

Chapter 21

THANKS, KP, BUT NO THANKS

'He [KP] wanted to know if I felt I could make myself available for the rest of England's one-dayers. He was trying to do what he had succeeded in doing with Harmy…'

If anyone had harboured concerns that the decision to end the guessing game over my future with England might have a negative effect on my performance as a Somerset player, I'd like to think my batting during the summer of 2008 dispelled them.

In fact, the announcement of my retirement brought a clarity and a relief that I thrived on. For too long the uncertainty over what was best for me, for the family and, a little further down the list, for England had been unsettling. Too many times the issue of whether I might be able to make myself available again, and when, had been raised, either in the press or gently by people connected to the England team, and I had spent too many hours agonising over it. Every time I indulged in the perhaps and maybe, or been seduced by kind words into thinking how much the team might actually need me, those sentiments were swiftly dispelled by the reality that, as far as making the huge commitment to throwing heart, soul, and, of course, mind into everything full-time international cricket entails and demands, it just wasn't possible. And, quite reasonably, though some people even raised the suggestion that England should consider me for home Tests only, there weren't too many takers in the set-up interested in that notion.

Deep down, as far as my ability to bat at the highest level was concerned, I still felt I was good enough; that if it was merely a matter of walking out on any given day to bat for England, I could do it. But, after having experienced seven years of all that goes with that and how it affected me in the end, I just knew, as far as a full-on comeback was concerned, I would be better off forgetting about England and they would be better off forgetting about me.

Once that had been laid to rest I could focus on playing for Somerset, knowing that at the end of the season, complete control over my life with my family would be ours, not someone else's. The way that thought enabled me to relax and start fully enjoying my life again made me think seriously about the level of personal sacrifice playing for England at all levels over a long period of time entails.

Now I look at other lads playing full-time at Test and one-day cricket, home and abroad, month after month, year after year and I marvel at how they can spend that amount of time away from home and their loved ones. Of course, everyone has a choice and the life of a professional cricketer beats work any time. But that doesn't make anyone any less of a dad. Cricketers don't love their wives or kids any less than people in other walks of life, nor are their feelings any less intense, but, now observing from the outside, the kind of compartmentalizing that goes with this job is just beyond me. Sometimes I look at what I did in my England career, the time I was away from Hayley and home and, even allowing for the kind of acute homesickness to which I was prone, I think 'How the hell did I do that?' And I say to myself quietly, 'Never again, not in a million years.'

Ellie is four years old now and when I consider how much of her growing up I might have missed, it makes me sad. And if I was still with England full-time, playing, travelling, playing, travelling, playing, travelling etc. how much of Millie would I be missing now? And how much of my life with Hayley? For me, too much. None of us would ever get it back. And that's when I realise that the benefit of my being ill is that it has given me the opportunity to stop before it was too late.

I'm extremely proud to have played for my country and to have scored hundreds and won the Ashes. I wouldn't have missed any of it for the world. But those priceless family moments I have enjoyed in the past year or so are worth more to me than anything I achieved on the cricket field – silly little things like taking Ellie to watch the film *Mamma Mia*, for instance.

She was massively into it, sang all the ABBA tunes, and knew all the words. When we were in the car she had to have the CD of the soundtrack playing, or else, and, at home, she acted out all the parts. Moments like that – or like picking her up from school and hearing what she learned today, watching her riding her bike – make me realize how lucky I am that I've experienced all of those memories that would otherwise have been lost to me. Occasionally I recall just how desperate I was at the lowest point and then think of how happy I can be now, and I absolutely know my decision to stop playing full-time for England was not just right but absolutely necessary.

And my plea to those who run international cricket is this: think twice about the demands you are placing on players. In many ways I was the lucky one. My illness turned out to be my cure. I had no choice but to get out and re-evaluate, and to take back my life. Please do everything you can to make sure others do not suffer as I did. When you are working out the bottom line, please take a moment to think about the human cost, and don't just pay lip service to the idea. You may not think players have an alternative. The global expansion of Twenty20 cricket means they have now.

Even though I thought I had made my intentions perfectly clear, my form in county cricket in 2008 meant that, from time to time, the old questions were still asked, and when Kevin Pietersen took over as England captain from Michael Vaughan towards the end of the summer, quite seriously.

Michael knew how I felt from the moment I announced my retirement. We spoke often on the phone as friends and he fully understood that, as far as I was concerned, the matter was closed. But that didn't deter KP, and, never one to hang about, his first enquiry came during Somerset's opening home championship match of the new season against Hampshire, on 7 May, with the ink on the official statement of my retirement from international cricket, on 22 March, barely dry.

I had already made runs in our first championship outing, against Lancashire at Old Trafford, where, incidentally, Freddie Flintoff bowled at the speed of light on a bouncy pitch and kept hitting Justin Langer for fun, a reminder of what a brilliant idea it is we won't be playing an Ashes Test there in 2009.

Then, after we folded to 126 against Hampshire, batting first, KP and John Crawley both scored hundreds, of which, initially at least, John's was the more fluent. I was interested to watch Kevin batting at close hand because we hadn't been on the same field for England for nearly a year and I wanted to see for myself how he had developed in that time. The truth was that in this innings he was struggling with his timing until Crawley, a vastly experienced batsman better maybe than his Test stats suggest, had a quiet word and suggested he concentrate on hitting much straighter, which seemed to do the trick.

Then, the morning after I made a decent 151 in our second innings, Kev sent me what turned out to be the first of several typically direct texts all bearing roughly the same message, as in 'Oi, c**k. Why aren't you playing for England?'

As the summer progressed, the number of jokey phone calls and texts increased. I took them all with a pinch of salt, until around the middle of August when the tone changed perceptibly. I had already made four hundreds for Somerset, two in the championship (against Hants and Kent), and two more which happened to be televised, one in a Twenty20 match against Worcestershire on 19 June and another in the Pro40 against Durham up at Chester le Street on 23 July. Then, when I followed up my second championship ton, against Surrey at Taunton on 12 August, with my third in the competition and sixth of the season in all, 184 in another televised Pro40 match against Gloucestershire at Taunton on 23 August, I exchanged messages with Kevin during which the joking stopped altogether.

Kevin had taken over as Test and one-day skipper from Michael by this time and had started brilliantly, England winning the fourth Test against South Africa at the Oval. His next success was in persuading Steve Harmison out of retirement from one-day international cricket, though the full significance of that didn't strike me at the time.

Then, when he led England to a resounding win in the first of the four-match one-day series against South Africa in a day/night game at Headingley, scoring an excellent 90 not out, I texted him to offer my congratulations and best wishes.

I ignored his first reply. It said something like, 'It would be a lot easier for me if you were playing.'

Then he sent another message, saying 'Answer the question.' To me, the meaning was clear. He wanted to know if I felt I could make myself available for the rest of England's one-dayers. He was trying to do what he had succeeded in doing with Harmy, and as Harmy had found a week or so earlier, when the captain of England asks you to play for him, it is bloody hard to say no.

But I simply had no choice. Much as I'd love to, I told him, and as much as I missed putting on an England shirt, it just couldn't happen.

Fair play to Kevin. He never raised the issue again and before long both he and I had enough on our plates to be going along with, enough indeed for him to end up losing the captaincy shortly after the turn of the year for reasons I still haven't quite got to grips with.

First came the Stanford Twenty20 fiasco in Antigua , then the interruption to the tour of India caused by the terrorist atrocity in Mumbai. Then the England management asked their captain what he felt he needed to help England win the Ashes in 2009 and when his honest assertion that he could no longer work with the coach Peter Moores was leaked, they sacked him for issuing them with an ultimatum. Answers on a postcard, please.

* * *

For me, from the moment I saw a copy of *Coming Back To Me* for the first time things changed in a rather better way.

The book had been serialised in the *Mail On Sunday* and the *News Of The World* for the previous couple of weekends so the story and the detail it contained were out there.

Prior to publication of the book and to the newspaper extracts I had felt some twinges of trepidation. I was not concerned about telling my story in the detailed way that I did, because all along I had wanted to produce something that would end all the speculation over the reasons for my returning from India and Australia; something that would attempt to explain my experience of the illness in such a way as to help those who, like me, have found it so cripplingly difficult to admit to or to come to terms with; and, perhaps most important of all, something to help those who have never suffered from it understand a little more about what it is like for those who do.

I did find reliving some of my experiences very difficult indeed. Once, on the train from Taunton to London, while re-reading the chapter about my early return from Australia, the events seemed so clear and vivid to me that I actually began to weep. I had taken myself back to the feeling so successfully that it hit me full on again. But in view of the seriousness of my illness and the responsibility I felt to do justice to it and those who suffer from it, it was important for me not only to be as candid as possible, but also to be as accurate as possible in my recollections of times, dates, places and events.

Given the circumstances and the way the illness gripped me at the time, that was hard enough because there were periods when I simply didn't know what day it was. When trying to piece together what went on in India, for example, and checking the blow-by-blow details, I had no recollection whatsoever of one entire innings that the record books proved I had played – not a single delivery. What was also tough, as much for Hayley as for me, was talking about the time I told the psychiatrist that I had thought about doing myself harm, because doing so now with her help meant she also had to relive some of the worst moments of our life together. One thing is not, nor has ever been, in dispute; namely the immense courage she has shown to help us both get to clearer water.

As the process continued, however, the weight I had been carrying around for so long began to lift. Some people have called it cathartic. I wouldn't disagree. It certainly helped the healing. For instance, whereas I still harboured residual feelings of guilt about having misled so many people for so long about the true nature of my problems, reliving all of what I went through helped me realise that was another symptom of the illness, not just me being devious for the sake of it.

Naturally, I did wonder how people might react to me personally after they read or were told of exactly what I went through and the nature of my symptoms.

I made it clear right from the start that I wasn't intending to write a self-help guide or a manual to depression and anxiety, but that if, by detailing my experiences, even one person was helped to come to terms with what they were going through, then the exercise would have been thoroughly worthwhile.

In the event, the response of the general public left me quite overwhelmed. Even before the book was published, the letters and messages began to arrive following the serialisations in mid-August.

When I began the round of book signings and interviews timed to coincide with publication, starting with a half-hour chat with Jonathan Agnew on BBC's *Test Match Special* in one of the many breaks for rain during the fourth one-day international on Sunday 31 August, the volume of mail increased substantially. Even now, in March 2009, seven months later, I am still receiving five or six letters per week.

They have come from fellow sufferers, thanking me for helping them make some kind of sense out of what they themselves have gone through, as in the following extract:

Dear Marcus,

I, like many others before me I'm sure, wondered just exactly what a stress related illness was when I watched the news. Let alone how it could happen to a young man like you or I. However, about the time it did happen to you it was happening to me, only I have just realised it. The reason I have realised it is because of your book. The symptoms, the feelings, nearly every word you wrote slapped me in the face and said 'this is you too'.

I marked the pages and left your book for my wife to read as I didn't have the courage to do it. I still don't fancy telling my family much either!

I won't go into detail, but as I'm sure you can imagine, things at home are not rosy at the moment. But I think realising that I am ill rather than just becoming a person I don't want to be, may just have set me on the road to saving my marriage and allowing my kids to grow up with a father they want to be around.

I have been to the doctors and despite wanting to escape and cover over the reason I was there and that I could do it on my own, I stayed and talked to the doctor. I persuaded him to refer me to a psychological colleague and although he was dead against medication unless things got worse (I'm not sure things could get any worse and hope to god they don't) I can at least know that something is being done.

Please keep up the good work in spreading the word about an illness that people just don't think will happen or is happening to them.

They have come from friends and relatives of sufferers, recounting similar experiences, like this one:

Thank you. You have saved my wife's life, and mine. My wife is bipolar and suffers from panic attacks and depression, which have steadily worsened over the last five years … The start of her darkest period was earlier in the year when I had to take her to A&E as she could not breathe, had chest pains and had trouble walking and seeing. We were told that this was just a little panic attack and wouldn't last more than a few moments. The first attack lasted three days. Her biggest problem was that she thought she was in a unique situation. No one really seemed to understand what she was going through and no one really seemed concerned. She was prescribed sleeping tablets but these had no effect on her. She even took five at one time to try and get some sleep, but did not even feel sleepy. She was convinced it was physical as she could not see how her head was doing this much damage and we had tests done to assure her that she did not face cancer or brain tumors. Then a few weeks ago, in the Sunday paper, we saw an excerpt from your book and she burst into tears, screaming: 'That's what I have, that's exactly how I feel!' The very next day she got a referral to a clinic and while she still has a very, very long way to go, the little changes in her are phenomenal. She no longer feels like a freak and now has hope she can master this. Just knowing that there are other people out there like you has made the world of difference to her. Thank you for showing us both that there is light at the end of the tunnel and thank you most of all for giving me back her laughter, even if it is only a little bit at a time.

And that, right there, was all I needed to tell me I had done the right thing.

They have also come from those offering me suggestions and ideas for helping me with my continuing recovery, like this one: 'I gather your postbag is full of messages from people who no longer feel alone now you've publicised your depression. This is just to remind you that you are not alone either.'

The extraordinary similarity of the shared experiences detailed in the letters underlined one very important point. Until and unless you have been through this illness I believe it is just impossible for you to understand fully how it feels to do so. Yet once you have that understanding the bond you share with fellow sufferers is real and strong.

How many letters and how many messages? Hundreds and hundreds. One would have been enough.

On the field, once the truth was out in the open, I was intrigued and a tad nervous as to how my team-mates and opponents might respond. What I wanted to reassure everyone was that, even though the graphic descriptions of what I had been through might be harrowing to read, they were about then and this is now. That, even though I will never be the same person as I was before I fell under the shadow of the black wings, there was no reason for any-one to treat me any differently from how they did before, good or bad. What I needed to see, and did very quickly, was an accept-ance from others that they could say, 'Well, he's been through it, but he's all right. He's still "Banger".'

It might have been better if one or two of the bowlers I came up against between them and the end of the season had taken pity on me because, unfortunately, the publication of the book coin-cided with my suffering my worst run of form with the bat for Som-erset for some time. As we tried our best to continue our push to win the county championship for the first time in our history, I ended with a top score of 19 from my last six innings as general fatigue set in, not exactly what the club had intended when they did me the honour of naming one of the stands at Taunton after me.

For me, though, the season had ended on a high because finally, and once and for all, the truth was in the public domain. People now had access to everything there was to know and I wasn't scared about the illness or talking about it anymore.

Chapter 22

DAYS IN
THE SUN

*'I knew that we had a responsibility to everyone
who had ever suffered these illnesses to try our
best to give proper voice to the experience'*

I had endured some nerve-wracking moments in my life as an England cricketer, none more so than during that fabulous Ashes winning series of 2005 when I joined the rest of the nation in wondering if Freddie was going to fall off the open-topped bus.

But not many come close to how I felt on 24 November 2008, the day of the announcement of the winner of the William Hill Sports Book of the Year.

Of course, I had hoped for the best from the moment *Coming Back To Me* was selected for the shortlist at the end of October because the book and all the work that went into it meant a great deal to me. But when I received the invitation to attend the award ceremony at Waterstone's in Piccadilly in November, the news that only one ghostwritten autobiography had ever won the award, Lance Armstrong's *It's Not About The Bike*, took the pressure off. Hayley and I decided the worst that could happen was that we would have a day out in London doing some early Christmas shopping.

All our attempts at casual detachment disappeared, however, when the train from Taunton pulled in at Paddington station that morning and the notion that we might actually win first took hold. Spookily, my collaborator Peter Hayter felt the very same feeling at the very same time his train was arriving at Euston and texted me to that effect. And that is when the nerves kicked in.

By the time Hayley and I reached Waterstone's I was in such a state that I began looking for clues. Fatal. On the ground floor I came across a display shelf containing all six of the shortlisted books, each taking up a shelf at a time. *Coming Back To Me* was on the top shelf, with the others* stacked neatly below.

'That's it, then,' I thought to myself. 'We've bloody won.'

When we got out of the lift at the top floor, where the ceremony was to take place, I spied another display unit. This time the book was on the bottom shelf. I stopped looking for clues.

One by one, all six authors went up on the stage to receive commemorative leather-bound copies of our books and the £2,000 betting vouchers supplied by the sponsors which Peter and I converted into hard cash by backing Paul Nicholls' horse Master Minded a few weeks later.

At about 2.30pm the BBC's John Inverdale addressed the audience in the room and said a few words about each book in turn and then we waited with growing edginess until the appointed time for the announcement of the winner of the cheque for £20,000, the biggest prize in sports book publishing, on Radio 5 Live, scheduled for exactly 3.04pm.

By now the nerves were shredded, though Peter had long since decided the best approach was to try and numb them with industrial quantities of the sponsors' white wine.

* *The Austerity Olympics* by Jennie Hampton, *Bad Blood* by Jeremy Whittle, *Bamboo Goalposts* by Rowan Simons, *Inverting the Pyramid* by Jonathan Wilson, and *Playing the Enemy* by John Carlin.

At 3.01pm, John was cued in. When he began by talking about a book that 'deals with one of the great taboos of team sports', I realised he was talking about us but also assumed he would be discussing the merits of each book in turn for the benefit of the listeners.

When about a minute passed without any mention of another book I then thought that he must be confining his comments to the two or three that had made it to the final choice and that, on the basis that ours was the first book being discussed, we could only be an also-ran. In my limited experience, the winner of any man-of-the-match award is never the first player mentioned. So-and-so scored a beautiful 92, whatshisname kept things tight with a great spell of three for 44 ...

'But the award goes to ...'

And then it dawned on me and Peter at the same time that, with only seconds to go before the 3.04pm deadline, John hadn't said a word about any of the other books at all. Then, from somewhere I heard John say, 'the award goes to *Coming Back* ...,' and all I could hear after that was my co-writer repeating over and over again one single word. That word was 'f**k'.

It is hard to describe the emotions that swept over me. Pride, of course, satisfaction, yes. But mainly relief. When we first under-took the project I knew that we had a responsibility to everyone who had ever suffered these illnesses to try our best to give proper voice to the experience, not only in order to remind them that they are not alone but also to offer non-sufferers an insight that might help them understand our world. Set alongside the correspon-dence I recieved, this award suggested those asked to judge our efforts considered, in this regard at least, we had achieved some degree of success.

Afterword

I had already enjoyed my other moment in the sun, the one that was supposed to happen on a September evening at the Oval, at Lord's in the spring of 2008, when I went with Ashley Giles to receive a special award from the sponsors Vodafone for my efforts as an England player. Ash called it the 'thanks-for-coming' award.

Just before the event began I went upstairs and popped my head round the door of the England and home dressing-room, the place I believed was the best in the world in which to be a cricketer. I closed my eyes and tried to connect with a few of the moments I had spent there playing for England, and I was overwhelmed by a profound sense of privilege that I had my chance to live the dream.

Was I sad? A little, perhaps. Bitter? Not at all. The memories of those great times representing my country with a bat in my hand and a ball to hit, of the nerves building up inside us before we went 'on stage', of the certain knowledge that, at the time I was doing it, I could not have imagined anything I would rather be doing or anywhere I'd rather be, far outweighed any feeling of remorse that I would never do those things again.

Do I miss it? Of course. When Fred bowls like he did on the second day of the third Test against South Africa's Jacques Kallis at Edgbaston in August 2008, and you connect with your own experience of what it felt like to be on the field when he bowled that fantastic over at Justin Langer and Ricky Ponting in 2005, how could you not? Part of me wonders whether I could still perform at the highest level, but, while there is no guarantee I could, I also understand the price I might pay in terms of my health and happiness is just too great. Writing this on the eve of the 2009 season, with the sights and sounds of spring and the promise of summer to come, that tingle of excitement is getting to me as much now as it did when I was a kid. But I've come too far and made too much progress to take unnecessary risks.

Of course I made mistakes, but if I have any regrets they are to do with how I behaved towards those closest to me, and Hayley in particular, when I put playing for England ahead of them for too long. I can only hope that those I misled along the way over the nature of my problems can now understand the reasons why.

As for lessons, I don't profess to be an expert on my own case, let alone anyone else's, but a few things have stuck; that depression is an illness, not a weakness, and that it can be cured, but that you may not be able to beat it just because you want to. That is what doctors and counsellors and medical science is for, so trust them. I also learned to seek help first and worry about what people might think of you later. And I learned not to be so quick to judge others.

I wouldn't have wished my illness on my worst enemy. But while I will be dealing with it for the rest of my life, forewarned is forearmed and I am a better person for having gone through it all.

I've spoken with people who've experienced similar feelings, and, whereas before I would have said, 'Just get on with it, we're all men, we're all missing home …,' now I understand how they feel and can say, 'How can we help those people before it's too late?'

As for me, the future can look after itself. For now, I can go home after a day's play, pick up my kids, give Hayley a squeeze and know I am so blessed that I have come back.

Career Highlights

Full name: Marcus Edward Trescothick
Born: 25 December 1975, Keynsham, Somerset
Age: 32 years
Nicknames: Banger, Tresco, Madfish
Major teams: Somerset (1993–), England Under-19s (1993–95), England (2000–06)
Batting: Left-hand opening batsman
Bowling: Occasional right-arm medium
Fielding position: Slip, occasional wicket-keeper
Height: 6ft 3in (1.91m)
Education: St Anne's Primary School, Sir Bernard Lovell Comprehensive
Family: Father Martyn, Mother Linda, Sister Anna. Married Hayley Rowse, 24 January 2004; children Ellie and Millie

Landmarks

First-class debut: Somerset v Lancashire, Taunton, May 1993
Test debut: England v West Indies, Old Trafford, Aug 2000
Final Test: England v Pakistan, The Oval, Aug 2006
ODI debut: England v Zimbabwe, The Oval, July 2000
Final ODI: England v Pakistan, Southampton, Sep 2006

Twenty20 International debut: England v Australia, Southampton, June 2005

Final Twenty20 International: England v Pakistan, Bristol, Aug 2006

Highest first-class score: 284, for Somerset v Northants, May 2007

Highest Test score: 219, for England v South Africa, The Oval, Sep 2003

Only Test wicket: Imran Nazir c Giles b Trescothick, England v Pakistan, Karachi, Dec 2000

Most runs in a season: 1,343 (av. 61.04) for Somerset, Division 2 Championship, 2007

Awards

Cricketer Magazine Young Player of the Year 1991

NBC Denis Compton Award 1996, 1997

Professional Cricketers' Association Player of the Year 2000

Wisden Cricketer of the Year 2005

MBE 2005

Somerset Benefit Season 2008

Winner, William Hill Sports Book of the Year 2008

Test Hundreds (14)

122	v Sri Lanka	Galle	22 Feb 2001
117	v Pakistan	Manchester	31 May 2001
161	v Sri Lanka	Birmingham	30 May 2002
219	v South Africa	The Oval	4 Sep 2003
113	v Bangladesh	Dhaka	21 Oct 2003
132	v New Zealand	Leeds	3 Jun 2004
105	v West Indies	Birmingham	14 Jul 2004
107	v West Indies	Birmingham	1 Aug 2004
132	v South Africa	Durban	26 Dec 2004
180	v South Africa	Johannesburg	13 Jan 2005
194	v Bangladesh	Lord's	26 May 2005
151	v Bangladesh	Chester-le-Street	3 Jun 2005
193	v Pakistan	Multan	12 Nov 2005
106	v Sri Lanka	Lord's	11 May 2006

One day Hundreds (12)

137	v Pakistan	Lord's	12 Jun 2001
121	v India	Kolkata	19 Jan 2002
109	v India	Lord's	13 Jul 2002
119	v Zimbabwe	Colombo	18 Sep 2002
108*	v Pakistan	Lord's	22 Jun 2003
114*	v South Africa	The Oval	28 Jun 2003
130	v West Indies	Gros Islet	1 May 2004
104	v West Indies	The Oval	25 Sep 2004
100*	v Bangladesh	The Oval	16 Jun 2005
104*	v Australia	Leeds	7 Jul 2005
113	v Ireland	Belfast	13 Jun 2006
121	v Sri Lanka	Leeds	1 Jul 2006

Batting and Fielding Averages

	M	I	NO	Runs	HS	Av	SR	100	50	Ct
Tests	76	143	10	5825	219	43.79	54.51	14	29	95
ODIs	123	122	6	4335	137	37.37	85.21	12	21	49
T20Is	3	3	0	166	72	55.33	126.71	0	2	2
First-class	239	412	21	14828	284	37.92	–	31	76	293
Twenty20	18	18	0	701	107	38.94	154.74	1	5	11

Bowling Averages

	M	I	Balls	Runs	Wkts	BBI	Av	SR	4w	5w
Tests	76	10	300	155	1	1/34	155.00	300.0	0	0
ODIs	123	13	232	219	4	2/7	54.75	58.0	0	0
T20Is	3	–	–	–	–	–	–	–	–	–
First-class	239	–	2674	1541	36	4/36	42.80	74.2	0	0
Twenty20	18	–	–							

Test Batting by Country

	Period	M	I	NO	Runs	HS	Av	SR	100	50	0
Australia	2001–5	15	30	0	1013	90	33.76	59.34	0	7	2
Bangladesh	2003–5	4	6	1	551	194	110.20	73.36	3	1	0
India	2001–2	4	8	2	355	99	59.16	59.86	0	4	0
New Zealand	2002–4	6	12	1	494	132	44.90	61.98	1	3	2
Pakistan	2000–6	12	22	0	743	193	33.77	46.26	2	3	2
South Africa	2003–5	10	20	2	935	219	51.94	54.23	3	3	3
Sri Lanka	2001–6	12	22	1	957	161	45.57	50.47	3	4	2
West Indies	2000–4	11	21	3	675	107	37.50	48.56	2	3	1
Zimbabwe	2003–3	2	2	0	102	59	51.00	46.15	0	1	0

Record by England Captain

	Spell	M	I	NO	Runs	HS	Av	SR	100	50	0
Atherton	2001	2	4	0	119	69	29.75	58.33	0	1	0
Flintoff	2006	3	5	0	188	106	37.60	49.86	1	0	1
Hussain	2000–3	31	57	5	2152	161	41.38	51.38	2	16	4
Stewart	2001	1	2	0	127	117	63.50	43.49	1	0	0
Strauss	2006	4	7	0	135	58	19.28	40.66	0	1	0
Trescothick	2004–5	2	4	0	286	193	71.50	57.08	1	1	0
Vaughan	2003–5	33	64	5	2818	219	47.76	58.81	9	10	7

2008 County Cricket Season

Competition	M	I	NO	Runs	HS	Av	100	50	Ct	St
Friends Provident Trophy	7	6	0	47	15	7.83	0	0	0	–
LV County Championship	16	28	1	1258	158	46.59	3	8	19	–
NatWest Pro40 League	8	8	0	556	184	69.50	2	2	1	–
Twenty20 Cup	8	8	0	306	107	38.25	1	1	6	–

Index

352 | Marcus Trescothick: Coming Back To Me